SpringerBriefs in Economics

SpringerBriefs present concise summaries of cutting-edge research and practical applications across a wide spectrum of fields. Featuring compact volumes of 50 to 125 pages, the series covers a range of content from professional to academic. Typical topics might include:

- A timely report of state-of-the art analytical techniques
- A bridge between new research results, as published in journal articles, and a contextual literature review
- A snapshot of a hot or emerging topic
- An in-depth case study or clinical example
- A presentation of core concepts that students must understand in order to make independent contributions

SpringerBriefs in Economics showcase emerging theory, empirical research, and practical application in microeconomics, macroeconomics, economic policy, public finance, econometrics, regional science, and related fields, from a global author community.

Briefs are characterized by fast, global electronic dissemination, standard publishing contracts, standardized manuscript preparation and formatting guidelines, and expedited production schedules.

Mantas Švažas

Energy Transformation in Lithuania

Analysis at the Municipal Level

Mantas Švažas
Vytautas Magnus University
Kaunas, Lithuania

ISSN 2191-5504   ISSN 2191-5512   (electronic)
SpringerBriefs in Economics
ISBN 978-3-032-02986-7   ISBN 978-3-032-02987-4   (eBook)
https://doi.org/10.1007/978-3-032-02987-4

This research was funded by the Lithuanian Research Council (LMTLT), grant number P-PD-22-135.

© The Editor(s) (if applicable) and The Author(s) 2026 . This book is an open access publication.

Open Access   This book is licensed under the terms of the Creative Commons Attribution-NonCommercial-NoDerivatives 4.0 International License (http://creativecommons.org/licenses/by-nc-nd/4.0/), which permits any noncommercial use, sharing, distribution and reproduction in any medium or format, as long as you give appropriate credit to the original author(s) and the source, provide a link to the Creative Commons license and indicate if you modified the licensed material. You do not have permission under this license to share adapted material derived from this book or parts of it.

The images or other third party material in this book are included in the book's Creative Commons license, unless indicated otherwise in a credit line to the material. If material is not included in the book's Creative Commons license and your intended use is not permitted by statutory regulation or exceeds the permitted use, you will need to obtain permission directly from the copyright holder.

The use of general descriptive names, registered names, trademarks, service marks, etc. in this publication does not imply, even in the absence of a specific statement, that such names are exempt from the relevant protective laws and regulations and therefore free for general use.

The publisher, the authors and the editors are safe to assume that the advice and information in this book are believed to be true and accurate at the date of publication. Neither the publisher nor the authors or the editors give a warranty, expressed or implied, with respect to the material contained herein or for any errors or omissions that may have been made. The publisher remains neutral with regard to jurisdictional claims in published maps and institutional affiliations.

This Springer imprint is published by the registered company Springer Nature Switzerland AG.
The registered company address is: Gewerbestrasse 11, 6330 Cham, Switzerland

If disposing of this product, please recycle the paper.

Introduction

The effects of climate change are increasingly felt around the world. Heatwaves, sudden snowfall and flooding are just some of the signs of changing weather patterns. One of the main causes of this phenomenon is the pollution generated by the energy system. The use of fossil fuels has revolutionized the world's environmental situation over the last 200 years. Growing economic prosperity has led to an increase in pollution. Late concern about the state of the environment makes action to halt climate change both necessary and urgent. This coincides with rapid urbanization and the deterioration of the economic and social situation of regions. The solution to both these problems can be comprehensive, involving energy transformation activities in regional areas. Renewable energy involves combining different technologies to increase green energy production. This creates a trend towards decentralization of the energy system, as in the case of electricity generation the influence of centralized sources of production is reduced. Energy transformation involves the combination of different technologies for energy production and storage. At the same time, new derivatives of energy production are emerging, such as the production of cooling by centralized heat generation plants. One of the key advantages of energy production based on renewable resources is the possibility of exploiting currently untapped resources. This includes the construction of wind and solar power plants on unused land, the use of biomass waste, the use of biomethane, and the use of renewable energy sources. Land resources and waste are concentrated in regions whose potential is currently not fully exploited. Harnessing these resources in the regions would create the conditions for new business activities such as profitable land rental, biomass exploitation and service provision. In addition, the regions have under-utilized electricity and gas grids, thus further boosting energy transformation.

The main obstacles to this process are lack of capital and political will. Capital can be raised by converting redundant assets into cash resources to be used to expand green energy capacity. The remaining funds can be borrowed from the market. However, political will can catalyze or constrain energy transformation. At present, there is a lack of decisive political action to achieve a coherent scale of energy transformation across countries. One of the reasons for political inaction is the lack of a methodology to achieve smooth energy transformation processes. This study provides a structured overview of the processes involved in implementing energy transformation based on the use of regional resources. The study is based on the example of Lithuania, with the addition of action plans focusing on non-fossil resource countries. For such countries, the transition to renewable energy would not only reduce environmental pollution but also strengthen their economies and regions. Lithuania's demonstrated progress in the energy transition provides a basis for translating the model into practice. The regional orientation reflects the objectives of decentralization of the energy system due to the availability of the necessary resources in the regions.

The Energy Transformation Plan covers the transition of municipal management companies towards circular economic activities, the use of synergies in energy production, the transformation of agriculture to promote recycling and the reduction of diesel fuel consumption. These actions would address both energy and economic/social challenges. Regions lacking management competences, progress more slowly than agglomeration. Changes in the energy system would allow regional companies to develop new business lines while greening the energy sector. The agricultural sector is characterized by high levels of environmental pollution at virtually all levels. On-farm energy production would help to reduce greenhouse gas emissions while creating strong community links and businesses. Achieving the integration of processes from resources will make the energy transformation process smooth and successful.

The energy transformation in developing and small countries has the potential to fundamentally change the geopolitical landscape. Countries that reduce or eliminate their dependence on fossil fuels would change the geopolitical situation on a large scale. Today, in the face of competition over the abundance of available resources, it is difficult to reorient the world towards the promotion of technological superiority. Consistent leadership and a drive to decarbonize the world would lead to deeper economic and social transformations. Pooling of expertise and financial resources, combined with a continued drive for efficiency, improves the chances of smooth implementation of transformation activities, while boosting local industry and resource use.

Competing Interests

The author has no competing interests to declare that are relevant to the content of this manuscript.

Contents

1	**The Need for Energy Transformation: Causes, Opportunities, and Barriers**	1
	1.1 New Horizons in Energy Strategy	1
	1.2 The Importance of ESG Indicators for Regional Energy Transformation	6
	1.3 Lithuanian Case Study Analysis	9
	1.4 Identification of Research Indicators	12
	1.5 Determination of Energy Transformation Priorities in the Regions	14
	References	19
2	**Practical Explorations for Energy Transformation Ways**	23
	2.1 The Potential of Energy System Conversion	23
	2.2 Impact of Energy Transformation on Different Economic Directions	26
	2.3 Identification of Problematic Regions in the Context of Energy Transformation Activities	29
	2.4 Regionalization Process	32
	2.5 Analysis of Problematic Municipalities from an Energy Transformation Perspective	34
	2.6 Asset Structure Analysis	40
	2.7 Action Plans and Solutions	44
	References	47
3	**Importance of Decentralization in Energy Transformation Process**	51
	3.1 Causes of the Decentralization Phenomenon	51
	3.2 Conversion Characteristics of Different Production Technologies	54
	3.2.1 Electricity Production	54
	3.2.2 Heat Production	56
	3.2.3 Gas Production	58

	3.3	The Importance of Biomass Cogeneration for Short-Term Transformation.	60
	3.4	Characteristics of Biomass Energy Sector.	62
	3.5	Methods for Estimating Cogeneration Parameters	66
	3.6	Investigation of Cogeneration Conditions in Rural Areas	67
		References.	73
4	**The Relation Between the Agricultural Sector and the Energy Transformation**		77
	4.1	Paradigm Shift in the Agricultural Sector from an Energy Perspective	77
	4.2	The Necessity of Renewable Energy for the Decarbonization of Farms	80
	4.3	Bioenergy Potential in the Agriculture Sector	83
	4.4	Agriculture and Energy Sector Synergy Model	90
		References.	96
5	**Modeling of the Energy Transformation Process**.		103
	5.1	The Main Risks of Energy Transformation	103
	5.2	Solutions to Promote Energy Transformation	105
		References.	112
References.			117

Chapter 1
The Need for Energy Transformation: Causes, Opportunities, and Barriers

1.1 New Horizons in Energy Strategy

The military conflict in Ukraine in 2022 encouraged developed countries to accelerate the transformation of the energy system. Rising energy prices have made wind and solar more competitive. In addition, investments in green hydrogen production as well as Power to X solutions have increased. These processes fundamentally change the economy of the country and regions—new jobs are created, available biological resources are better used, and electricity storage solutions are developed. Hydrogen production technologies allow the use of cheaply produced energy at a time when its demand is reduced. Later, hydrogen can be used to produce either as electricity or fuel for other equipment with hydrogen engines. The new energy concepts are fundamentally different from the energy canons established in the last century. The traditional model of an energy system, based on fossil fuels, was built on the following principles:

- Centralized production of electricity and heat and transport management
- Limited central planning and energy policy
- Restrictions in the supply of fuels
- Limitations on the number of energy producers and passive consumers
- Growing demand for energy, targeted production [1]

The transformation of renewable energy in the regions fundamentally changes their economic situation. Next to production development, the service sector is expanding, the quality of life is improving, and parallel businesses serving energy facilities are emerging. The main developer of renewable energy in the world is currently the European Union. It produces the greenest energy in terms of consumption. The development of renewable energy promotes the emergence of new businesses and economic development. The EU assists member states to develop these businesses by providing subsidies and grants. The approved European Green

Deal is aimed at energy transformation based on renewable energy. The following directions of support and promotion are provided:

- Clean energy and energy-efficiency technologies
- Regeneration, decontamination, renaturalization, and land redevelopment
- Strengthening the circular economy
- Diversification and creation of new enterprises, including start-ups
- Support for employees
- Digitization and digital communications
- Research, innovation, and technology transfer [2]

When studying the directions of renewable energy development, there is a need to gather different data groups. In the initial stages of research, clustered groups of data are selected, according to which more detailed data is later unified. The links between renewable energy and social integration encourage the study of broader datasets. This is because it aims to demonstrate to prospective investors not only the economic returns, but also the wider factors that could encourage investment in green energy production. By associating the cluster themes derived from both social innovation–energy transition and social innovation–circularity cluster themes, it could be proposing five key elements that need to receive attention and be put forward as future agenda directions: policy for climate change, circular justice, energy business models, transition innovation, and sustainability [3]. Energy transformation can be considered an integral part of circular bioeconomy. It is a rapidly growing field that has been gaining traction in recent years. It is an interdisciplinary field that combines biology, economics, and technology to create sustainable solutions to produce food, energy, and materials [4].

A wide spectrum of synergistic effects exists in the field of renewable energy. Synergies arising from the combination of different energy types help to increase competitiveness in the context of fossil fuels. Harmonizing different energy technologies can ensure sustainable energy production without harming the environment. At the same time, competitive energy prices and uninterrupted energy supply are ensured. To produce large amounts of energy, different types of production are combined, various wastes are used, or several production processes are developed at the same time. Key synergies in renewable energy are the following:

- Wastewater management (mixing sewage sludge with grass, leaves, and food waste, and extracting biogas)
- Animal waste and oil in the extraction of biogas
- Biomass waste in cities and regions used to produce heat and electricity
- Secondary processing of used oil into biofuel 2.0
- Utilization of municipal waste
- Power to X production from wind and solar energy

When going deeper into the directions of synergy and the data required for more detailed research, it is necessary to single out those types of energy that will have the greatest potential for municipal energy transformation. Rising concerns about global warming are driving investment in green energy solutions. Depending on the climatic conditions and the abundance of available natural resources, the countries of the world choose different methods of green energy production. As for traditional sources of energy production, biomass energy occupies the main part of investments [5]. The structure of the biomass energy sector is determined by the specifics of the origin and development of biomass. Economic output is related to the natural processes that produce biomass resources. Certain natural processes form different types of biomasses that can be used for heat, electricity, or biogas production. A business structure is formed according to the type of biomass and the type of its occurrence, the purpose of which is to convert biofuel into energy and achieve a positive economic effect.

Traditional energy companies face extensive challenges related to energy transformation. It is especially related to the use of alternative types of fuel, with the help of which green energy would be extracted. One such type of fuel can be municipal waste. Municipal solid waste (MSW) is a solid waste that is commonly described as trash or garbage that is generated daily by households, commercial establishments, industries, and others. It is regarded as an inevitable and valueless by-product due to community activities. The MSW is one of the main waste source streams beside commercial and industrial waste and construction waste [6]. Responsible management of municipal waste is one of the main indicators that segment developing and developed countries. Municipal waste can be managed in several ways. In one case, they can be burned to produce heat or electricity. Otherwise, if they are buried in landfills, the gas is extracted. In the latter case, new innovations are observed, allowing to produce a larger amount of energy. Landfill methane is a potential resource, but allowing its release into the environment has a lot of environmental implications [7]. Municipal waste management can be linked to the creation of the so-called eco-cities. This concept is related to the maximum reduction of pollution in agglomerated areas. In eco-cities, it is possible to localize the sources of waste, use them more efficiently for recycling, and from the rest efficiently extract the energy needed to meet the needs of the city. However, this concept is still fairly new and carries some risks. It is also noted that "eco-cities," often created as implementations of experimental technological solutions for adaptation to the phenomena of global warming, are also places where, under the guise of the need for "green growth," social inequalities are often deepened. As a remedy for this situation, support is most often indicated for individual eco-enterprises and sustainable lifestyles, i.e., developing (broadly defined) mechanisms for resilience to external crises and dwindling resources [8].

The concept of eco-cities is very similar to the concept of a smart city. In the latter case, the synergy of urban planning and IT solutions is emphasized. Investments in IT solutions in cities can create conditions to save resources and increase the level of ecology in the most polluted areas. Previous research by scientists has shown that smart city management can be based on big data management for energy prosumption in residential buildings and electric vehicles (EV). Furthermore, secondary data could be employed to show the applications of the developed IT solutions in promoting energy prosumption. Findings suggest that the IT architecture provides interoperable open real-time, online, and historical data in facilitating energy prosumption [9]. The use of big data is one of the main components with which it is possible to carry out energy transformation in municipalities. Since renewable resources cannot yet ensure uninterrupted energy production, smart grid management can assist distribute energy correctly to consumers, and demand-side management would reduce pressure on energy producers.

One of the main trends in renewable energy is the development of Power to X technologies [10]. In this case, hydrogen is extracted from different renewable energy technologies, which can later be used for different directions in manufacturing, consumption, or energy balancing. According to the information presented in Fig. 1.1, there are many different ways to use the energy obtained by electrolysis.

Previous studies of the economic impact on emissions were characterized by abstraction, confirmation of a certain fact [12]. Foreign direct investment can play an important role in the transformation [13]. In some cases, they can stimulate investment, and in other cases, as consumption grows, there is a need to produce more energy. As quick results are sought, energy production capacity can be developed using fossil fuels. Previous research has revealed the effects of different aspects of transformation [14,15]. Using several indicators of financial development, the empirical results reveal that financial development measured using broad money, domestic credit to the private sector, and domestic credit to private sector by banks increase carbon emissions, while foreign direct investments (FDI), liquid liabilities, and domestic credit to private sector by financial sector do not affect carbon emissions [16,17]. The results show that none of the financial development indicators exerts a significant nonlinear effect on carbon emissions. The results further indicate that FDI moderates economic growth to reduce carbon emissions but does not moderate energy consumption to affect carbon emissions [18]. The relationship between financial development and environmental pollution is presented in Fig. 1.2.

Other scientific studies have analyzed empirical aspects to obtain answers to fundamental questions. For this, different statistical methods are used, which allow finding causal relationships between the analyzed phenomena. In one case, results based on a Panel Granger causality test showed a unidirectional causality running from energy prices, gross domestic product (GDP), the quadratic term of GDP, and

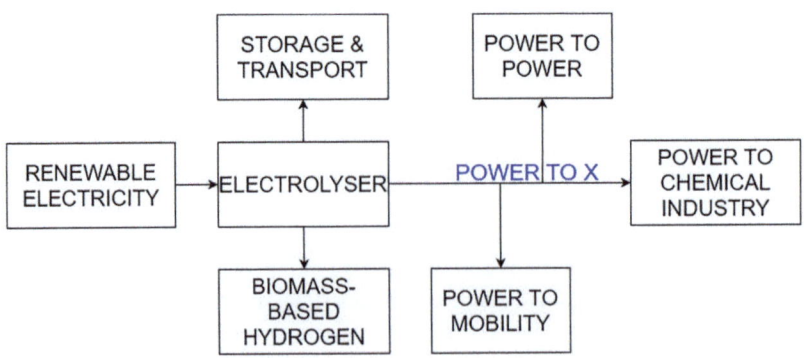

Fig. 1.1 Possible applications of green hydrogen [11]

1.1 New Horizons in Energy Strategy

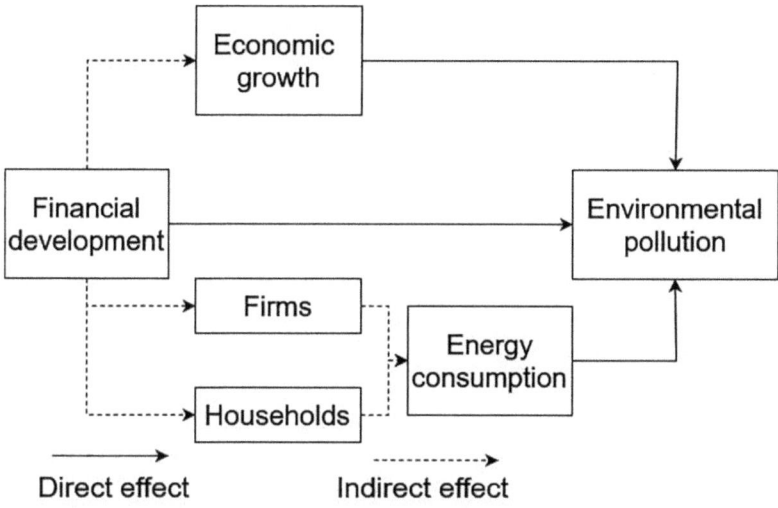

Fig. 1.2 Connections between financial development and environmental pollution [18]

trade to CO_2 emissions. The results further revealed no evidence to support the causal relationship between renewable energy consumption and CO_2 emissions; however, renewable energy consumption was found to indirectly affect CO_2 emissions through its direct effect on energy prices [19–21]. This justifies the direct link between GDP dynamics and CO_2 emissions. Other studies describe abstract aspects that are poorly supported by analytical information [22,23]. Since financial development improves environmental quality, it can play a constructive and important role in improving environmental quality around the world, as increased development of the financial sector can encourage further borrowing at lower cost (as the nation's financial institution is controlled by commercial banks, whose main aim is to give loans to both the private and public sectors for various development projects), including for investment in environmental programs [24–26]. The lack of analytical directions encourages further research, which would allow expanding scientific knowledge in evaluating the energy transformation and the effects it creates [27–29]. The collected scientific information, as well as the elaboration of previous research, allows to single out the main groups of data and sources that would help to study the possibilities of energy transformation:

- Volumes of sewage sludge formation (from water treatment companies)
- Annual energy potential of biomass
- Power of wind and solar power plants by region
- Volumes of communal waste generation
- Amount of unprocessed municipal waste
- Free power in electrical networks
- Volumes of green purchases

The indicated data groups will allow to assess the perspective of each region to contribute to the strengthening of the country's energy system using different renewable energy sources. Currently, there is a lack of information, which is presented in the form of data groups, because the process of energetic transformation is not yet precisely defined. These datasets are related to the regional dimension, as the regional waste dynamics are assessed, as well as the share of regional budgets for green initiatives. This group of data covers the interface between economic and environmental factors, thus aiming to explore the possibilities of developing new ecological activities in the regions, strictly based on the principles of sustainable development.

In conclusion, with the right political will and mobilization of resources, the energy transformation goals can be achieved in terms of infrastructure. The variety of energy production methods allows adaptation to climatic or geographical conditions while simultaneously extracting energy. To achieve energy transformation, it is important not only to change the infrastructure but also to change the governance. Investment management based on industrial methods is no longer relevant, as the current aim is to involve society and protect the environment. The following data group consists of social and governance indicators that are significantly related to economic activity. It allows to ensure the profitability of the projects, the speed of execution, and the creation of a positive impact.

1.2 The Importance of ESG Indicators for Regional Energy Transformation

Investments in renewable energy are inseparable from the application of environmental, social, and governance (ESG) principles. This type of investment can assist with quoting green bonds for sustainable projects. It involves investment in companies and governments that the investor believes best holds values of importance to the investor. These include the environment, consumer protection, religious beliefs, employees' rights and human rights, among others. These areas of concern can be summarized as "Environmental, Social, and Governance" and is referred to as ESG investing (Environmental, Social, and Governance). In addition, Socially Responsible Investing includes shareholder advocacy and community investing [30]. ESG investments have attracted wider attention from both investors and customers worldwide. These investments largely follow a triple-bottom-line approach that combines financial returns with environmental and social norms. In addition, it emerges from the analysis that companies have performed relatively better in policy disclosure and governance parameters of ESG integration than in environmental and social factors [31]. Compliance with ESG criteria ensures that the investment project will fulfill social needs, be economically profitable, and protect the environment. The management dimension allows for the continuous, sustainable support of the investment in the future. ESG risk management is becoming an increasingly important aspect of the economic agenda. In order to secure public trust and orderly revenue growth, an ESG component is included in risk assessment plans. ESG risk is currently one of the leading risks in terms of its impact and probability of occurrence. Practical actions to reduce ESG (Environmental, Social, and Governance) risk are necessary because the link between ESG risk and financial performance has been documented [32]. Recently, ESG application actions are clearly visible in the energy sector. This sector is going through two transformations—infrastructural and corporate. It creates the conditions for qualified business model development.

To assess the influence of ESG on energy transformation, it is necessary to distinguish the responsibilities of the energy sector. The energy sector is on the path of decarbonization—investments are being made in clean environment solutions, while creating new areas of activity. It is a global trend. The information presented in Table 1.1 confirms that the implementation of these components significantly contributes to the development of ESG. However, these indicators are quite difficult to measure and express numerically—only some indicators are suitable for objective assessment.

Previous studies by Baran et al. [33] have examined different alternatives for ESG assessment. It is generally agreed that the application of ESG principles ensures ethical and environmental interests for future generations. The management component enables the development of human resource intelligence, thereby increasing economic performance and social impact [34]. The need for the environmental, social, and governance-firm value (ESG-FV) relationship is gaining momentum in Asia, as investors believe that firms following sustainable practices are good for value creation in the long run [35]. This is especially important when it comes to strategic planning and risk management. The energy sector is one of the most important users of ESG principles, as the sector is undergoing transformation. Business integration with the internal and external world is gaining momentum in the light of Environment, Social, and Governance factors (ESG score) linking to corporate financial performance (CFP). However, the impact of the ESG–CFP relationship varies across economies, industries, and institutional frameworks due to

Table 1.1 Areas of responsibility in energy sector [33]

Social responsibility	Environmental responsibility	Economic responsibility
1. Personnel's welfare, skills, and motivation 2. Open interaction with stakeholders 3. The quality of energy supply 4. Good business practices and cooperation with the stakeholders, networking with other companies 5. The correct price for energy	1. Measuring environmental impact 2. Awareness and reduction of environmental impacts of energy production and transfer 3. Minimization of use of fossil fuels 4. Reduction of pollution and emissions 5. Development of renewable sources 6. Controlling systems for waste and pollution	1. Cost-effective operations 2. Fair prices and good service 3. Investing in new technologies 4. Reliability of energy supply 5. Financial risk management

varying legal, social structures and expectations from stakeholders [36]. This is especially visible when comparing developed and developing countries. ESG (environmental, social, and governance) factors have, in recent decades, gained attention from different investors and investment strategies. As a result, asset managers are considering and incorporating the financial materiality of ESG factors (including environmental factors, such as risk of climate change, greenhouse gas emissions, biodiversity, and pollution of water and waste; social factors, such as human rights and safety in the workplace; and governance factors, such as ethics, bribery, and corruption) in the investment management process [37]. However, this strategy has so far been applied mostly at the private or public level. At the level of municipalities, where there is a lack of qualified human resources, these ideas hardly make their way. This situation is continuous—the application of ESG requires constant monitoring, accountability to social partners, and the application of the latest environmental protection ideas. It requires constant financial resources and control. Smaller municipalities often do not consistently implement the necessary actions, which is why they avoid ESG projects. However, the application of ESG in the case of renewable energy would ensure a reduction in environmental pollution and an increase in the income of the local population. The most straightforward motivation for ESG investing comes from a preference function that loads positively on the goals of a given ESG fund [38]. ESG also forms the prerequisites for the longevity of companies. The sustainable development spheres are interconnected to create a circular value chain of supply in the company [39]. Balancing positions creates the greatest positive impact on the environment and society.

In the previous works of researchers, an ESG index was created, with the help of which possible investment risks are assessed when investing in this type of companies. This index can also be used to assess the possibilities of investing in harmonious business units as an alternative direction of investment. Authors segmented the detailed dependence structures into four groups (ESG/The Wilder Hill New Energy Global Innovation Index; ESG/The Wilder Hill Clean Energy Index; ESG/The S&P Global Clean Energy Index; ESG/The European Renewable Energy Total Return Index) and compare their performances compared with merely investing in the renewable energy index (as the current renewable energy index fund/ETF). Overall, the results suggest that investors could trust the ESG index in hedging investment risk and increasing the profitability level in fund management [40]. However, the ESG index cannot fully assess the element of transformation when aiming to orient the energy system towards self-sufficient production using renewable resources. Saygili et al. [41] conducted research to investigate the correlations between certain topical phenomena. The results showed that there was a positive correlation between stakeholder-oriented governance practices and financial performance measures, such as accounting measures for both financial and non-financial companies. Besides, shareholder protection policies have a negative impact on accounting performance measures, especially for non-financial industries, while the corporate practices that are referred to board of directors and public disclosure vary between financial and non-financial entities. Balanced management of energy companies will speed up energy transformation, as expanded competences will allow municipalities to make the necessary decisions. Improving governance based on ESG principles will both save monetary resources and increase the pace of transformation.

Based on the collected scientific information, clear weaknesses in information evaluation have been identified. There is a lack of research that would enable the evaluation of organic production volumes, sustainable use of the environment in agriculture, and the management of municipal enterprises. It creates a situation where the results of the conducted research are superficial, focused on quantitative assessment, thus excluding important qualitative aspects. The following data groups are distinguished, which are relevant for the evaluation of energy transformation in terms of social/environmental aspects:

- Number of employees in the renewable energy sector in the regions
- Production of biological fertilizers
- Number of boards in municipal companies
- Approval of ESG plans in municipal companies
- Areas of organic farms, ha

In conclusion, the application of ESG criteria is inseparable from the success of the implementation of energy transformation. The application of ESG principles enables the implementation of projects that would allow the production of green energy at the lowest costs. This is a huge difference compared to fossil fuels or nuclear power, where projects can take decades and exceed planned budgets. An example of energy transformation in the heat sector is Lithuania, which created a completely new biomass energy sector in a couple of years. In 2022, economic and political unrest created an incentive to invest in other types of energy as well, strengthening electricity production. In both cases, the intentions of the regions to progress by initiating new activities that are important for the climate and social structure have a huge influence.

1.3 Lithuanian Case Study Analysis

The need for an initial analysis includes a case study. This was necessary to be able to identify the initial trends that merit analysis. At present, the allocation of resources for renewable energy development is uneven and fragmented. The clarification of the directions based on current successful examples of development would allow a model to be developed that could be applied to a wider range of countries and regions.

The results of the study are significantly related to the analysis of the Lithuanian sample. Changes made in the heat energy sector during the global financial crisis (2008–2011) significantly increased energy self-sufficiency and reduced the level of social problems (Fig. 1.3). However, there are some problems with electricity production. Lithuania's electricity generation is predominantly fueled by natural gas, with a smaller portion coming from renewable sources such as wind, solar, and

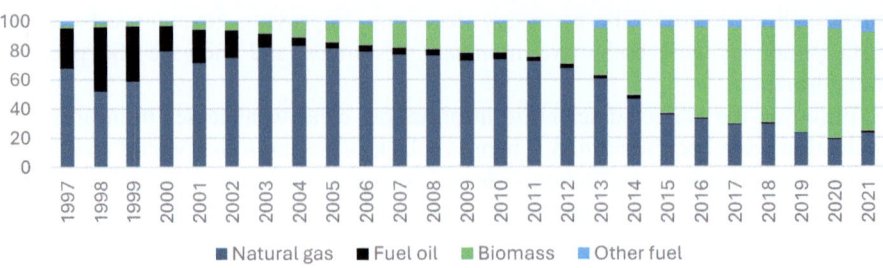

Fig. 1.3 Lithuanian heat energy balance 1997–2021 [42]

hydropower. The country has significant potential for wind energy, particularly in offshore wind farms in the Baltic Sea, and several large-scale wind energy projects are currently under development. Lithuania has made significant progress in improving energy efficiency in recent years, particularly in the building sector. The country has implemented energy efficiency standards for buildings and has invested in retrofitting older buildings to improve their energy efficiency.

Lithuania was heavily reliant on energy imports, particularly from Russia. To reduce its dependence on Russian energy, the country has diversified its energy sources, investing in renewable energy and building interconnections with neighboring countries to facilitate energy trade. Lithuania's energy policy is focused on achieving energy independence and reducing greenhouse gas emissions. The government has set ambitious targets for renewable energy and energy efficiency and has implemented policies such as feed-in tariffs and energy performance standards to incentivize the adoption of renewable energy and energy-efficient technologies.

The country has a history of nuclear energy, with the Ignalina Nuclear Power Plant being a major source of electricity until its closure in 2009. The government has expressed interest in developing a new nuclear power plant, but this has been met with opposition from environmental groups and concerns over the cost and safety of nuclear energy. However, the government has set a goal of achieving 100% renewable energy by 2050, and significant investments are being made in renewable energy sources such as wind, solar, and biomass.

The country's transition to renewable energy sources was catalyzed by actions taken in the past. The negative example is the abolishment of district heating (DH) networks after independence. At that time, the price for heating using gas boilers was much higher than that for individual gas boilers. A massive reconstruction project was done by replacing DH with individual natural gas and electric boilers. However, the development of this plan has turned against users, because after a decade, price for natural gas and oil has increased dramatically and consumers have started to reconstruct natural gas heating systems and replace gas boilers with biomass boilers [43]. This millennium has seen clear progression in the use of biomass. One can notice that significant progress has been achieved in implementing renewable energy systems (RES) and energy efficiency improvement targets by all Baltic countries. For example, in Lithuania, the use of biomass doubled during 2004–2013 [44]. Almost all the fuel used to produce energy is local—wood and industrial waste extracted from forests, soilless areas, and the wood industry were used. This situation made it possible not only to manage waste, but also to turn it into a product with financial value. The need to convert the country's energy system significantly served the breakthrough of biomass utilization in Lithuania. The reasons for the conversion to biomass were unambiguous. Such results seem to be logical, as a biomass power plant using renewable energy sources plays an important role in ensuring the country's autonomy in the energy generation potential, and these technologies are efficient and attractive from the environment protection point of view [45]. The country's need to switch to cheaper fuel in this case was perfectly aligned with the goals of sustainable development. During this period, biomass is the main renewable source used for energy production in Lithuania. Štreimikienė et al. [46] studied the effect of using different fuels on electricity production. The results of the conducted research showed that the lowest electricity generation costs are for new nuclear power plants followed by biomass and hydro power plants. Otherwise, the biomass could also be used to fulfill other needs of industry and citizens. Wood and biofuel are two most perspective fuels of renewable energy potential [47]. The national energy independence strategy contains clear principles where the Lithuanian energy system must be improved. The development of RES in Lithuania must be carried out in accordance with the following principles [48]:

- Gradual integration of RES in the market
- Affordability and transparency
- Proactive participation of energy users

The Lithuanian energy system has achieved great progress in the field of heat production. However, there is a lack of electricity production capacity, and the potential of biogas is also underutilized. The development of renewable energy resources encourages the adoption of complex solutions that would allow combining energy production capacities. This paves the way for a fundamental transformation of the energy sector. When exploring the possibilities of transformation, first, cooperation is done with innovative Lithuanian municipalities, which tend to follow the path of transformation. In this way, objective criteria will be approved, which will later allow comparing municipalities with each other.

The primary research actions are conducted based on the "research by design" formula. In this case, it builds on good practice from previous research, while identifying key areas for improvement. The selected data groups will enable the creation of a database, which will enable the comparison of the regions of the countries. Research by design is any kind of inquiry in which design is a substantial part of the research process. In research by design, the design process forms a pathway through which new insights, knowledge, practices, and products come into being. Research by design generates critical inquiry through design work that may include realized projects, proposals, possible realities, and alternatives. Research by design produces forms of output and discourse proper to disciplinary practice, verbal and non-verbal that make it discussable, accessible, and useful to peers and others [49]. In the case of energy transformation research, knowledge will be collected about the resources available to municipalities, the possibilities to manage projects, and information on loans and borrowing. Energy systems are changing, and it is important to quantify and assess those variations, measuring the progress toward the established goals. Indicators can be a useful tool to achieve that purpose. Indicators can analyze energy systems globally, such as the energy mix for a given country, considering the different sources of energy: fossil (fuel, coal, and gas), nuclear, biofuels and waste, renewable (hydro, solar, wind, geothermal, etc.), or parts of the energy system (renewable energy sources). Another indicator is energy dependence, which is important because it can significantly affect the development of countries since it increases their vulnerability to price instability and supply ruptures. Share of renewable energy in the gross final energy consumption is an important indicator since it can represent the pathway to lower carbon energy systems [50]. At the same time, specific solutions will be sought to achieve a positive impact on energy with the lowest costs. Finally, the investment plans of municipally run companies will be reviewed in order to bring them closer to the principles of sustainable development.

A team of researchers are currently cooperating with four Lithuanian municipalities, which are provided with consultations on energy transformation issues. Communication was carried out in February–December 2022. During the consultations, specific transformation plans are drawn up, which include specific solutions that promote the growth of green energy. This is related to increasing the efficiency of asset utilization, applying new technologies, and improving governance in municipal enterprises. At the same time, the main disturbances in the transformation process, which prevent municipalities from accelerating the pace of change, are analyzed. The disturbances will later be standardized to find correlations between municipalities. This will be followed by an assessment of the impact of disruptions in monetary terms, as well as the impact of certain transformation decisions on individual territories. When drawing up transformation plans, there is communication with the management of the municipal administration, the boards of municipally managed companies, and public associations. This is aimed at extracting the expectations of all interested parties, then evaluating them according to economic, social, and environmental logic. The initial results revealed the main aspects of the energy transformation analysis, as well as the main obstacles to the development of green energy in municipalities.

1.4 Identification of Research Indicators

Energy transformation implies major changes both in the municipal infrastructure and in changing public life. In order to achieve optimal investments, it is necessary for institutions, financiers, and society to focus on a common goal. The energy transformation in Lithuania is hindered due to the lack of cooperation between science and business, low competences of the public sector, and the influence of interest groups. Working with innovative municipalities and company boards allows applying scientific knowledge to strengthening regions and solving social problems. At the same time, it allows for the identification of the main directions of change,

1.4 Identification of Research Indicators

which can later be used to promote the development of economically weaker municipalities.

The first discussions with stakeholders formed the problem of the situation. There is a clear divide between the previous, post-Soviet management and the new corporate culture. The latter enables all employees to propose relevant ideas, the decision-making process is decentralized, and the influence of the board is proactive, promoting progress. This is fundamentally different from centralized, post-Soviet governance, where the assumptions of corruption are possible. During the discussions, indicators were singled out that will allow us to assess the current state of the municipality, as well as the prospects for transforming unused assets into sources of energy production. Municipal companies are engaged in the following services, which are relevant in the energy transformation process:

- Heat production
- Water supply and sewage treatment
- Transportation of passengers by bus
- Waste management
- Housing and environmental care

In principle, all these areas either use or have the potential to use renewable resources. Some sectors generate waste that can be used as fuel (wastewater treatment, waste management, environmental care). This situation makes it possible to search for joint activities and carry out circular economic activities in the municipality. Since these companies are made up of municipal capital, proper corporate governance is a prerequisite for the success of the processes. The problems of the management of municipal enterprises formed the initial assumptions of the research. The main directions of the researchers' assessment are related to the following aspects:

- How could companies, managed by municipalities, contribute to energy transformation?
- What synergies could be possible between the activities carried out in the municipality?
- How is organic waste generated in the municipality used?
- How could the management of municipal companies influence the pace of change?
- How are assets by the municipality and its companies used?

During communication with the municipalities, clear areas for improvement emerged, to which the management's attention and investments must be directed. These directions will allow generating the necessary data, thus creating a comparative base with other municipalities. All the municipalities investigated are managed by companies that are engaged in the previously mentioned communal activities. Management of municipal activities allows obtaining standardized answers about the prevailing situation in municipalities. When studying the municipalities of Lithuania, the main problem was encountered:

- Assets of municipalities related to energy activities are managed through municipal companies. While studying these companies, it was noticed that some of the companies do not have a board. This reduces the accountability of company managers and creates conditions for inefficient project management or corruption. The absence of boards stifles innovation, creating the risk of a slower pace of change.
- Synergies between water treatment and heat production companies are not yet sufficiently exploited. The resulting dried sewage sludge is not sufficiently used as renewable fuel. In addition, not all sludge is properly dried, so it cannot be used either as fuel or as fertilizer
- The municipality has not always approved specific plans, which areas are priority for the development of renewable energy
- The majority of municipalities do not undertake energy efficiency projects that would allow them to produce electricity independently, as well as heat-saving projects that are implemented at a slow pace
- There is not enough synergy between private and public business, e.g., biogas from agricultural waste is not used for city buses or heat production and supply.

1.5 Determination of Energy Transformation Priorities in the Regions

Complex challenges are faced to transform regional energy systems. In one case, it is necessary to secure the necessary financing for the installation of new facilities. Otherwise, human competences are required for the successful implementation of projects. However, the most important component of energy transformation is prioritization. Resource constraints make it difficult to complete all the necessary projects at once. Mitigation scenarios focusing on wind and solar power are more effective in reducing human health impacts compared to those with low renewable energy, while inducing a more pronounced shift away from fossil and toward mineral resource depletion. Conversely, non-climate ecosystem damages are highly uncertain but tend to increase, chiefly due to land requirements for bioenergy [51]. In working with municipalities, the following main priorities were established in the tactical period (1–3 years):

- Changing management structures (professional boards with a majority of independent members)
- Approval of energy transformation plans
- Electricity production for own needs is increased up to 100%
- Solar power parks are being created to serve municipal entities
- Specific energy transformation plans are being developed in the heat, water, and utility sector

The impact of renewable energy is unique in that the first steps can be taken already in the tactical period. This applies to the assessment of solar energy—the design of solar parks is much simpler than in the case of wind, biomass, or biogas. In this case, a stable supply of equipment, land, or a roof is required. In Lithuania, in 2022, a solar park on the roof, including the necessary permits, is installed in an average of 9 months [52]. Currently, half of the examined municipalities are engaged in the use of solar energy either for their own needs or in the implementation of solar park projects. The change in the situation was prompted by the increase in electricity prices, when in 2022 in May, the price of electricity per MW on the NordPool Spot exchange was EUR 400. At the same time, the hourly price record was reached—4000 EUR/MWh [53]. The actions of the municipalities to control the sudden rise in prices were quite limited due to the lack of free monetary funds. The behavior of municipal enterprises differed due to the type of boards. In the case of political trust boards, action was significantly slower than in professional boards with independent members. In the latter case, specific actions were taken:

- Ordinances have been established to ensure the permeability of electricity networks in the case of new solar power plants
- To finance new solar power plants by selling unnecessary assets not used in the main activity
- Carry out energy efficiency projects, identifying energetically inefficient activity chains

These specific actions have created a dual effect. First, it made it possible to increase the energy independence of companies, while saving the financial resources of shareholders—municipalities. These could have been directed towards the solution of social problems, covering part of the electricity prices for budgetary institutions. Second, the energy difficulties made it possible to review the asset structures of companies, discarding unnecessary assets that were not realized for unknown reasons. This made it possible to mobilize funds and order the components needed for solar power plants. IQ of 2023. The studied municipalities have 700 kW power generation capacity, which allows to produce 750,000 kWh of electricity. Currently, projects are being initiated that would increase the solar energy production capacity by another 3 MW. The use of electricity is most relevant in water treatment companies, which need electricity to service sewage treatment plants and ensure water supply. Due to a sharp increase in electricity prices, all Lithuanian water supply companies in 2022 became unprofitable [54]. Currently, in three of the analyzed municipalities, the installation of solar power plants on the roofs of buildings is being considered. In one municipality, it is planned to install power plants in water production lands where there are large areas of unused land.

Currently, several municipally managed companies have set goals either to produce 100% of the required electricity or to acquire a remote solar park that would meet part or all of the energy needs. At the same time, the possibilities of asset conversion are constantly being investigated, realizing assets that are not needed in the main activity. Synergies with other municipal companies are being sought by combining activities (common waste collection, hot water production, etc.).

During the tactical period, energy transformation actions can be implemented particularly smoothly. Due to the smooth design process and fast delivery of components, the development of solar power plants is significantly faster compared to other types of renewable or fossil fuels. Further stages of the energy transformation include wider infrastructure conversion and better utilization of waste. These processes require significantly longer time, especially due to design and bureaucratic constraints. The latter are related to both municipal and state restrictions, inefficient bureaucratic process.

In the strategic period (approximately 5 years), after properly exploiting the opportunities to expand solar energy, necessary decisions related to better utilization of municipal assets are needed. The discussions envisage the pursuit of complex actions—not only the development of infrastructure, but also the increase of operational efficiency. For that purpose, it is planned to expand the scope of hybrid work, to reduce the number of buildings used in the activity. Funds received for excess premises can be used to strengthen energy independence.

Lithuania has a strong biomass processing sector, which concentrates the entire supply chain from biomass processing to the production of biomass power plants. However, there is a relatively small number of cogeneration power plants in Lithuania. In strengthening energy self-sufficiency, it is necessary to develop biomass cogeneration capacities in medium-sized cities (> 20,000 inhabitants). The cycle of biomass power plants is 15–25 years. The peak of biomass energy development in Lithuania was in 2010–2012. Working with municipal companies made it possible to clarify priorities when investing in heat production. The aim is to turn central biomass power plants into cogeneration plants capable of producing heat and electricity at the same time. This would make it possible to reduce the electricity production problems prevailing in Lithuania, while at the same time making better use of biomass.

In addition to the heat production sector, which is relatively developed, the focus is on the further development of other sectors. In the strategic period, it is necessary to increase the contribution of municipal enterprises to the implementation of the European Green Deal. The task plan is established based on communication with municipalities. The financial plan will be determined in future research, when data on potential operating income and incurred costs will be collected. The following challenges of the strategic period have been identified:

- Utilization of synergistic effects (combining different technologies, production of several types of energy, and governance transformations)
- Adaptation of the heat sector to clean production
- Adaptation of water treatment facilities for sludge preparation
- Reorganization of the transport system using biomethane, hydrogen, and other sustainable fuels
- Development of the waste collection mechanism, including food waste
- Modernization of lighting systems
- Application of geothermal heating combined with solar energy
- Appropriate use of electrical power

Exploitation of synergistic effects is associated with better utilization of energy resources. Currently, one municipality is working on a pilot project in which sewage sludge and urban green waste would be treated in one facility. The extracted biogas would be converted into biomethane, which is then used for city buses. The remaining dried sewage sludge would be used either for fertilizing land areas or as fuel for the only cement factory in Lithuania, replacing coal. In the latter case, the use of fossil coal in Lithuania would be reduced to a minimum. The wider use of sludge as a renewable fuel requires the improvement of legal acts in Lithuania. Likely, different opinions will not be avoided until generally accepted strategic goals can mobilize various stakeholders and unify justification for the transition towards a sustainable energy sector [55].

Another important segment of changes is the improvement of lighting systems in municipalities by installing LED lighting solutions. Several municipalities in Lithuania apply the ESCO model, which allows the modernization of city lighting systems with private funds. An investment contract is concluded between the municipality and a private investor, which stipulates that the municipality will pay the investor the difference between the electricity price paid and the savings received during a certain period. The investor undertakes investing in municipal lighting systems by installing LED solutions. In this case, energy savings are achieved, thus enabling the installation of smaller power generation capacities.

In addition, it is necessary to develop charging stations for electric cars, using the free power available in the networks at a certain moment. When installing LED lighting, it is possible to install devices on lighting poles that would provide the opportunity to charge a car in a parking lot, on the streets, near public buildings, etc. This would make it possible to make better use of the electricity network and reduce excess investments in increasing the power of certain selected objects. Power management would be done with the help of software. In Lithuania, this technology has already started to be implemented in the capital city of Vilnius, when the power of offices or lighting poles is used with the help of software at a time when this power is not used for the main activity [56].

In order to achieve further synergistic effects, it is necessary to make waste collection more efficient, by producing solid recovered fuel from solid waste and extracting biomethane from biological waste. Solid recovered fuel is suitable for waste incineration power plants. Of course, to achieve the principles of sustainable development, it is necessary to ensure the largest possible volumes of waste processing. In addition, it is necessary for Lithuania to use the potential of geothermal energy. Lithuania is characterized by large geothermal water resources. In Western Lithuania, geothermal water resources up to a depth of 2 km in the mentioned area amount to 1450 EJ [57]. A combination of geothermal energy and solar energy can produce large amounts of green energy for households. By utilizing the available resources, municipalities can fully supply urban areas with energy. In addition, with economic and practical incentives, municipal residents living in non-urbanized areas can switch to using clean and ecological solutions.

Data analytics is a key factor in achieving rationality in the energy transformation process. Determining clear investment directions allows faster implementation of energy transformation ideas. The focus on public sector companies was chosen because it is these companies that can mobilize public resources and initiate the necessary changes. Private entities naturally choose investments with the highest profitability and lowest costs, which become profitable in the shortest possible period. To fundamentally transform the region's energy system, it is necessary to assess the situation comprehensively. This will require significant time and one-time financial resources. For this reason, the municipal government must initiate changes that will be implemented through municipal companies. The primary task is the reorganization of their internal structures and inventory of assets. Later, to achieve a greater economic effect, the municipality can transfer unused assets to them, which would later be converted into energy production, storage, or saving units.

The initial assessment of investments is inseparable from the transformation of municipal enterprises. The changing technological situation suggests that municipal enterprises should be much better integrated. Different utilities have common directions that can be combined with each other. One of the best examples is the synergy of the water from heat farms. In the heating sector, hot water is produced using water purchased from water sector companies. Today's technologies allow the exploitation of heat from wastewater, which is later redistributed to heat networks. It makes sense to combine the activities of these companies. During sewage treatment, the formed sludge releases gases. This gas may be suitable for city buses. Utility companies can provide the materials needed to produce gas. With the right technologies, green waste can be mixed with sludge. Meanwhile, waste suitable for incineration can be utilized in thermal power plants. The use of solar energy for electricity production is acceptable to all parties. The synergy map in Fig. 1.4

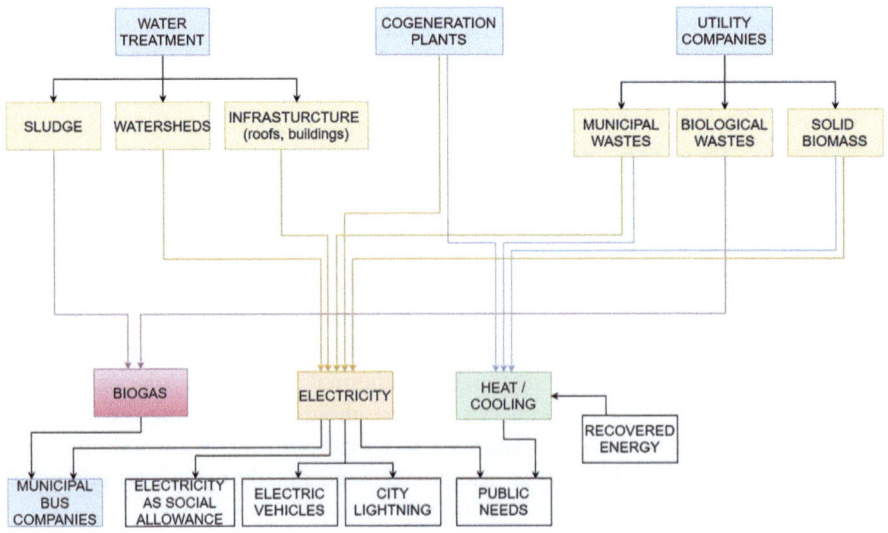

Fig. 1.4 Map of synergies between municipal companies

creates the conditions to highlight the main areas of municipal business in the regions, while also identifying areas of cooperation. This allows better use of local resources, monetary savings, and the creation of new businesses.

The primary objectives of the energy transformation identified enable regions and the companies they manage to seize the opportunity to create new economic activity. Positive examples from public companies can encourage private companies in the regions to upgrade their energy systems, thus contributing to local decarbonization. In this context, the State has a responsibility to ensure the smooth operation and development of the grid in cases of power shortages. Resource and time constraints make it necessary to identify not only areas for development, but also the regions with the greatest problems in terms of energy structure. This action is what is being done in the next stages of the study.

References

1. Bazan-Krzywoszańska, A., Skiba, M., Mrówczyńska, M., Sztubecka, M., Bazuń, D., & Kwiatkowski, M. (2018). Green energy in municipal planning documents. In *E3S web of conferences* (Vol. 45, p. 00006). EDP Sciences.
2. European Commission. (2020). *Proposal for a regulation of the European Parliament and of the council establishing the just transition fund; COM/2020/22 final*. European Commission.
3. Popescu, C., Hysa, E., Kruja, A., & Mansi, E. (2022). Social innovation, circularity and energy transition for environmental, social and governance (ESG) practices—A comprehensive review. *Energies, 15*(23), 9028.
4. Piccinetti, L., Rezk, M. R. A., Kapiel, T. Y., Salem, N., Khasawneh, A., Santoro, D., & Sakr, M. M. (2023). Circular bioeconomy in Egypt: The current state, challenges, and future directions. *Insights into Regional Development, 5*, 97–112.
5. Pilusa, T. J., & Muzenda, E. (2014, April 15–16). Municipal solid waste utilisation for green energy in gauteng province-South Africa: A review. In *Proceedings of the International Conference on Chemical, Integrated Waste Management & Environmental Engineering (ICCIWEE'2014), Johannesburg, South Africa*, pp. 174–179.
6. Zulkifli, A. A., Mohd Yusoff, M. Z., Abd Manaf, L., Zakaria, M. R., Roslan, A. M., Ariffin, H., et al. (2019). Assessment of municipal solid waste generation in Universiti Putra Malaysia and its potential for green energy production. *Sustainability, 11*(14), 3909.
7. Johari, A., Ahmed, S. I., Hashim, H., Alkali, H., & Ramli, M. (2012). Economic and environmental benefits of landfill gas from municipal solid waste in Malaysia. *Renewable and Sustainable Energy Reviews, 16*(5), 2907–2912.
8. Cała, M., Szewczyk-Świątek, A., & Ostręga, A. (2021). Challenges of coal mining regions and municipalities in the face of energy transition. *Energies, 14*(20), 6674.
9. Anthony Jnr, B. (2020). Smart city data architecture for energy prosumption in municipalities: Concepts, requirements, and future directions. *International Journal of Green Energy, 17*(13), 827–845.
10. Bogdanov, D., Ram, M., Aghahosseini, A., Gulagi, A., Oyewo, A. S., Child, M., et al. (2021). Low-cost renewable electricity as the key driver of the global energy transition towards sustainability. *Energy, 227*, 120467.
11. Guarieiro, L. L., Anjos, J. P. D., Silva, L. A. D., Santos, A. Á., Calixto, E. E., Pessoa, F. L., et al. (2022). Technological perspectives and economic aspects of green hydrogen in the energetic transition: Challenges for chemistry. *Journal of the Brazilian Chemical Society, 33*(8), 844–869.

12. Adawiyah, W. R., Rahajuni, D., & Kadarwati, N. (2022). Economic growth and environmental degradation paradox in ASEAN: A simultaneous equation model with dynamic panel data approach. *Environmental Economics, 13*(1), 171.
13. Makarenko, I., Bilan, Y., Štreimikienė, D., & Rybina, L. (2023). Investments support for sustainable development goal 7: Research gaps in the context of post-COVID-19 recovery. *Investment Management and Financial Innovations, 20*(1), 151–173.
14. Boros, A., Lentner, C., Nagy, V., & Tőzsér, D. (2023). Perspectives by green financial instruments – A case study in the Hungarian banking sector during COVID-19. *Banks and Bank Systems, 18*(1), 116–126.
15. Tsaurai, K. (2022). Effect of foreign direct investment on domestic investment in BRICS. *Investment Management and Financial Innovations, 19*(4), 260–273.
16. Al-Faryan, M. A. S. (2022). Nexus between corruption, market capitalization, exports, FDI, and country's wealth: A pre-global financial crisis study. *Problems and Perspectives in Management, 20*, 224–237.
17. Tite, O., Ogundipe, O. M., Ogundipe, A. A., & Akinde, M. A. (2022). Analysis of foreign capital inflows and stock market performance in Nigeria. *Investment Management & Financial Innovations, 19*(4), 51.
18. Dar, J. A., & Asif, M. (2018). Does financial development improve environmental quality in Turkey? An application of endogenous structural breaks based cointegration approach. *Management of Environmental Quality: An International Journal, 29*(2), 368–384.
19. Ike, G. N., Usman, O., Alola, A. A., & Sarkodie, S. A. (2020). Environmental quality effects of income, energy prices and trade: The role of renewable energy consumption in G-7 countries. *Science of the Total Environment, 721*, 137813.
20. Streimikiene, D. (2022). Renewable energy technologies in households: Challenges and low carbon energy transition justice. *Economics and Sociology, 15*(3), 108–120.
21. Streimikiene, D. (2022). Energy poverty and impact of COVID-19 pandemics in Visegrad (V4) countries. *Journal of International Studies, 15*(1), 9–25.
22. Endri, E., Hania, B. T., & Ma'ruf, A. (2022). Corporate green Sukuk issuance for sustainable financing in Indonesia. *Environmental Economics, 13*(1), 38.
23. Bertrand, N. A. S., & Etienne, K. L. (2022). Increasing the productivity of manufacturing firms in Cameroon in a sustainable way: Renewable or non-renewable energy? *Environmental Economics, 13*(1), 28.
24. Kirikkaleli, D., & Adebayo, T. S. (2021). Do renewable energy consumption and financial development matter for environmental sustainability? New global evidence. *Sustainable Development, 29*(4), 583–594.
25. Alsmadi, A. A., Alrawashdeh, N., Al-Gasaymeh, A., Al-Malahmeh, H., & Moh'd Al-hazimeh, A. (2023). Impact of business enablers on banking performance: A moderating role of Fintech. *Banks and Bank Systems, 18*(1), 14–25.
26. Lantara, D. (2022). Indonesian Islamic banks: A review of the financial state before and after the COVID-19 pandemic. *Business Perspectives, 17*(4), 12–24.
27. Naumenkova, S., Mishchenko, V., & Mishchenko, S. (2022). Key energy indicators for sustainable development goals in Ukraine. *Problems and Perspectives in Management, 20*(1), 379–395.
28. Ginevičius, R. (2022). The efficiency of municipal waste management systems in the environmental context in the countries of the European Union. *Journal of International Studies, 15*(4), 63–79.
29. Štreimikienė, D. (2021). Externalities of power generation in Visegrad countries and their integration through support of renewables. *Economics and Sociology, 14*(1), 89–102.
30. Hys, K. (2015, June 4–5). Respect index stock exchanges in Poland as the corporate social responsibility tool. In *Proceedings of the International Scientific Conference, Nitra, Slovakia*, pp. 119–126.
31. Sarangi, G. K. (2021). *Resurgence of ESG Investments in India: Toward a sustainable economy*. Asian Development Bank Institute.

References

32. Zioło, M., Bąk, I., & Spoz, A. (2023). Incorporating ESG risk in companies' business models: State of research and energy sector case studies. *Energies, 16*(4), 1809.
33. Baran, M., Kuźniarska, A., Makieła, Z. J., Sławik, A., & Stuss, M. M. (2022). Does ESG reporting relate to corporate financial performance in the context of the energy sector transformation? Evidence from Poland. *Energies, 15*(2), 477.
34. Xie, C. L. (2020). *Institutional investors, shareholder activism, and ESG in the energy sector* (Wharton research scholars). University of Pennsylvania.
35. Alsayegh, M. F., Abdul Rahman, R., & Homayoun, S. (2020). Corporate economic, environmental, and social sustainability performance transformation through ESG disclosure. *Sustainability, 12*(9), 3910.
36. Behl, A., Kumari, P. R., Makhija, H., & Sharma, D. (2022). Exploring the relationship of ESG score and firm value using cross-lagged panel analyses: Case of the Indian energy sector. *Annals of Operations Research, 313*(1), 231–256.
37. Kuzmina, J., Atstaja, D., Purvins, M., Baakashvili, G., & Chkareuli, V. (2023). In search of sustainability and financial returns: The case of ESG energy funds. *Sustainability, 15*(3), 2716.
38. Cohen, L., Gurun, U. G., & Nguyen, Q. H. (2020). *The ESG-innovation disconnect: Evidence from green patenting*. National Bureau of Economic Research.
39. Domanović, V. (2022). The relationship between ESG and financial performance indicators in the public sector: Empirical evidence from the Republic of Serbia. *Management: Journal of Sustainable Business and Management Solutions in Emerging Economies, 27*(1), 69–80.
40. Liu, G., & Hamori, S. (2020). Can one reinforce investments in renewable energy stock indices with the ESG index? *Energies, 13*(5), 1179.
41. Saygili, A. T., Saygili, E., & Taran, A. (2021). The effects of corporate governance practices on firm-level financial performance: Evidence from Borsa Istanbul Xkury companies. *Journal of Business Economics, 22*, 884–904.
42. Lithuanian District Heating Association (LDHA). (2021). *Šilumos Tiekimo Bendrovių 2020 Metų Ūkinės Veiklos Apžvalga*. Lietuvos Šilumos Tiekėjų Asociacija.
43. Klevas, V., Biekša, K., & Murauskaitė, L. (2014). Innovative method of RES integration into the regional energy development scenarios. *Energy Policy, 64*, 324–336.
44. Štreimikienė, D. (2016). Review of financial support from EU structural funds to sustainable energy in Baltic States. *Renewable and Sustainable Energy Reviews, 58*, 1027–1038.
45. Sliogeriene, J., Turskis, Z., & Streimikiene, D. (2013). Analysis and choice of energy generation technologies: The multiple criteria assessment on the case study of Lithuania. *Energy Procedia, 32*, 11–20.
46. Štreimikienė, D., Šliogerienė, J., & Turskis, Z. (2016). Multi-criteria analysis of electricity generation technologies in Lithuania. *Renewable Energy, 85*, 148–156.
47. Katinas, V., & Markevicius, A. (2006). Promotional policy and perspectives of usage renewable energy in Lithuania. *Energy Policy, 34*(7), 771–780.
48. Government of the Republic of Lithuania. (2018). *National energy independence strategy*. Government of the Republic of Lithuania.
49. Hauberg, J. (2011). Research by design: A research strategy. *Revista Lusófona de Arquitectura e Educação, 5*, 46–56.
50. Martins, F., Felgueiras, C., Smitkova, M., & Caetano, N. (2019). Analysis of fossil fuel energy consumption and environmental impacts in European countries. *Energies, 12*(6), 964.
51. Luderer, G., Pehl, M., Arvesen, A., Gibon, T., Bodirsky, B. L., De Boer, H. S., et al. (2019). Environmental co-benefits and adverse side-effects of alternative power sector decarbonization strategies. *Nature Communications, 10*(1), 5229.
52. Environmental Projects Management Agency. *Saulės Elektrinės Namų Ūkiuose*. https://www.apva.lt/saules-elektriniu-irengimas-namu-ukiuose/
53. NordPool Group. *Market data*. https://www.nordpoolgroup.com/en/Market-data1/Dayahead/Area-Prices/ALL1/Hourly/?view=table
54. BNS. *Vandens Įmonėms Prakalbus Apie Nuostolius, Jo Tiekimas Vartotojams Brangs*. https://www.bns.lt/topic/1912/news/66233633/

55. Genys, D., & Pažėraitė, A. (2022). Mapping Lithuanian transition towards sustainable energy: Sociological account on a waste-to-energy case. *Entrepreneurship and Sustainability Issues, 10*(2), 527.
56. Vilniaus Apšvietimas. *Vilniuje—Pirmosios Elektromobilių Įkrovimo Stotelės Nuo Apšvietimo Stulpo.* https://naujas.vilniausapsvietimas.lt/vilniuje-pirmosios-elektromobiliu-ikrovimo-stoteles-nuo-apsvietimo-stulpo-2/
57. Lithuanian Geological Survey. *Geoterminės Energijos Tyrimai.* https://www.lgt.lt/index.php?view=article&id=344:geotermines-energijos-tyrimai&catid=233/

Open Access This chapter is licensed under the terms of the Creative Commons Attribution-NonCommercial-NoDerivatives 4.0 International License (http://creativecommons.org/licenses/by-nc-nd/4.0/), which permits any noncommercial use, sharing, distribution and reproduction in any medium or format, as long as you give appropriate credit to the original author(s) and the source, provide a link to the Creative Commons license and indicate if you modified the licensed material. You do not have permission under this license to share adapted material derived from this chapter or parts of it.

The images or other third party material in this chapter are included in the chapter's Creative Commons license, unless indicated otherwise in a credit line to the material. If material is not included in the chapter's Creative Commons license and your intended use is not permitted by statutory regulation or exceeds the permitted use, you will need to obtain permission directly from the copyright holder.

Chapter 2
Practical Explorations for Energy Transformation Ways

2.1 The Potential of Energy System Conversion

In the twentieth century, the developed energy system was based on the use of fossil fuels, essentially without limiting the production of energy or the use of resources. In the twenty-first century, faced with serious challenges caused by climate change, the functioning of the energy system must be fundamentally changed. New concepts such as demand-side management and energy storage in batteries are emerging, and the need for energy system balancing has increased significantly. When looking for opportunities to implement energy transformation, the use of existing infrastructure can significantly contribute to the speed of implementation of the transformation.

The dynamics of the energy system are characterized by extensive connections between different methods of energy production. Renewable energy is no exception; there are clear examples of interaction. In the case of biogas, it can be used to produce electricity or heat, to fuel cars, or to supply main gas pipelines. The use of renewable resources makes it possible to create a multidirectional impact on different branches of business. Overall, the shift toward renewable energy sources can have a tangible impact on the economy by promoting workplace creation, reducing environmental costs, enhancing energy security, and fostering innovation and economic growth [1]. However, the specific economic effects can vary depending on factors such as government policies, market conditions, and the scale of renewable energy adoption.

One of the ways to increase the positive impact created by renewable energy is to search for relevant connections. Different types of fuel can be produced from one type of green energy, which would be used to supply the necessary aggregates. Figure 2.1 shows that interactions between different technologies can enable the energy system to operate dynamically in a competitive environment. In cases of overproduction in one energy sector, the energy produced can be transferred to

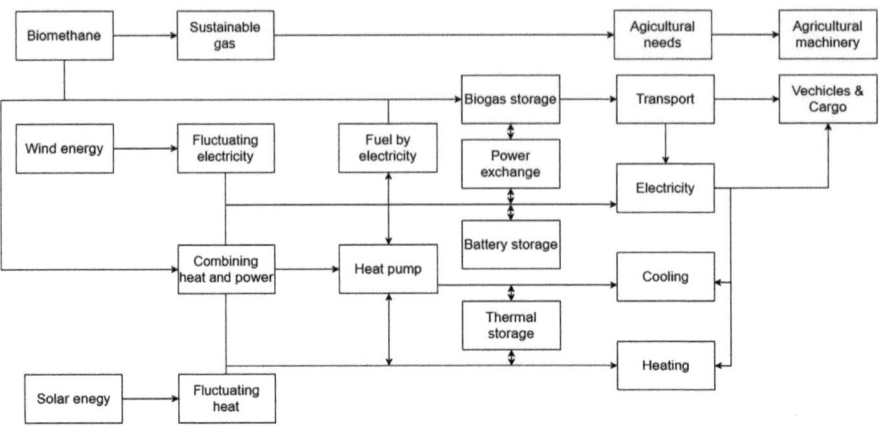

Fig. 2.1 Interaction between different technologies in the energy system

fulfill the needs of other sectors. The shaded boxes demonstrate the key technological changes required.

The potential of energy conversion is inseparable from successful political implementation. Political will is inevitably necessary to achieve the most effective implementation of transformation projects. When implementing policy decisions, potential synergies must be sought, as well as key factors that save taxpayers' funds. The policy decisions to accelerate the energy transition will need to be aligned with the development of enabling infrastructure. More attention is needed for emerging infrastructure issues such as smart charging of EVs, distribution grid reinforcements, and the role of shifting demand and smart grids. In addition, important synergies exist between higher energy efficiency and higher shares of renewable energy; both solutions should therefore be pursued jointly [2]. Due to the specifics of energy production, it is necessary to look at the transformation process in an extremely complex manner. When correcting one part of the energy system, it is necessary to consider other parts as well, since this can lead to the potential of saving energy and financial resources. Energy efficiency is inseparable from the success of the transformation process; infrastructure development to meet current needs is pointless and costs significant financial and time resources. Meanwhile, the negative consequences of climate change are already being felt. The expansion of renewable energies for power generation is a key element on the development path to combine low costs with low emissions. In the industrial sector, emission reductions in high-temperature heat generation exclusively require electrification, whereas for medium and especially low industrial heat generation, biomass can be a vital part of possible decarbonization pathways. In the transport sector, battery-powered passenger vehicles and electric overhead freight trucks are gradually replacing conventional combustion engines. The electrification of the transport sector is also reflected in the expansion of electric rail transport [3]. In the case of rail transport, greater synergies are possible—instead of sound-absorbing walls, vertical solar modules can be installed to provide energy to the railway system [4]. The reduction of pollution caused by industry and transport will essentially define the success of the energy system transformation process, since these sources of pollution have a particularly negative impact on the quality of the environment.

In addition, there are certain risks associated with implementing the energy transformation process. Conversion potential varies across countries and continents. This may hinder the faster development of the consumption of renewable resources, despite the positive political will. The need for conversion using existing assets is recognized at a global level. However, in order for decisions to be made smoothly, it is necessary to manage all the necessary processes. Clearly, the differences in energy conversion efficiency cannot be neglected. In some regions (e.g., Africa), such differences go up while the overall trend is downward. However, through the implementation of pertinent measures, there could still be scope to reach greater convergence toward a higher efficiency level in energy transformation [5]. Increasing energy efficiency would reduce the pressure on the budgets of countries and regions, while accelerating the pace of investment implementation. The importance of conversion is particularly visible in the international documents that have already been adopted. The Kyoto Protocol and the Paris Climate Change Agreement clearly regulate the actions that must be taken to avoid a climate catastrophe. The first period, according to which the achieved global progress of the energy transformation will be evaluated, is the year 2050. Today, the directions of the future transformation are already known. The energy system of the future will be based on electricity consumption. The greening of electricity production will be an essential condition for energy transformation. Figure 2.2 shows that, based on conservative estimates, the transformation of the electricity and heat sectors would ensure the implementation of the essential goals of the transformation. It is intended that these projects will be implemented under market conditions. A subsidy system was used for new projects at the beginning of this century. Today, the subsidy system is no longer such an effective tool, with negative effects in some cases. The system of feed-in tariffs stifles competition among renewable energy producers and creates perverse incentives to lock into existing technologies [7]. As there is clear opposition from countries developing conventional energy, the promotion of renewable energy can hold back projects. In addition, promotion directions may not necessarily be chosen for those technologies that would have the greatest positive impact on society. In order to develop new concepts, it is necessary to look for unused resources of state or regional enterprises, the conversion of which would allow the development of new innovations, especially in electricity production.

The necessity of energy transformation is presupposed by the fact that it is fundamentally necessary to stop using fossil fuels. For now, it is based on the hope that it will be possible to develop productive and cost-effective electricity generation technologies. This process can take decades, so today it is necessary to act "from below" by initiating regional changes. Energy transformation based on the use of renewable resources creates a clear and calculable impact on different economic structures. In this case, it is necessary not only to establish the directions of positive impact, but also to show solutions that allow for the practical benefits of using renewable energy.

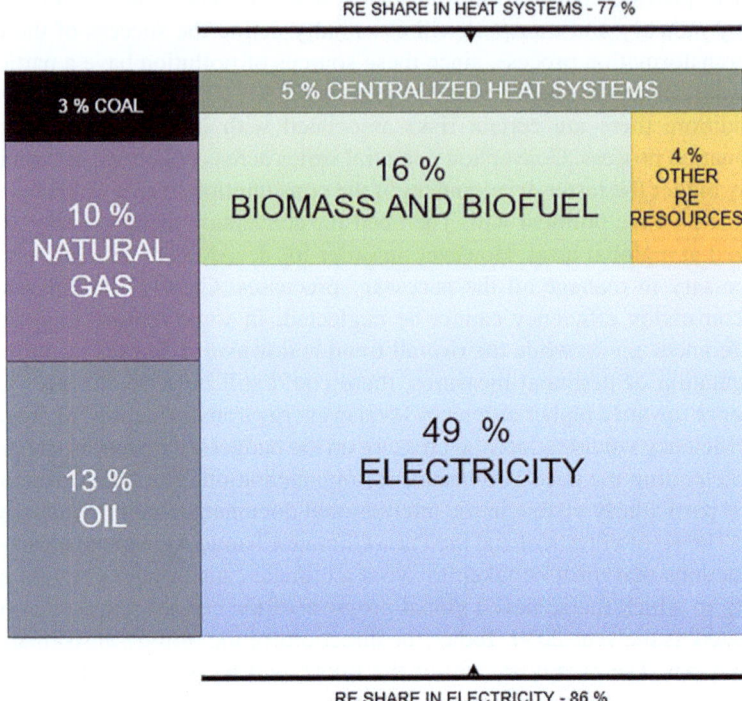

Fig. 2.2 Total final energy consumption breakdown by energy carrier (%) system, projected in 2050 [6]

2.2 Impact of Energy Transformation on Different Economic Directions

The use of renewable resources fundamentally changes the economic situation of countries and the competitive advantages that have arisen. Early innovation creates more synergistic effects that contribute to economic growth. The impact on the economy can be assessed both numerically and qualitatively. However, the current progress in renewable energy is insufficient due to the negative impact of climate change. In order to achieve a breakthrough in energy transformation, the possibilities of further strengthening the leading branches of energy must first be evaluated and only then engaged in the development of new concepts.

One of the main positive effects of renewable energy production is the creation of new jobs. Jobs in renewable energy are related to the maintenance of power plants, the supply and cultivation of biomass, the collection of biological waste, and the development of new technologies. Renewable energy technologies are significantly more complex than the technologies of thermal power plants and biomass boilers. Their development requires deep knowledge of human capital, as well as the work of scientific institutions. The impact on countries transitioning to renewable energy is assessed from various perspectives [8]. The contribution of renewable investment and job generation in the Czech Republic was investigated. The findings suggested the resilient dependence of employment enhancement on investment in the renewable industry of the Czech Republic. The Czech Republic is characterized by its own coal resources, but the country has a clear goal of transforming the energy system toward the use of renewable resources. Workplace creation within a country creates multi-scale impacts that are felt both regionally and nationally. Benefits occur when workers spend part of their income in the local economy, generating spin-off benefits known as the "multiplier effect." This increased spending creates economic activity (jobs and revenues) in other sectors such as retail, restaurants, leisure, and entertainment. The number of jobs also depends on how many stages of production are carried out in the region, as more jobs will be created if the materials and technologies are processed and manufactured locally [9]. Over time, the importance of workplace creation has increased as more opportunities have become available to produce energy at a competitive price. As the payback of new energy capacity accelerates, the pace of workplace creation has increased significantly. The largest workplace growth is recorded in the power plant design, construction, and maintenance sectors. The example of the Netherlands is also relevant for workplace creation. This country makes a significant contribution to environmental protection by developing new, climate-friendly technologies. Renewable energy has the potential to stimulate growth and jobs in the Dutch economy. Other scientists expect that an additional 0.85% of gross domestic product will be created by 2030 as a result of the shift toward a renewable energy mix, with the largest effect seen in investment growth. In terms of job creation, the projection is around 50,000 new full-time jobs by 2030. This positive impact is explained by the relatively higher labor and capital intensity of wind and solar technologies compared to gas and coal plants. This creates growth opportunities primarily for domestic, but not imported, products [10]. Also, countries that excel in renewable energy technology can export their expertise and products to the global market [11]. Trends increasing the use of renewable energy resources are visible around the world. Recently, the volume of production of components using renewable resources has increased rapidly in Asian countries. These countries have favorable conditions for renewable energy; the population is growing rapidly, and the existing energy system is not yet strong enough to meet the current needs of the population. Renewable energy in Asian countries is stimulating different directions. Gross fixed capital formation, renewable energy consumption, and the labor force are valid determinants of economic well-being in Malaysia. Renewable energy consumption enhances energy efficiency and encourages growth through upgraded technology transfer and resource distribution [12]. In the case of Malaysia, consistent decisions are being made to reduce the impact of fossil fuels while making better use of available local resources. The goal is to increase the use of solar energy by installing modules on buildings. This avoids the use of land for energy needs. Other Asian countries, especially China, have concentrated solar panel production capacities and competencies. The impact on the labor market is an important catalyst for the development of renewable energy and the energy transformation. The renewable energy sector creates a substantial number of workplaces in manufacturing, installation, maintenance, and research and development. These workplaces often offer stable employment opportunities and can stimulate local economies [13]. However, in certain countries, e.g., in coal-rich Poland, the energy transition has the potential to create a short-term decline in unskilled workplaces. Due to the avoidance of this condition, retraining solutions or the promotion of parallel businesses (biomass energy, agroforestry) are necessary [14].

The impact of renewable energy use can also be described using more general elements. One of the most important is the connection between renewable energy and economic growth. In order to justify the huge expenditure on renewable energy, the element of economic growth is one of the essential arguments. Several studies have been conducted that point to a general relationship between renewable energy and economic growth. In one case, the results provide evidence of the nonlinear impact of renewable energy consumption on economic development under different country risks (composite risk, political risk, financial risk, and economic risk). Countries with a lower composite risk have a more stable environment, and renewable energy consumption has a greater promotional effect on economic development. Similarly, a stable political environment helps renewable energy consumption play a larger role in promoting economic development [15]. An abstract conclusion is formed that there is a positive relationship between these two elements. In this study, the components of the political situation are distinguished. Politically unstable states can discredit energy transformation projects, thus undermining the development of this idea around the world. In other countries, combined studies have been conducted, investigating the synergy between different economic and social elements. In the case of Morocco, the overall figures for the economic impact on GDP range from 1.21% to 1.99% at the end of the forecasting period covered (2040), with a full-time equivalent employment effect of between 269,252 and 499,000 jobs. In conclusion, the alternative that produces the most benefits in terms of impact on GDP and employment growth would be the installation of windmills, whatever framework of exports and imports is observed [16]. Specific directions for energy transformation allow for better performance results. In the case of Morocco, energy production is possible both onshore and offshore. In the case of developed countries, similar studies have been carried out, which provide a general overview of the essential advantages of renewable energy. The cases of OECD countries also show clear causal relationships. Estimations indicate that a 1% increase in renewable energy consumption will increase GDP by 0.105% and GDP per capita by 0.100%, while a 1% increase in the share of renewable energy to the energy mix of the countries will increase GDP by 0.089% and GDP per capita by 0.090% [17]. Another aspect is related to environmental pollution from using biomass or other bioenergy products. It is not uncommon to try to justify the negative effects of using biomass because burning biomass releases CO_2 that was previously recorded in trees. In the case of biogas, CO_2 is also released, but it comes from burning the even more polluting methane gas. For the production of biomass, low-value wood is used, which does not have a high oxygen production potential. This situation makes it possible to obtain positive environmental and economic effects. The statistics illustrate that bioenergy production, biomass production, energy import, energy export, and economic development have a negative association with the carbon emissions of ASEAN countries. The results show that bioenergy production, biomass production, energy import, energy export, and economic development have a negative association with carbon emissions or a positive association with the environmental quality of the ASEAN countries [18]. The use of biomass is relevant in heat production, while biogas can be converted into different types of energy according to demand.

Combining energy transformation measures can significantly reduce the consequences of climate change while supporting economic growth. This fundamentally contradicts the hitherto prevailing narrative that only the use of fossil fuels can ensure satisfaction of economic needs. The lack of political will and the need for professional project management are holding back the breakthrough of renewable energy. At a time when it is necessary to focus resources as consistently as possible, primary research is essential. They must be focused on the problem points that, together, have the greatest potential for transformation. A clear focus on problem regions would allow resources to be concentrated, thereby maximizing economic, social, and environmental benefits.

2.3 Identification of Problematic Regions in the Context of Energy Transformation Activities

To explore the potential of the regions, data related to the current situation in the regions and prospects are used. The research is based on the principles of sustainable development, as it aims to base the impact of energy transformation on all these dimensions. First, data groups are selected that represent the energy and management activities taking place in the regions, as well as the opportunities to develop such activities on a larger scale (Table 2.1). The information presented in the table will allow to find out objective directions where it is possible to achieve the fastest positive impact by utilizing the resources available in the regions.

To assess the potential of regions, cluster analysis is used. During the analysis, the regions will be grouped according to the identified characteristics to explore their potential for the first stage of transformation. In this study, the clustering method will be able to effectively identify regions that have energy system problems. Based on this, short-term investment decisions can be made. Such regions require primary attention. The efficiency of identification is directly related to the quality of the selected indicators. Cluster analysis does not allow for econometric estimates but is designed to group objects in the space of selected indicators [27].

Table 2.1 Research indicators [19–26]

Social indicators	Environmental indicators	Economic indicators
Number of boards with independent members Approval of ESG plans of municipal companies	Forest coverage projects, ha Unused lands, ha Forestry sector incomes, thousand EUR Area of organic farms, ha Biomass potential, toe Sludge potential, t	Wind and solar power plants, MW Municipal wastes for energy needs, t. Free power in electricity grid, MW Biomass consumption, % Electricity production incomes, thousand EUR

Cluster analysis has a wide range of applications, depending on the available data and the purpose of using it. This is related to the specifics of cluster analysis. Clustering is the process of grouping a set of objects based on some similarity measure. Each group of partitioned objects is known as a cluster. The partitioning is performed by clustering algorithms. Clustering algorithms can be categorized into partitioning methods, hierarchical methods, grid-based methods, and density-based methods. Clustering techniques are widely used in data mining, information retrieval, classification, pattern recognition, data analysis, etc. [28]. In addition to these basic methods, there are several alternatives for performing cluster analysis. One of the main alternatives is K-means analysis, which helps group different elements into groups according to previously selected parameters. K-means clustering is a method that attempts to partition existing data into two or more groups. This method partitions data into groups (clusters) so that data with the same characteristics are included in the same cluster and different data are grouped into other clusters. The iterative concept of the FCM method is the same as the K-means method, which is based on minimizing the objective function [29]. The application of cluster analysis will enable the grouping of municipalities according to their possible energy transformation potential and speed, thus creating a basis for further transformation research.

Data from 60 Lithuanian municipalities are used for cluster analysis. According to the data in Table 1.1, which represents the main characteristics of municipal enterprises, the aim is to group municipalities in such a way that it is possible to identify directions of immediate impact. According to the wide data coverage, the objective direction of the primary transformation actions is determined since it focuses on those regions where the short-term potential will be the highest. Potential is assessed not only through physical indicators but also through governance and ESG dimensions. This will project the speed of implementation of changes and determine the reasons why changes are not happening at this time. The data analysis aims to identify the guiding directions where the energy transformation model should first be applied. After forming the core of the investigated municipalities, the main characteristics of the municipalities will be systematized. According to this, a universal energy transformation model will be developed, which will allow municipalities to move toward the use of renewable energy faster and more sustainably.

The purpose of the cluster analysis in this case is to identify the municipalities that have the most obstacles to the implementation of the transformation, and based on their example, to create a financing mechanism for the transformation. The most relevant, 2022, is used for the study data, arguing that today's energy sector environment is extremely volatile. It is pointless to use older data because, during 2015–2022, the country invested more in purchasing building permits and equipment. Data is drawn from different databases as they cover a wide range of items.

With cluster analysis data, asset analysis is undertaken. Asset analysis in prospective municipalities will allow us to find out the possibilities of financing as well as asset conversion. Financing of the energy transformation will be carried out from the own funds of entities in municipalities (by converting assets or developing profitable activities) and borrowed funds (by taking loans, issuing bonds, etc.). The asset analysis method is useful to systematize the structure of the entity's assets while investigating borrowing possibilities. Asset structure illustrates the amount of assets that can be used as collateral [30]. In this study, asset analysis is used for a specific task: to identify unused assets of municipalities, inefficiently used energy production plants, and borrowing potential. This is considered the basis of the energy transformation since the efficiency of the structure of the assets in the regions allows for reducing or even eliminating the need for state investments. In the selected regions, a detailed analysis of the assets of municipally managed utility companies is carried out, identifying the strengths of the companies and the assets that can be converted into new energy production units.

Asset analysis is a less frequently used research method focused on very clear and specific goals. It is suitable for analyzing the asset structure of both the private and public sectors. Asset analysis is a critical process in financial management, involving the evaluation and assessment of various assets to make informed investment decisions. This analytical approach employs quantitative and qualitative methods to gauge the potential risks and returns associated with different asset classes. The primary goal is to optimize portfolio performance and achieve specific financial objectives. Asset analysis extends to various asset classes, including stocks, bonds, real estate, and commodities. Each asset class has unique risk and return characteristics, necessitating tailored analytical approaches. In the case of municipalities, based on the principles of sustainable development, the focus is on the search for convertible assets and the utilization of borrowing potential. These actions would allow the energy transformation processes to be significantly accelerated with the smallest capital investments.

Asset analysis is significantly related to asset management. This practice is particularly used in the private sector, but responsible asset use practices are also seen in cutting-edge municipalities and states. One of the most important rules is the constant review of available assets and the assessment of the efficiency of their use. At the same time, other factors are also important. Tangibility (asset structure) is an important factor in corporate funding decisions because tangible assets act as collateral, provide guarantees for lenders in the event of financial difficulties, and provide a comparison between fixed assets and total assets [31]. Considering these factors, it is possible to create an adequate asset structure that allows the implementation of energy transformation ideas [32–34]. Property reviews in selected municipalities will be conducted based on public data. The focus is on municipally managed companies, their infrastructure, and their borrowing potential.

After the formation of certain asset groups, a structure is finally created that allows controlling the energetic transformation processes of this stage. The structure is created based on a generic system diagram. It includes key performance aspects such as external and internal factors, action tactics, and value creation [35]. This diagram will outline opportunities and challenges that occur during the energy transformation in problematic regions of the country. Because the diagramming approach is systematic, it allows for a more accurate prediction of possible risks and possible directions of impact [36]. This diagram will serve as a basis for further research, allowing for an empirical assessment of the potential of energy transformation.

2.4 Regionalization Process

Data from 2023 are used during the cluster analysis—data summarizing 60 Lithuanian municipalities. The R package is used for analysis. Since the data groups are sufficiently different, the indicator values are converted according to the Z-score to unify them. By unifying the values of the indicators, distortion of the results will be avoided. When performing cluster analysis, an important result is achieved: municipalities are evaluated not only through the economic definition of sustainability, but at the same time, the social and environmental impact of sustainable initiatives on the regions is consistently presented. This solves an important scientific problem: sustainability is often evaluated only according to economic form, without emphasizing the importance of social aspects or the public's interest in living in a clean and transparent environment. Figure 2.3 presents the main results of the cluster analysis, expressed according to the regions of Lithuania, showing a clear regional distribution and direction of activity priorities.

The figure shows that all municipalities are divided into three clusters. Cluster 1 includes municipalities that are characterized by a relatively well-developed heat economy sector, but there are unexploited opportunities to develop electricity production (based on the data on free power in the electricity grids). These municipalities have relatively smaller governance problems; most of the municipal enterprises have boards with independent members. In the cluster, municipalities have above-average forest resources and relatively small areas of abandoned land. The energy progress of these municipalities is largely related to the development of their own electricity generation, especially in terms of solar and wind energy.

Only one municipality participates in cluster 2, the city of Vilnius. It is a capital city municipality characterized by high energy consumption and other opportunities to develop its own energy capacities compared to other clusters. In this municipality, there are no large vacant land areas for solar and wind energy, as well as abandoned lands and forests. However, this municipality has fundamentally different

2.4 Regionalization Process

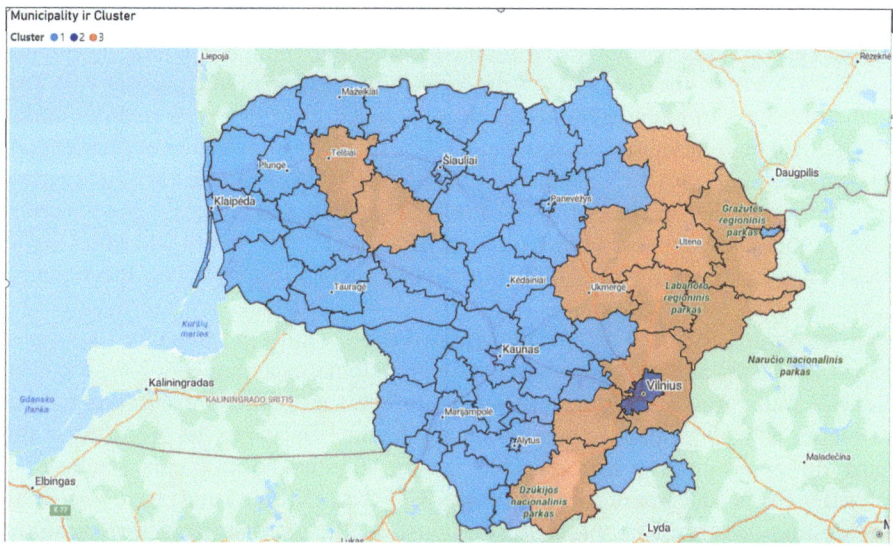

Fig. 2.3 Results of cluster analysis in the case of Lithuania

possibilities for energy transformation. Building roofs and walls can be used for local energy production. In addition, political projects are already being developed in the municipality that allow for the recovery of heat from the sewage network. There are various energy-saving options related to power balancing, heat utilization of servers, and the development of cooling networks. The municipality of the second cluster has an exceptional corporate culture; all companies in this municipality have independent board members, and ESG plans are prepared and strictly followed. The waste generated in the municipality already meets a significant part of the energy needs. Greater development of green cogeneration would enable faster achievement of energy self-sufficiency goals.

Cluster 3 municipalities have a huge perspective for the implementation of short-term energy transformation goals. The third cluster shows concentrated problems, the solution of which would create a positive impact on the whole country. First, most municipalities still use imported fossil fuels for heat production. The municipalities of the cluster have all the conditions to provide themselves with local biomass—the forest cover of the municipalities is higher than the national average, and the amount of abandoned land is five to seven times higher than the indicators of the rest of the country. In the latter case, it is possible to exploit biomass resources that are not useful for industry. In these regions, there are fundamental governance problems: municipal companies either do not have boards or do not have independent members. ESG plans are also not in place. Due to the complex negative situation, electricity grids are not fully utilized, and thus wind and solar energy are not developed. The number of organic farms in the cluster is higher than average, but their potential to produce biogas is not fully exploited. These complex problems basically prevent the municipalities of the cluster from achieving an energy breakthrough and solving current social problems. The unexploited potential of internal resources leads to the fact that, in the long term, cluster municipalities will lose competitiveness in the context of the entire country. Energy transformation initiatives should be focused on these municipalities since the elimination of problems in this cluster would provide valuable experience for solving problems in other regions or countries. In this and the following studies, the focus will be on solving the problems of municipalities belonging to the third cluster. This action will allow us to focus on a clear sample and study the complex positive impact on the regional economy and social cohesion.

In the future, focusing on energy transformation actions in Lithuania, two-speed transformation plans must be drawn up. The municipalities of cluster 3 must implement the transformation faster, as they have complex infrastructure and resource use problems, as well as management problems. As the solution to the problems of the third cluster progresses, it is possible to start solving the problems of cluster 1 related to the production of local electricity. Cluster 2 (Vilnius) must have a separate energy transformation plan focused on housing efficiency projects, decentralized production, and better utilization of local waste.

In the next phase of the research, the focus is on the municipalities in the third cluster, which have structural development problems. In order to identify opportunities for financing and expanding the use of renewable energy, an analysis of assets managed by municipalities is carried out. The purpose of this analysis is to identify opportunities for short-term energy transformation initiatives, while creating a basis for long-term actions. Carrying out the transformation based on the principles of sustainable development creates the need to first analyze not the development of new production volumes but to study greener alternatives for the use or conversion of existing assets. The study of the property structure of the most energetically inefficient municipalities will create conditions for understanding the extent of the efficiency of the energy system and finding even single possible cases of the use of inefficient assets.

2.5 Analysis of Problematic Municipalities from an Energy Transformation Perspective

Quantitative data on the regional energy transformation process primarily covers resources that are not yet fully exploited. From the volume of hot water sold, the volume of energy recovered can be determined, and from the volume of waste generated, the volume of solid fuels recovered can be determined. It is somewhat more difficult to determine the volumes of biogas and biomethane generation, as there is a lack of objective research assessing the synergies between the water management sector and other sectors of the economy. This has led to a greater focus on agricultural waste and municipal biowaste such as grass, leaves, and other biodegradable

2.5 Analysis of Problematic Municipalities from an Energy Transformation Perspective

wastes. Food waste plays a key role in the biogas production process—the success of its collection is directly linked to the volumes of biogas produced.

The research will use data summarizing three main groups—the raw material potential in the regions, the current energy situation, and the efficiency opportunities through the realization or better use of existing assets. All the indicators used for the study are presented in Table 2.2.

The study focuses on the 13 least energy-efficient municipalities in Lithuania identified in previous studies. The overall transformation plan focuses primarily on the progress of these municipalities. As the data was collected on the basis of an extreme negative case, the model can be adapted to other regions. This will allow for the creation of a comparative basis. A universal assessment will make it possible to identify the priorities where short-term investment should be directed first, while also allowing the model to be adapted for other countries. The study uses multi-criteria assessment methods to examine a wide range of factors. This approach is particularly suitable for both energy system studies [41] and renewable energy systems analysis [42–44]. This type of assessment allows for the analysis of different datasets at different scales, thus providing objective and meaningful results. This approach will generate results that will be used to develop the final energy transformation model for short-term solutions. This will be a key task for future research.

The initial stage of the study is diagnostics of indicators, which will allow the identification of indicators suitable for further research on energy transformation. The indicators that have been discarded may be suitable for assessing future transformation processes, but for short-term action, it is necessary to focus on aspects that have a more immediate positive impact. This will help to address the gap created by the lack of short-term solutions. The study included 17 indicators that characterize the studied regions in terms of the use of potential energy resources and possibilities to transform the regional energy system. Not all indicators will be used in subsequent analyses. The indicators should be characterized by high variability to discriminate between individual areas (groups) and should not be strongly related to each other. Therefore, the coefficients of variation were checked to see if they were

Table 2.2 Main indicators of the research [37–40]

Potential	Perspective	Efficiency
Biogas potential	Amount of public buildings	Value of unused real estate
Organic waste potential	Amount of free capacity of grid	Value of unused movable property
Municipal waste potential	Energy consumption	Municipal companies' debt
Amount of unused lands	The total amount of electricity consumed in municipal institutions	The value of shares of municipally owned companies
Farms with biogas production potential	Used heat production equipment	Municipal companies' creditworthiness
Biomass potential		
Sludge potential		

high enough (Vz > 10%) and if the correlation was not too high. Basic descriptive statistics of the studied indicators are given in Table 2.3.

After analyzing the coefficients of variation, all indicators can be taken into the study because they are all characterized by appropriate variability. The second stage of selecting the indicators was the correlation analysis. The indicators taken into the study should not be strongly correlated with each other because this would mean transferring the same information. The correlation matrix is presented in Table 2.4. In the correlation matrix, there are two correlation coefficients that take high values, and so between biogas potential, MWh and farms with biogas potential, the

Table 2.3 Basic descriptive statistics of the studied indicators

		Mean	Median	Min	Max	Std. Dev.	Coef. Var.
X_1	Biogas potential per thousand people, MWh	1787.5	1503.6	215.9	4168.3	1325.1	74.1
X_2	Organic waste potential per thousand people, t	157.8	156.3	101.2	217.0	38.3	24.3
X_3	Municipal waste potential per thousand people, t	313.5	296.5	219.0	448.6	80.2	25.6
X_4	Amount of unused lands per hundred kilometers, ha	95.1	101.5	22.8	167.0	49.9	52.5
X_5	Used heat production equipment per hundred thousand people, MW	2.0	1.8	0.2	5.4	1.3	64.6
X_6	Biomass potential per thousand people, ktoe	5.9	3.8	1.8	13.9	4.1	69.5
X_7	Annual sludge potential per thousand people, t	17.2	14.5	7.4	33.6	7.6	44.2
X_8	Amount of unused public buildings per thousand people	1.3	1.1	0.3	2.1	0.5	40.9
X_9	Amount of free capacity of grid per thousand people, MW	3.4	2.7	0.1	8.1	2.6	74.5
X_{10}	Energy consumption per thousand people, toe	731.0	764.8	380.2	1003.8	225.1	30.8
X11	*Farms with biogas potential per thousand people*	*0.6*	*0.6*	*0.1*	*1.7*	*0.4*	*69.0*
X_{12}	Value of unused real estate per capita, EUR	307.3	284.2	153.7	609.7	128.9	41.9
X_{13}	Value of unused movable property per capita, EUR	5.7	4.5	2.7	10.5	2.5	44.3
X_{14}	The total amount of electricity consumed for municipal needs per thousand people, MWh	32.8	31.7	14.4	55.9	11.5	35.1
X_{15}	Value of shares of municipally owned companies per capita, EUR	212.4	184.4	92.6	448.8	100.9	47.5
X_{16}	Municipal companies debt per capita, EUR	9.6	7.9	4.0	21.0	5.2	54.3
X17	*Municipal companies creditworthiness per capita, EUR*	*106.2*	*92.2*	*46.3*	*224.4*	*50.4*	*47.5*

2.5 Analysis of Problematic Municipalities from an Energy Transformation Perspective

Table 2.4 Correlation matrix between the studied indicators

	X1	X2	X3	4	5	6	7	8	9	10	11	12	13	14	15	16	17
1	1	−0.34	−0.61	0.07	−0.01	0.09	0.01	0.14	−0.15	0.22	0.95	−0.14	0.14	0.23	−0.21	0.12	−0.21
2	−0.34	1	0.51	−0.32	−0.09	−0.29	0.44	−0.01	0.18	0.41	−0.32	−0.08	−0.05	−0.16	0.07	0.00	0.07
3	−0.61	0.51	1	0.04	0.19	0.05	0.21	0.02	−0.08	0.37	−0.40	0.01	0.24	0.01	0.08	−0.14	0.08
4	0.07	−0.32	0.04	1	−0.28	0.02	−0.23	0.26	0.09	0.38	0.18	0.53	0.20	0.09	0.38	−0.17	0.38
5	−0.01	−0.09	0.19	−0.28	1	0.62	0.02	0.02	−0.42	−0.19	0.03	−0.25	−0.29	0.59	−0.71	−0.21	−0.71
6	0.09	−0.29	0.05	0.02	0.62	1	−0.03	0.66	0.28	−0.27	0.12	0.39	0.05	0.85	−0.30	−0.35	−0.30
7	0.01	0.44	0.21	−0.23	0.02	−0.03	1	0.19	0.28	0.51	0.03	−0.03	0.12	−0.01	0.13	0.67	0.13
8	0.14	−0.01	0.02	0.26	0.02	0.66	0.19	1	0.70	0.15	0.20	0.80	0.17	0.48	0.05	−0.25	0.05
9	−0.15	0.18	−0.08	0.09	−0.42	0.28	0.28	0.70	1	−0.11	−0.21	0.68	0.29	0.17	0.43	−0.08	0.43
10	0.22	0.41	0.37	0.38	−0.19	−0.27	0.51	0.15	−0.11	1	0.38	0.08	0.08	−0.11	0.18	0.30	0.18
11	0.95	−0.32	−0.40	0.18	0.03	0.12	0.03	0.20	−0.21	0.38	1	−0.14	0.18	0.30	−0.29	0.10	−0.29
12	−0.14	−0.08	0.01	0.53	−0.25	0.39	−0.03	0.80	0.68	0.08	−0.14	1	0.17	0.11	0.46	−0.24	0.46
13	0.14	−0.05	0.24	0.20	−0.29	0.05	0.12	0.17	0.29	0.08	0.18	0.17	1	−0.03	0.42	0.09	0.42
14	0.23	−0.16	0.01	0.09	0.59	0.85	−0.01	0.48	0.17	−0.11	0.30	0.11	−0.03	1	−0.41	−0.34	−0.41
15	−0.21	0.07	0.08	0.38	−0.71	−0.30	0.13	0.05	0.43	0.18	−0.29	0.46	0.42	−0.41	1	0.24	1.00
16	0.12	0.00	−0.14	−0.17	−0.21	−0.35	0.67	−0.25	−0.08	0.30	0.10	−0.24	0.09	−0.34	0.24	1	0.24
17	−0.21	0.07	0.08	0.38	−0.71	−0.30	0.13	0.05	0.43	0.18	−0.29	0.46	0.42	−0.41	1.00	0.24	1

correlation coefficient was 0.95, while between value of shares of municipally owned companies, EUR and municipal companies' creditworthiness, EUR, the correlation coefficient is equal to 1. Therefore, one indicator from each relationship should be removed from further studies. The indicator with the lower coefficient of variation will be excluded from the study, and the lower standard deviation will be taken into account second.Based on the correlation analysis, two indicators were removed from the study:Farms with biogas potential per thousand peopleMunicipal companies' creditworthiness per capita, EURTherefore, 15 indicators will be taken for further analysis. Based on the selected indicators, a taxonomic analysis was performed to distinguish groups of regions similar to each other in terms of the analyzed indicators responsible for energy potential. The Ward method was used for research, which is based on the analysis of variance. The plot of linkage distances across steps chart (Fig. 2.4) can be used to decide on the number of clusters (clusters, groups) to be created. It allows for selecting the appropriate division on the cluster tree. In this case, the suggested division is three groups.The division into groups is presented in Fig. 2.5:

(A) Anyksciai DM, Kelmë DM, and Trakai DM
(B) Moletai DM, Ignalina DM, Varena DM, and Zarasai DM
(C) Rokiskis DM, Svencionys DM, Telsiai DM, Ukmerge DM, Utena DM, and Vilnius district

To characterize individual clusters, the group average method was used. The values of individual indicators are presented in Fig. 2.6. The worst group is

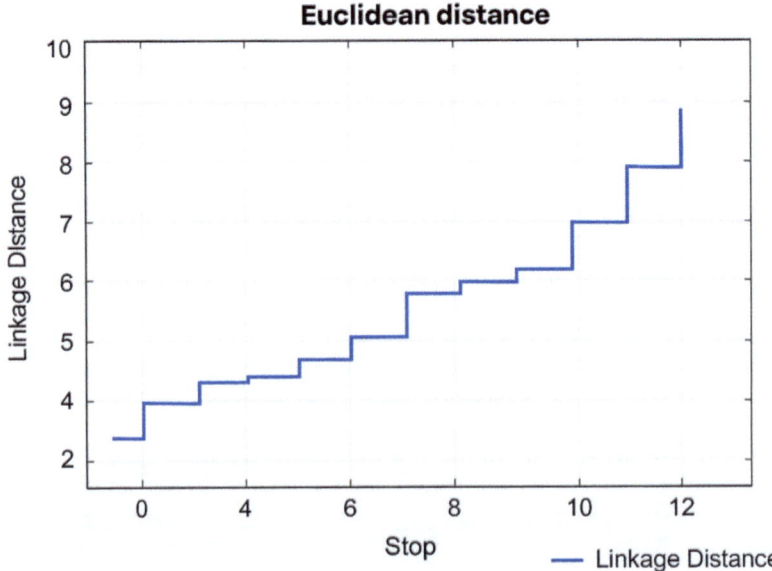

Fig. 2.4 Plot of linkage distances across steps

2.5 Analysis of Problematic Municipalities from an Energy Transformation Perspective

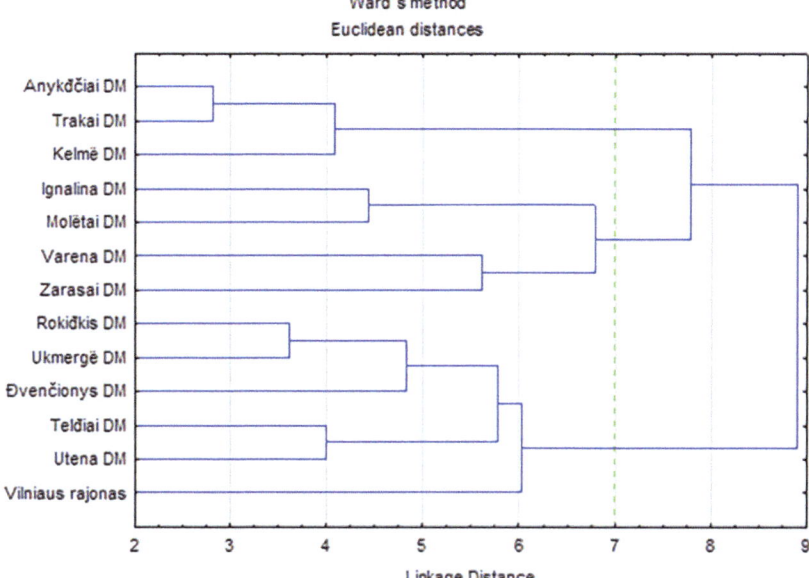

Fig. 2.5 Diagram tree

definitely group A, where almost all indicators have values below the global average. The municipal waste potential indicator has the lowest level of the groups created, as well as the amount of unused land, annual sludge potential, unused public building, amount of free capacity of grid, energy consumption, value or unused real estate, value of unused movable property, and value of shares of municipally owned companies. This group includes: Anykščiai DM, Kelmë DM, and Trakai DM. The best of the groups created is group B. The districts that are in this cluster are Moletai DM, Ignalina DM, Varena DM, and Zarasai DM. Most of the indicators adopted for research (9) have maximum values compared to the other clusters.

The lowest value was taken by the municipal companies' debt indicator, which in the case of this indicator indicates a positive side The areas that were in the third cluster are Rokiskis DM, Svenčionys DM, Telsiai DM, Ukmerge DM, Utena DM, and Vilnius district, and they present an average level in the studied area. Some of the indicators are at a high level and some have values close to the average. Based on the selected 15 features, a ranking of regions was also created, which is presented in Table 2.5.

The research shows that the regions that were included in the worst cluster A were placed at the end of the ranking and occupy ninth, 10th, and 13th places, respectively. The regions from the best cluster occupy the first, fourth, fifth, and 7.5th places in the ranking, respectively. The last group defined as the average included six regions that occupy second, third, sixth, seventh and fifth, 11th, and 12th places in the ranking..

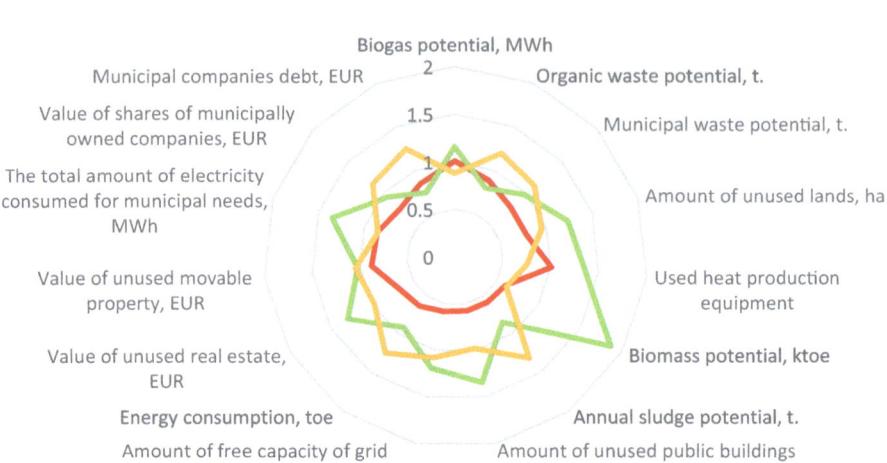

Fig. 2.6 Graph of group means of the resulting clusters in the diagram tree

Table 2.5 Ranking of regions and results of cluster analysis

	Ranking	Results of cluster
Ignalina DM	1	B
Svenčionys	2	C
Rokiskis DM	3	C
Varena DM	4	B
Zarasai DM	5	B
Utena DM	6	C
Vilnius	7,5	C
Moletai DM	7,5	B
Anykščiai	9	A
Trakai DM	10	A
Ukmergė DM	11	C
Telđiai DM	12	C
Kelmė DM	13	A

2.6 Asset Structure Analysis

Asset analysis is focused on assessing the asset structure of problematic Lithuanian municipalities (cluster 3). In this case, the possibilities of converting existing property units are analyzed, alongside investing and using borrowed capital. Asset conversion involves the realization of unnecessary infrastructure as well as the sale of unprofitable municipal enterprises.

The structure of the analyzed Lithuanian municipality properties is quite similar. It consists of real estate managed by municipalities, shares in municipal companies, movable units, and other smaller groups of assets. This is a grateful situation for evaluation, since these municipalities are characterized by a similar area, number of inhabitants, and problems. Analyzing the financial statements of companies managed by municipalities shows that the income from assets is relatively low. When

2.6 Asset Structure Analysis

examining individual cases, it was noticed that municipal companies not only have a lot of depreciated assets but also assets that are not related to the main activities of the companies (apartments, recreation rooms, etc.). This allows for significant asset conversion potential.

The initial stage of asset analysis consists of the identification of assets suitable for energy transformation. After reviewing the public data of the municipalities, the potential for using the existing assets is high, and the existing assets can be put to good use. Figure 2.7 presents the main actions that would accelerate the potential of transformation into problematic municipalities. These actions are condensed into action groups, according to which a specific asset management plan will be developed. The scope of the first task (SELL) includes the sale of all possible redundant assets. These assets are of a particularly wide spectrum; they can be unused equipment, unused premises, old power plants, unsuitable for conversion, or other assets not used in direct activities. A concrete and objective review of the assets of companies managed by municipalities would allow for the formation of sustainable initial capital for further sustainable investments. These assets must be immediately realized at the moment when the investment plan is prepared. Realization is recommended to be carried out through public electronic auctions. Another group (CONVERT) is directly related to sustainability; the possibilities to convert or improve the existing infrastructure are analyzed to switch to green energy production. This can include the use of old coal power plants or upgrading gas power plants by building facilities suitable for storing and burning biomethane. Another

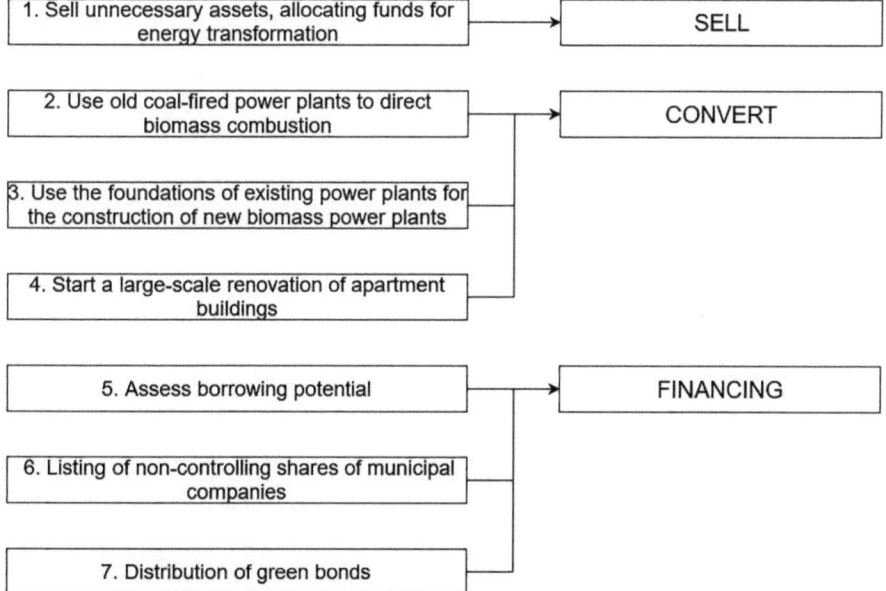

Fig. 2.7 Tactics that enable the formation of the potential for the use of assets by municipally managed enterprises

option is also possible: the use of existing foundations for new construction after they have been substantially strengthened. However, the conversion of energy production will not be fully successful without a large-scale renovation program. With its assistance, ecological insulation materials could be used, and more efficient houses would consume less energy. In addition, other alternatives (FINANCING) are necessary, related to the distribution of shares of municipally managed companies and better use of borrowing potential. This would allow for the attraction of additional capital, which would be invested exclusively in renewable energy. This will be guaranteed by the distribution prospectus of shares or bonds and approved investment plans.

According to these tasks, a plan for the use of existing assets is prepared, including the use of borrowed capital. The plan is created based on a generic system diagram. When creating an asset management plan, internal and external factors are included that affect the scope of asset utilization and, at the same time, the timing of the start of the energy transformation. Connections are formed between the components. This will allow to focus on the most important tasks while identifying the areas of greatest change. The plan presented in Fig. 2.8 is complex, but its implementation requires consistency; without mobilizing all available resources, transformation activities may be delayed, thus further contributing to higher levels of environmental pollution.

Based on the asset management tactics selected in Fig. 2.5, an asset management system is created, including three internal factors: capacity, governance, and efficiency. Bold lines show relationships between internal factors, while lighter lines define relationships between all other factors and their directions. In this case, it is considered that proper governance can help achieve the goals of energy transformation. Cluster 3 municipalities do not lack unused assets, have excess energy production capacities, or have adequate opportunities to finance projects. They are also rich in local resources and energy production competencies. The main obstacle to better progress is the governance of municipal companies, the improvement of which would allow both achieving the primary goals of energy transformation and extracting synergistic effects. The phenomenon of governance can also lead to an increase in efficiency, and governance can also affect capacity (well-managed municipal companies can expand to surrounding regions or companies, supplying them with energy). Important external factors—local resource potential and grid—are related to the possibilities of developing renewable energy activities in the municipality. Automation trends can further accelerate transformation activities. The equipment market significantly affects construction and development prices. Competence in the regions can be used both to transform the energy system and to talk about new future activities. Political will from the municipal administration can lead to changes in governance. At the same time, it allows for the monitoring of the entire transformation process, removing possible administrative obstacles.

Property transformation in municipalities creates a complex effect that is not only economic. First of all, the perception is formed within the municipalities that the property must be used efficiently, and if there are no opportunities for its use, it must be converted. In addition to business development and emerging technological

2.6 Asset Structure Analysis

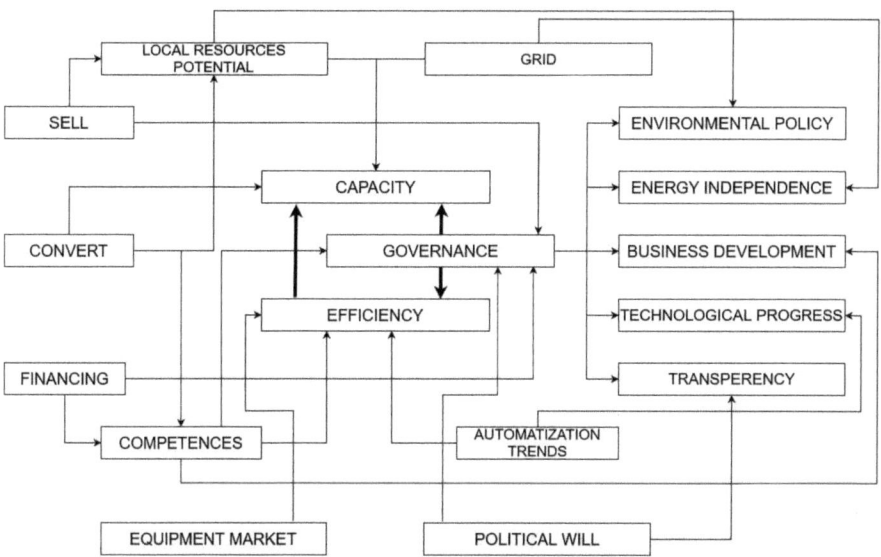

Fig. 2.8 The asset management system in cluster 3 municipalities

progress in municipally managed companies, there are more directions for positive impact. Environmental progress is perhaps the most important of these—when the burning of coal and natural gas is abandoned, the state of the environment improves. If biogas energy is developed, particularly harmful methane gas will not enter the environment. Another element that is particularly relevant for countries without fossil fuels is energy independence. Decentralized energy systems will make it possible to supply energy to customers more efficiently and reduce energy transmission losses. At the same time, it will be a safe measure to avoid cyber or physical incidents. Ultimately, good governance practices will ensure transparency, thus preventing opportunities for corruption and the waste of resources. The developed model is universal and can be applied to a wide range of regions. Internal factors and created benefits are not finite; in the case of both positively and negatively evaluated municipalities, achieving these aspects would allow for the creation of analogous benefits.

Cluster and asset analysis showed that the initiation of change must start in those regions with the greatest energy problems. Focusing on these regions allows us to distinguish objective action tactics, internal and external factors, and possible positive effects on the transformation of the energy system. According to the selected municipalities, after the analysis of their assets, clear directions for transformation were formed. Their final results are presented in the newly created asset management system. Further stages of energy transformation will be formed on the basis of this system. It is necessary to emphasize that the transformation process has many directions, which in turn can create additional synergistic effects. This would allow us to further expand the transformation potential, thus strengthening the regions and improving their environmental status.

2.7 Action Plans and Solutions

The solutions for determining the directions of energy transformation presented in this study will allow decision-makers to structure the process and argue the initial directions of the transformation. Without optimizing the existing asset structure, the transformation will take more time and require greater financial resources. In addition, it is necessary to emphasize the fact that the transformation must comply with the principles of sustainable development. The destruction of convertible infrastructure must be avoided, and the use of secondary raw materials and waste must be focused on, as this will reduce the need for expensive technologies. The use of existing resources will allow for reduced intervention in new areas of land when they are prepared for wind or solar energy needs. Although these species are compatible with the principles of sustainable development and sustainable farming, the sale or conversion of redundant assets will have a greater impact on the sustainable transformation of already existing infrastructure. The directions presented in this study clearly focus on better utilization of existing infrastructure, existing assets, and the existing business environment. Once these steps are completed, it will be possible to objectively assess the possibilities of further development.

This work differs from other works as it clearly links the sustainability component and regional economic development through energy business development. Due to the centralization of the energy business, not every region is suitable for conventional energy activities. Renewable energy enables each region to contribute to the strengthening of the country's energy independence by using available renewable resources for energy activities. This creates conditions for improving municipal businesses and empowering communities to engage in the business of fuel supply and environmental management.

Energy transformation will form clear directions of influence. First, it will empower the regions. This is related to both economic and social changes. The role of independent boards is particularly important; this can not only help enrich the regions economically but also stimulate the progress of the education system, since responsible management would become a good example for the progress of the regions. Strengthening the economic condition of the regions will reduce grants from the national budget and allow for the solving of long-standing problems related to unused and undemanded assets, lack of alternatives, and non-transparent management.

Orientation to energy transformation related to these ways:

- **An algorithm for implementing sustainable internal operational efficiency is developed.** Due to a lack of knowledge, insufficient political will, and, in many cases, the absence of a clear national direction, it is not clear how best to start transforming the energy system. This study proposes a clear algorithm for the implementation of sustainable energy transformation based on improving internal efficiency and better use of internal resources. The algorithm is based on the use of concrete data and can be used both at the national level (identifying problem areas) and at the regional level (identifying sustainability-based efficiency

priorities). The solutions presented in the study allow the measurement of both quantitative and qualitative indicators related to green energy production, regional economic viability, and governance transparency.
- **A clear focus on achieving mid-term results.** While the world's countries, enterprises, and organizations are working hard to develop the latest technologies, the challenges posed by climate warming are getting worse. The commercialization of the latest technologies may lead to a situation where this milestone is reached too late. The solutions proposed in this study highlight the urgent need to address the challenges of energy transformation in the electricity and heat generation sectors. The emphasis on the regional level ensures speed of decision-making, as key decisions would be taken at the local rather than national level. Once the pollution problems in the electricity and heat sectors have been solved, soon, the commercialization of the latest technologies will make a significant contribution to solving the problems in the transport sector.
- **Emphasizing governance as a central axis in the mid-term energy transformation processes.** The study highlights the fact that, despite the abundance of resources available in the regions, it is first necessary to depoliticize the municipally owned companies, allowing them to be managed by professionals. This must be done both at the level of the management team and the board. This will make it possible to implement all the transformation measures set out in the study, which are intended to cover an intermediate period until cost-effective mass production technologies are developed.

Comparing this study with the opinions of other authors, the lack of intermediate solutions becomes apparent. Other research by scientists focuses on conceptual solutions that will create huge positive impacts in the future. The most talked about is hydrogen technology and its influence on future energy [45,46]. A common opinion is that the transition to hydrogen will happen directly—fossil fuels will be immediately replaced by hydrogen production [47]. However, cost-effective hydrogen production has not yet been achieved, and this process may take time. Until then, environmental pollution will not be stopped, and the elimination of the consequences will only become more difficult. This study proposes intermediate solutions until the breakthrough of hydrogen technology, which would significantly solve environmental pollution problems in the short term. In addition, some conceptual hydrogen projects do not talk about wastewater but about the use of groundwater. This would go against the principles of sustainable development. The solutions proposed in the study for the beginning of the energy transformation correspond to the principles of sustainable development in all aspects.

Although other studies talk about empowering communities [48], in this case, the focus is on regional policy changes, encouraging the more efficient functioning of municipal enterprises. This would allow us to catalyze the energy transformation since, unlike in the case of communities, municipal entities have many unused assets that can be invested in the energy sector. Existing studies on regional aspects of transformation are incomplete, either focusing on resources within the region [49], on financing issues [50], or on a single transformation technology [51]. The lack of integral solutions makes it difficult to identify the benefits of using intermediate solutions in the energy transformation process. Decision-makers, especially at the regional level, lack the information and arguments that are needed to understand that they are a key part of the whole energy transformation process. This study clearly identifies this problem and proposes integral and coherent solutions to initiate energy system transformation.

Governance in energy transition processes is perhaps the least addressed topic. This study proposes a rather novel approach, not in terms of recommendations for adjusting governance but in terms of the fundamental necessity of this action for achieving the goal. Previous studies have mainly examined governance through the prism of sustainability [52–54]. These studies have looked at changes in governance that would lead to improvements in the achievement of the sustainable development goals (SDGs). However, the directions for change they provide are prescriptive. Moving on to governance aspects, specific regional examples are used, and inter-institutional cooperation structures are presented [55]. There are studies that analyze the prospects for European governance [56]. There is a dearth of research in the scientific field that proposes concrete solutions to the issue of governance and points to the clear role of governance in energy processes. This study establishes the importance of governance in energy transformation, distinguishing it from other relevant processes.

Another aspect of the transformation is subsidies. Although renewable energy solutions have become significantly cheaper, the impact of subsidies is still emphasized. This is to encourage energy transformation initiatives. Previous research has emphasized the impact of subsidies on the transformation until 2050 [57], as well as the theoretical implications of innovation [58–61]. This study focuses on avoiding subsidies, especially in the short term. Starting the transformation based on efficiency would allow better use of public finances instead of distorting the free market. The solution proposed in the study would be better in line with the principles of sustainable development—excess funds that would be allocated to subsidies can be directed to promote other sustainable development initiatives.

Suggestions for municipal policymakers:

- Promotion of professional and independent corporate boards
- Quotation of shares of municipal companies on the stock exchange
- Sales of shares of non-priority municipal companies
- Enlargement of municipal companies in at least one direction—by consolidating companies from one municipality or by consolidating companies operating in the same sector of different municipalities

Research directions for energy transformation have various aspects that must be evaluated. Incorrectly chosen transformation priorities can not only not bring positive results but also discredit the idea of energy transformation in general. For that purpose, it is necessary to find out the problematic points at the national level from which active transformation actions could be started. In this study, the analysis of Lithuanian municipalities is chosen since the country is currently actively transitioning toward renewable energy. When analyzing problem areas, cluster analysis was used, for which different data proving sustainable development were used. Cluster analysis identified those municipalities that have difficulties transitioning to green heat and electricity production. Based on this, the groups of assets they have that can serve to achieve less polluting energy production were analyzed. The asset analysis made it possible to form an asset management system, which will be used in future research. In the absence of appropriate management competencies, critical thinking, and the desire to change the nature of activity, energy transformation is not possible. The axis of the newly created asset management system is ensuring internal governance factors. With the help of this action, it will be possible to achieve both energy and environmental goals. Another important aspect is ensuring the decentralization of the energy system. A stably operating decentralized energy system allows to protect yourself from the influence of external factors, while creating conditions for more entities to get involved in energy activities. Decentralized production allows to reduce the negative consequences of renewable energy related to unstable production. The abundance and integration of technologies strengthens both regions and the state, while creating conditions for achieving energy independence from external entities and conflicting structures.

References

1. Connolly, D., Lund, H., & Mathiesen, B. V. (2016). Smart energy Europe: The technical and economic impact of one potential 100% renewable energy scenario for the European Union. *Renewable and Sustainable Energy Reviews, 60*, 1634–1653.
2. Gielen, D., Boshell, F., Saygin, D., Bazilian, M. D., Wagner, N., & Gorini, R. (2019). The role of renewable energy in the global energy transformation. *Energy Strategy Reviews, 24*, 38–50.
3. Bartholdsen, H. K., Eidens, A., Löffler, K., Seehaus, F., Wejda, F., Burandt, T., et al. (2019). Pathways for Germany's low-carbon energy transformation towards 2050. *Energies, 12*(15), 2988.
4. Nazir, C. P. (2019). Solar energy for traction of high speed rail transportation: A techno-economic analysis. *Civil Engineering Journal, 5*(7), 1566–1576.
5. Duro, J. A., & Padilla, E. (2011). Inequality across countries in energy intensities: An analysis of the role of energy transformation and final energy consumption. *Energy Economics, 33*(3), 474–479.
6. Gielen, D., Gorini, R., Wagner, N., Leme, R., Gutierrez, L., Prakash, G., & Renner, M. (2019). *Global energy transformation: A roadmap to 2050*. International Renewable Energy Agency (IRENA).
7. Frondel, M., Ritter, N., Schmidt, C. M., & Vance, C. (2010). Economic impacts from the promotion of renewable energy technologies: The German experience. *Energy Policy, 38*(8), 4048–4056.
8. Dvořák, P., Martinát, S., Van der Horst, D., Frantál, B., & Turečková, K. (2017). Renewable energy investment and job creation; a cross-sectoral assessment for the Czech Republic with reference to EU benchmarks. *Renewable and Sustainable Energy Reviews, 69*, 360–368.
9. Akella, A. K., Saini, R. P., & Sharma, M. P. (2009). Social, economical and environmental impacts of renewable energy systems. *Renewable Energy, 34*(2), 390–396.
10. Bulavskaya, T., & Reynès, F. (2018). Job creation and economic impact of renewable energy in the Netherlands. *Renewable Energy, 119*, 528–538.

11. Sharma, R., Shahbaz, M., Kautish, P., & Vo, X. V. (2021). Analyzing the impact of export diversification and technological innovation on renewable energy consumption: Evidences from BRICS nations. *Renewable Energy, 178*, 1034–1045.
12. Haseeb, M., Abidin, I. S. Z., Hye, Q. M. A., & Hartani, N. H. (2019). The impact of renewable energy on economic well-being of Malaysia: Fresh evidence from auto regressive distributed lag bound testing approach. *International Journal of Energy Economics and Policy, 9*(1), 269–275.
13. Elia, A., Kamidelivand, M., Rogan, F., & Gallachóir, B. Ó. (2021). Impacts of innovation on renewable energy technology cost reductions. *Renewable and Sustainable Energy Reviews, 138*, 110488.
14. Szpor, A., & Ziółkowska, K. (2018). *Transformation of the polish coal sector*. International Institute for Sustainable Development.
15. Wang, Q., Dong, Z., Li, R., & Wang, L. (2022). Renewable energy and economic growth: New insight from country risks. *Energy, 238*, 122018.
16. Naumenkova, S., Mishchenko, V., & Mishchenko, S. (2022). Key energy indicators for sustainable development goals in Ukraine. *Problems and Perspectives in Management, 20*(1), 379–395.
17. Ginevičius, R. (2022). The efficiency of municipal waste management systems in the environmental context in the countries of the European Union. *Journal of International Studies, 15*(4), 63–79.
18. De Arce, R., Mahía, R., Medina, E., & Escribano, G. (2012). A simulation of the economic impact of renewable energy development in Morocco. *Energy Policy, 46*, 335–345.
19. Inglesi-Lotz, R. (2016). The impact of renewable energy consumption to economic growth: A panel data application. *Energy Economics, 53*, 58–63.
20. Sibuea, M. B., Sibuea, S. R., & Pratama, I. (2021). The impact of renewable energy and economic development on environmental quality of ASEAN countries. *AgBioforum, 23*, 12–21.
21. Lithuanian District Heating Association (LDHA). (2023). *Šilumos Tiekimo Bendrovių 2022 Metų Ūkinės Veiklos Apžvalga*. Lietuvos Šilumos Tiekėjų Asociacija.
22. NordPool Group. *Market data*. https://www.nordpoolgroup.com/en/Market-data1/Dayahead/Area-Prices/ALL1/Hourly/?view=table
23. Governance Coordination Centre. *List of MOEs*. https://governance.lt/en/apie-imones/svi-sarasas/
24. State Forestry Service. *Lietuvos Miškų Rodikliai*. https://amvmt.lrv.lt/lt/atviri-duomenys-1/lietuvos-misku-rodikliai/
25. Agricultural Data Center. (2023). *Lietuvos Respublikos Žemės Fondas 2023 m. Sausio 1 d.* Žemės ūkio Duomenų Centras.
26. Official Statistics Portal. *Indicators database*. https://osp.stat.gov.lt/statistiniu-rodikliu-analize#/
27. Litgrid. Renewable Energy Integration Centre. https://www.litgrid.eu/index.php/renewable-energy/renewable-energy-integration-centre/32092
28. LŽŪMPRIS. *Ekologinių Ūkių Statistika*. https://www.vic.lt/zumpris/statistine-informacija/
29. Capece, G., Cricelli, L., Di Pillo, F., & Levialdi, N. (2010). A cluster analysis study based on profitability and financial indicators in the Italian gas retail market. *Energy Policy, 38*(7), 3394–3402.
30. Chen, J., Qi, X., Chen, L., Chen, F., & Cheng, G. (2020). Quantum-inspired ant lion optimized hybrid k-means for cluster analysis and intrusion detection. *Knowledge-Based Systems, 203*, 106167.
31. Sari, I. P., Al-Khowarizmi, A. K., & Batubara, I. H. (2021). Cluster analysis using K-means algorithm and fuzzy C-means clustering for grouping students' abilities in online learning process. *Journal of Computer Science, Information Technology and Telecommunication Engineering, 2*(1), 139–144.
32. Brigham, E. F., & Houston, J. F. (2001). *Financial management* (8th ed., p. 39). Erlangga.

References

33. Yunusa, D. A., & Prasetyob, K. (2020). Company type, asset structure and capital structure listed on LQ-45 index. *International Journal of Innovation, Creativity and Change, 13*(8), 1251–1261.
34. Mukhtarov, S., Aliyev, J., Borowski, P. F., & Disli, M. (2023). Institutional quality and renewable energy transition: Empirical evidence from Poland. *Journal of International Studies, 16*(3), 208.
35. Štreimikienė, D. (2021). Externalities of power generation in Visegrad countries and their integration through support of renewables. *Economics and Sociology, 14*(1), 89–102.
36. Streimikiene, D. (2022). Energy poverty and impact of COVID-19 pandemics in Visegrad (V4) countries. *Journal of International Studies, 15*(1), 9–25.
37. State data agency. *Official statistics portal.* https://osp.stat.gov.lt/
38. Eurostat. *Portal of statistics.* https://ec.europa.eu/eurostat/
39. Agricultural Data Center. *Data from the agricultural sector.* https://zudc.lt/statistika/
40. Lithuanian Energy Agency. *Data.* https://www.ena.lt/aktuali-aei-statistika/
41. d'Amore-Domenech, R., Santiago, O., & Leo, T. J. (2020). Multicriteria analysis of seawater electrolysis technologies for green hydrogen production at sea. *Renewable and Sustainable Energy Reviews, 133*, 110166.
42. Bortoluzzi, M., de Souza, C. C., & Furlan, M. (2021). Bibliometric analysis of renewable energy types using key performance indicators and multicriteria decision models. *Renewable and Sustainable Energy Reviews, 143*, 110958.
43. Şahin, M. (2021). A comprehensive analysis of weighting and multicriteria methods in the context of sustainable energy. *International Journal of Environmental Science and Technology, 18*(6), 1591–1616.
44. György, O. (2024). Cluster grouping of EU member states according to some economic performance and circular economic indicators. *Management/Vadyba (16487974), 40*(1).
45. Hermesmann, M., & Müller, T. E. (2022). Green, turquoise, blue, or grey? Environmentally friendly hydrogen production in transforming energy systems. *Progress in Energy and Combustion Science, 90*, 100996.
46. Capurso, T., Stefanizzi, M., Torresi, M., & Camporeale, S. M. (2022). Perspective of the role of hydrogen in the 21st century energy transition. *Energy Conversion and Management, 251*, 114898.
47. Baquero, J. E. G., & Monsalve, D. B. (2024). From fossil fuel energy to hydrogen energy: Transformation of fossil fuel energy economies into hydrogen economies through social entrepreneurship. *International Journal of Hydrogen Energy, 54*, 574–585.
48. Coy, D., Malekpour, S., & Saeri, A. K. (2022). From little things, big things grow: Facilitating community empowerment in the energy transformation. *Energy Research & Social Science, 84*, 102353.
49. Igliński, B., Kiełkowska, U., Pietrzak, M. B., Skrzatek, M., Kumar, G., & Piechota, G. (2023). The regional energy transformation in the context of renewable energy sources potential. *Renewable Energy, 218*, 119246.
50. Ding, W., Du, J., Kazancoglu, Y., Mangla, S. K., & Song, M. (2023). Financial development and the energy net-zero transformation potential. *Energy Economics, 125*, 106863.
51. Kikuchi, Y., Nakai, M., Kanematsu, Y., Oosawa, K., Okubo, T., Oshita, Y., & Fukushima, Y. (2020). Application of technology assessments to co-learning for regional transformation: A case study of biomass energy systems in Tanegashima. *Sustainability Science, 15*, 1473–1494.
52. Beck, S., Jasanoff, S., Stirling, A., & Polzin, C. (2021). The governance of sociotechnical transformations to sustainability. *Current Opinion in Environmental Sustainability, 49*, 143–152.
53. Pickering, J., Hickmann, T., Bäckstrand, K., Kalfagianni, A., Bloomfield, M., Mert, A., et al. (2022). Democratising sustainability transformations: Assessing the transformative potential of democratic practices in environmental governance. *Earth System Governance, 11*, 100131.
54. Sovacool, B. K., Hook, A., Sareen, S., & Geels, F. W. (2021). Global sustainability, innovation and governance dynamics of national smart electricity meter transitions. *Global Environmental Change, 68*, 102272.

55. Hoppe, T., & Miedema, M. (2020). A governance approach to regional energy transition: Meaning, conceptualization and practice. *Sustainability, 12*(3), 915.
56. Knodt, M., Ringel, M., & Müller, R. (2020). 'Harder' soft governance in the European energy union. *Journal of Environmental Policy & Planning, 22*(6), 787–800.
57. Taylor, M. (2020). *Energy subsidies: Evolution in the global energy transformation to 2050* (pp. 10–14). International Renewable Energy Agency.
58. Shao, Y., & Chen, Z. (2022). Can government subsidies promote the green technology innovation transformation? Evidence from Chinese listed companies. *Economic Analysis and Policy, 74*, 716–727.
59. Wang, Z., Li, X., Xue, X., & Liu, Y. (2022). More government subsidies, more green innovation? The evidence from Chinese new energy vehicle enterprises. *Renewable Energy, 197*, 11–21.
60. Ginevičius, R. (2022). The efficiency of municipal waste management systems in the environmental context in the countries of the European Union. *Journal of International Studies, 15*(4), 63–79.
61. Svazas, M., Navickas, V., Paskevicius, R., Bilan, Y., & Vasa, L. (2023). Renewable energy versus energy security: The impact of innovation on the economy. *Rynek Energii, 1*, 60–71.

Open Access This chapter is licensed under the terms of the Creative Commons Attribution-NonCommercial-NoDerivatives 4.0 International License (http://creativecommons.org/licenses/by-nc-nd/4.0/), which permits any noncommercial use, sharing, distribution and reproduction in any medium or format, as long as you give appropriate credit to the original author(s) and the source, provide a link to the Creative Commons license and indicate if you modified the licensed material. You do not have permission under this license to share adapted material derived from this chapter or parts of it.

The images or other third party material in this chapter are included in the chapter's Creative Commons license, unless indicated otherwise in a credit line to the material. If material is not included in the chapter's Creative Commons license and your intended use is not permitted by statutory regulation or exceeds the permitted use, you will need to obtain permission directly from the copyright holder.

Chapter 3
Importance of Decentralization in Energy Transformation Process

3.1 Causes of the Decentralization Phenomenon

Climate change, energy crises, military actions in the world, and unstable oil prices create enormous challenges for the world's nations. The need to use less fossil fuels opens opportunities for new or somewhat neglected green technologies. To reform the energy sector, it is necessary to have a clear and measured strategy. This allows for the identification of the potential of renewable resources in each space, while finding sources of financing for the transformation. The use of renewable resources makes it possible to solve an actual problem of the developed world—as the population of cities grows, the economic vitality of regions drops significantly. By creating new energy production capacities in the regions, social exclusion is reduced, and the main resources of the regions are better used—land areas, farms, and biomass sources. Nowadays, mankind is experiencing the third significant transformation that converts from conventional fossil fuels to new energy. The future development will go along with the three major trends—resource-type carbon reduction, production technology intensification, and utilization method diversification [1]. Based on these directions of transformation, the main investment decisions will be made, which will promote the progress of the energy system. Humanity is so far the least advanced in carbon collection and burial technologies, but the development of other trends allows for tangible progress.

Recently, a process of decentralization of energy production has been observed, when large local power plants are abandoned. Instead, the focus is on solar or wind parks, modular biomass power plants, and the potential of using biogas. This is related to the changing energy sector—the increase in the number of generating consumers, the construction of efficient houses, and the increase in the number of wind and solar power plants. The year 2030 is predicted to be the turning point of new energy development, in which the cost of new energy will drop to be able to compete with fossil energy; new energy will be promoted and applied on a large scale from 2030 to 2050, and the downward trend of carbon emissions will accelerate [1]. The idea of decentralization has been explored by global leaders in renewable energy but is now becoming a global trend. Promotion of decentralized power generation includes small-scale renewable energy systems, combined heat and power (CHP), and microgrids [2]. In addition, transformation solutions are complex and inseparable from each other. To increase the use of renewable energy resources, it is necessary to adapt the energy distribution networks. Although the concept of smart grid is not fundamentally new, its practical application is gaining momentum. Implementation of smart grid technologies could enhance grid flexibility and reliability. In addition, encouraging demand response programs helps adjust energy consumption patterns based on supply and demand fluctuations [3]. The complexity of the transformation determines the fact that the process of transition to the use of renewable resources is complex and requires maximum involvement from politicians, business, and society.

Another trend is the development of energy storage technologies. As the energy production method changes, energy consumption solutions also change. Instead of continuous, polluting energy production, renewable but unstable energy is relied upon. The effect of instability is reduced by the activities of hydro accumulation power plants and battery parks. Even more progress in energy storage solutions is expected soon. To address the global challenge of environmental pollution and energy crisis, power devices, such as fuel cells, metal-air batteries, lithium-air batteries, lithium-ion batteries, lithium-sulfur batteries, water electroliers, electrochemical production of ammonia, supercapacitors, and photovoltaic devices, are important energy conversion and storage technologies, which have caused widespread concern due to their merits of energy-efficient, eco-friendly, sustainable, and clean systems [4]. The development of energy storage solutions would improve the prospects for the use of renewable energy, especially in those countries where energy consumption is the highest. This includes utilizing advanced energy storage systems, including batteries, pumped hydro storage, and thermal storage, to store excess energy and address intermittency issues [5]. The main obstacles to progress are the lack of infrastructure and unwillingness to abandon old production and consumption habits. The lack of infrastructure can be compensated for by rigorous planning. Energy storage technologies are combined with demand-side management. Reducing the need for energy storage requires contracts with consumers to adapt their consumption or production processes to surges in energy supply. The goals of all mentioned innovations are lower use of fossil fuels, more stable energy prices, and the ability to create innovations on a wider scale than is currently the case. The innovations mentioned can significantly contribute to the realization of these goals, as they are focused on decarbonization and wider inclusion of regions in economic processes.

The global energy sector is characterized by an increasing use of synergistic effects and the interaction of different technologies. It becomes possible to produce different types of energy from one type of fuel, depending on the energy demand. As hydrogen technology expands, an even greater breakthrough in energy is possible. This includes developing a hydrogen economy through green hydrogen production using renewable energy sources, and exploring hydrogen as a clean fuel for various sectors, including transportation and industry [6]. This will increase the volume of electricity production. However, hydrogen energy is a long-term and extremely ambitious project with an uncertain financial payback period. Until hydrogen solutions become cost-effective, it is important to discover those opportunities that ensure the transition to green energy now. In addition, it is necessary to combine technological and tax aspects to achieve faster transformation. Previous studies have shown that the environmental tax and green technology are important drivers for improving energy efficiency and productivity and lowering energy intensity [7]. At the same time, there is agreement that regions are a favorable environment for energy transformation [8]. Fiscal aspects and political activity are important factors in the case of transformation, as certain social risks are encountered, at least in the short term. In the case of another study, it is stated that achieving transformation from the economic and power structure based on nonrenewable energy resources to one based on renewable energy resources is processed at the cost of diminishing economic activities [9]. Such a risk may arise if energy transformation actions are carried out recklessly, without thinking about the possible social consequences— jobs eliminated, employee qualifications not changed, etc. In the future, the situation will be the opposite. The contribution of RES to changes in the future employment levels are quite significant for the short to medium term, while those coming from nonrenewables are significantly smaller in comparison, partly because most of the jobs from nonrenewable energy deployment are generated in countries outside the EU, particularly Asian countries [10]. One of the opportunities to create workplaces in renewable energy is the green supply chain. It can be another aspect of energetic transformation. Green supply chain plays an important role in promoting enterprise energy conservation and consumption reduction, optimizing energy consumption structure and other aspects [11]. Efficiency components are a particularly important part of energy transformation. In addition, it is necessary to emphasize the aspect of promoting the improvement of energy efficiency, which is related to increasing the rationality of energy use in the places of its consumption, as well as limiting losses in the process of its transmission [12]. Public policies aimed at improving environmental awareness should be directed first towards those regions where the exposure of the citizens to pollution is lower [13]. The European Union understood these risks—the European Green Deal sets out guidelines on how to make Europe the first climate neutral continent by 2050 and provides the most comprehensive package of measures enabling Europe's inhabitants and businesses to benefit from a sustainable ecological transformation [14]. The abundance of renewable energy technologies encourages to review the directions of transformation from a sustainability perspective. Previously applied solutions for the use of renewable resources today may not be compatible with the perspective of energy transformation. In previous studies, it was established that solar energy is the most appropriate and sustainable one followed by biomass energy. Otherwise, hydro energy is the worst and least sustainable renewable energy resource [15]. The phenomenon of energy transformation originates primarily from an environmental perspective. To achieve a faster transformation, a focus on households has emerged, as it is possible to test certain technologies and avoid the shock of changes. Commonly available technologies generating energy from renewable sources for households and enterprises solve problems associated with the systematic increase in energy demand and a limited amount of traditional energy sources, which are becoming increasingly expensive and cause significant environmental degradation. The problem of energy transformation is a key issue related to the possibility of further development of world economies [16]. The inclusion of consumers in the energy system also includes the concept of producing consumers, or in other words—civil power engineering. In this case, residents' investments in independent energy production are encouraged. Civic power engineering is a vision in which the citizen becomes an entity and is not subject to the energy market and additionally has a virtual advisor in the form of smart grid and data processing technologies in a "digital cloud" [17]. In this case, it is necessary to strengthen the grid so that they can withstand sudden spikes in energy production. However, this does not eliminate the problems created by sudden changes. To avoid the shock of changes, two main directions are currently applied. Based on China's example, it is necessary to promote renewable energy and electricity through various effective policies, e.g., accelerating the "coal to electricity" and "coal to gas" projects [18]. However, the choice of gas as an intermediate fuel will only delay the prospects of energy transformation based on renewable resources. This study will look for possible perspectives that would allow the use of renewable sources in the interim period to ensure a stable energy supply and balancing functions.

3.2 Conversion Characteristics of Different Production Technologies

3.2.1 Electricity Production

The electricity generation process is traditionally carried out in high-power coal and gas power plants, as well as in nuclear power plants. In recent years, there has been an increase in energy production from wind or solar energy. It should be noted that electricity continues to be stably produced in biofuel cogeneration power plants and biogas power plants.The electricity sector plays a pivotal role in modern society, serving as the backbone of economic development and daily life. Over the years, this sector has witnessed transformative changes driven by technological advancements, environmental imperatives, and shifting energy policies [19]. To change the way electricity is produced to a more ecological one, a clear technological change is necessary. This is related to the choice of another fuel or a radical technological change. The decline of coal and the challenges facing nuclear power have reshaped the global power generation landscape. The rise of natural gas as a transitional fuel, coupled with the exploration of hydrogen as a clean energy carrier, further adds to the complexity of the sector [20]. In some countries, there is an attitude about the possibilities of natural gas to become an intermediate fuel for the final transformation. However, this approach is not correct. First, it is a fossil fuel, and its use would only marginally reduce global pollution. Second, as in the case of oil, gas resources are concentrated in a dozen countries of the world, some of which are not characterized by clear political stability.

To properly utilize renewable energy resources for electricity production, it is necessary to solve the problem of unstable production. This can be done in two ways. In the first case, it is necessary to expand the practice of demand-side management, when large electricity consumers adapt their ongoing production operations to the surges in electricity production. In the second case, it is necessary to expand energy storage capacities in hydro accumulation power plants and battery parks. In the latter case, the efficiency of battery parks is still relatively low. The construction of hydroelectric power plants fundamentally changes the landscape and requires the destruction of natural biotopes. Dams may obstruct fish migration routes and lead to the degradation or loss of fish habitats, affecting local fish populations [21]. These actions are hardly compatible with today's environmental policy. While the sector undergoes positive transformations, it faces challenges such as intermittency of renewable sources, aging infrastructure, and evolving cybersecurity threats. The importance of energy security increases significantly in crisis situations [22]. Opportunities lie in addressing these challenges through innovation, policy support, and international collaboration [23]. The innovation element is inseparable from political will. With sufficient political support, the transformation of electricity generation can be accelerated. For the effective fulfillment of political will, it is necessary to consider expert knowledge related to the use of renewable energy technologies.

To find the most suitable short-term energy transformation methods, it is necessary to compare different production alternatives. Table 3.1 presents the main renewable energy solutions, compared to essential characteristics. Technology is fundamentally different, characterized by continuous technological progress. The presented technologies are universal and can be developed in various countries of the world. The table shows those solutions that are applied on a mass scale and use renewable energy resources. It does not include some types of production in which electricity is extracted as a by-product. Such a decision was made considering the

Table 3.1 The most common renewables-based electricity generation alternatives

Type	Onshore wind energy	Solar energy	Offshore wind energy	Biomass energy
Type of fuel	Local renewable	Local renewable	Local renewable	Local renewable
Product of energy	Electricity	Electricity/hot water	Electricity	Heat/electricity/biogas
Time of power plant construction, years	5–7	2–3	7–10	1–3 (conversion of fossil fuel power plants)
Efficiency of power plant, %	50	29	70	40 (part of electricity)
Price, mln. EUR/MW	2.5	0.8	3.5	0.5 (part of electricity)
Service time, years	25	25	30	25
The need of balancing	Necessary	Necessary	Requirable	Can be used of balancing

possibility of supplying electricity to large residential areas, while certain technological solutions would not allow this to be done.

In the case of electricity, the transition towards renewable energy is fundamentally about changes in consumption. When using unstable energy sources (in the case of wind and solar), balancing solutions and production adapted to the energy supply are necessary. Biomass power plants can perform the balancing function themselves. This potential is not yet sufficiently exploited. The production of electricity is related to the process of heat production. Technology synergy exists not only in evaluating the use of fossil fuels, but also in renewable energy technologies.

3.2.2 Heat Production

The heat production process is related to electricity production. The heat production sector encompasses a diverse range of processes and technologies that generate heat for various industrial, residential, and commercial applications. This sector plays a critical role in meeting energy demands and often intersects with broader energy systems. There are different production methods that have not changed over the past decades. The heat production sector is relatively carbonized, i.e., clear alternatives to fossil fuels are still lacking. One of the main reasons is the impact of direct combustion on the heat sector. Combustion of fossil fuels, including coal, oil, and natural gas, is a primary method for heat production. Combustion involves the exothermic reaction of fuel with oxygen, releasing thermal energy. While fossil fuel combustion is a major contributor to heat production, it raises environmental concerns due to greenhouse gas emissions and air pollutants [24]. Decoupling economic growth and greenhouse gas (GHG) emissions will be one of the key challenges of the future [25]. Adequate solutions have not yet been developed that would allow profitable use of wind and solar energy for heat production. One of the alternatives is the use of electric heat pumps. As for district heating systems, green heat can be produced from biomass or geothermal energy. In the case of biomass, it can be used in both urban and regional areas. Biomass power plants can be decentralized, adapting to heat demand in certain regions. The main advantage of using biomass is the locality of the fuel. Biomass resources are widely distributed in almost all countries of the world. In the case of geothermal energy, utilizing the Earth's natural heat, geothermal heat pumps extract warmth from the ground for heating applications [26]. Renewable heat technologies offer sustainable alternatives to fossil fuel-based systems, reducing carbon footprints and dependence on finite resources. The infrastructure of the district heating sector can also be used to meet the demand for district cooling. Similar to district heating, district cooling involves the distribution of chilled water for air conditioning [27]. District energy systems enhance efficiency and can integrate renewable and waste heat sources.

The heat production sector is a dynamic and multifaceted domain, involving various processes and technologies. As society seeks sustainable and efficient energy solutions, ongoing scientific research and innovation in heat production are essential for achieving environmental and energy goals. In the case of heat energy, synergies can be obtained when biomass cogeneration plants are built instead of coal or gas burning facilities. Combined heat and electricity production based on cogeneration technology is carried out in larger urban areas. In this case, next to the main product—thermal energy, a by-product—electricity is extracted. The conversion of pollution power plants complies with the principles of sustainable development, as there is no need to build new foundations and pipelines or to fundamentally change the terrain. In addition, the project is implemented much faster since it is not necessary to obtain building permits for new construction.

Analogously in the case of electricity, Table 3.2 presents alternative options for heat energy production. Heat production technology has not changed fundamentally for some time. However, important improvements have been made in recent decades in terms of operational efficiency and smooth power plant management. New technologies that have appeared allow the use of already produced types of energy by converting them into heat production. The technological development of heat production has been slower than that of electricity technology for reasons of demand—heat production is needed in countries with a climate characterized by cold autumns and winters. However, the production of centralized heat creates conditions in synergy with the supply of centralized coolness. This technological breakthrough creates conditions for the diffusion of these technologies on a wider scale.

Due to less developed technological research, the dominant heat production technologies are related to the use of biological waste. They replace the coal and gas-fired power plants that currently dominate. The use of biomass and biogas is competitive due to the construction time of the power plants and relatively lower costs per megawatt. The main advantage of such power plants is the ability to produce several types of energy at once or depending on the demand for different types of energy. However, due to the more convenient use of imported natural gas, this production method was somewhat forgotten.

Table 3.2 The most common renewables-based heat generation alternatives

Type	Geothermal energy	Electricity (heat pumps)	Biogas	Biomass energy
Type of fuel	Local renewable	Local/imported renewable/non-renewable.	Local renewable	Local renewable
Product of energy	Heat/electricity.	Heat	Heat/electricity/biomethane	Heat/electricity/cool
Time of power plant construction, years	5–6	1–2	2–3	1–3 (conversion of fossil fuel power plants)
Efficiency of power plant, %	50[a]	70	85 (part of heat)	105 (part of heat)[b]
Price, mln. EUR/MW	1	0.8	0.7 (part of heat)	0.3 (part of heat)
Service time, years	25	25	20	25

[a]Depending on the temperature of the geothermal water
[b]If a condensing economizer is installed

Thermal energy production is characterized by flexibility and the ability to simultaneously produce several different types of energy. To use the possibilities of transformation, it is necessary to assess the perspective of gas consumption. Currently, the market is dominated by natural gas and petroleum gas, but in the future, gas consumption will fundamentally change. It is noticeable that a large part of scientific research and technological progress is directed specifically to new generation gas production technologies. In some cases, energy converted into gaseous form would allow to reduce the overloads of the energy system, when a large amount of energy is produced at the same time.

3.2.3 Gas Production

Even today, natural gas is considered the least polluting fossil fuel. In some cases, it is proposed to include gas in energy transformation plans as an intermediate fuel in the transition to full decarbonization. This does not stop scientific and applied research—alternatives to natural gas have already been developed. The main strength of the alternatives is the ability to utilize existing gas transportation networks with certain technical adjustments.

One of opportunities to replace natural gas is biomethane production. Biomethane, also known as renewable natural gas (RNG), is a type of biogas that is upgraded to a quality similar to fossil natural gas. It is produced through anaerobic digestion or other biological processes of organic materials, such as agricultural residues, food waste, sewage, and energy crops. Biomethane is considered a sustainable and low-carbon energy source, contributing to efforts to reduce greenhouse gas emissions and promote the use of renewable energy [28]. Biogas is produced from organic materials consisting mainly of methane (CH4) and carbon dioxide (CO_2), along with trace amounts of other gases. Biomethane is obtained by removing impurities and increasing the methane concentration to levels comparable to natural gas [29]. The impact of biomethane is clearly visible on livestock farms—they collect particularly polluting methane gas, which is then cleaned and burned. In this way, they do not enter the atmosphere, and the process of raising animals becomes more ecological. New technologies allow this gas to be used as fuel for agricultural machinery. There are already mass-produced tractors that use this gas [30]. Initiatives have emerged in EU countries that supply purified biomethane to common main gas pipelines. Biomethane can be injected into natural gas pipelines, used as vehicle fuel, or utilized for electricity generation. Its versatile applications make it a valuable renewable energy resource with potential benefits for reducing dependence on fossil fuels. This will partially improve the situation in the gas sector, but the amount of animal waste is lower than the demand for gas. However, in countries where alternative fuels are used for heat or electricity production, biomethane can help minimize the need for natural gas.

The main likely alternative to natural gas and transport fuel is hydrogen. Currently, the possible cost price of hydrogen and the possible commercial price

3.2 Conversion Characteristics of Different Production Technologies

have already been calculated. In recent years, hydrogen has gained significant attention as a clean and versatile energy carrier with the potential to play a crucial role in the transition to a sustainable energy system. This is determined by the chemical properties of hydrogen—it can be extracted from water, the by-product is oxygen, and hydrogen itself is perhaps best suited for energy storage. Hydrogen can be produced through various methods, including steam methane reforming (SMR), electrolysis, and gasification of biomass. SMR is currently the most common method, using natural gas as a feedstock [31]. As the production of green hydrogen increased, the divide between black, gray, and blue types of hydrogen became apparent. It is widely accepted that the development of green hydrogen, where the gas is produced using renewable energy sources, is the goal. The most suitable for this is electricity obtained from wind farms, especially from the sea. This is due to the large amount of electricity generated. Hydrogen is then extracted by electrolysis, which is supplied to modified main gas pipelines. Hydrogen can store and deliver energy, making it an energy carrier. It can be used in fuel cells to produce electricity through an electrochemical reaction with oxygen, and it can also be burned for heating and power generation [32]. In the case of the success of the development of hydrogen technologies, this would especially affect the transport sector, creating competition for electric cars.

Table 3.3 presents a comparison of the characteristics of biomethane and hydrogen. As these technologies are still largely in the development stage, some elements cannot be precisely defined. When developing gas technologies, preventive actions are important, primarily by changing the electricity and heat sectors. Significantly reduced gas demand for heat and electricity production will facilitate the transformation of the gas sector, but progress in replacing natural gas in the long term is completely dependent on hydrogen production development.

While examining electricity, heat, and gas alternatives for the short term, it was decided to further analyze the use of biomass. Biomass can be considered as a transition fuel due to the relatively high level of technological development and the possibility of producing all the mentioned types of energy from this fuel. Biomass technologies overlap with traditional heat and electricity generation technologies. In this way, cogeneration will be considered as a transitional technology, allowing to produce several types of energy from one type of fuel. In addition, the use of biomass will ensure social inclusion in those regions that will have problems with the closure of coal plants.

Table 3.3 The most common renewables-based gas generation alternatives

Type	Biomethane	Hydrogen
Type of fuel	Local renewable	Local renewable
Product of energy	Heat, gas for household needs, fuel for agriculture needs	Car fuel, gas for manufacturing
Time of power plant construction, years	2	?
Efficiency of power plant, %	65	?
Price, mln. EUR/MWh	136	20
Service time, years	20	?

3.3 The Importance of Biomass Cogeneration for Short-Term Transformation

The use of biomass for cogeneration has grown significantly in recent years. This is especially true for Eastern European countries that do not have their own natural gas resources. After realizing the availability of gas and the emergence of price instability, it turned to the use of local biomass. Biomass fully complies with the principles of sustainable development. In the case of incineration, wood waste or waste generated during production is used. Low-value plants that have no prospect of growing into large, environmentally valuable trees can also be used. In the case of biogas, only biological waste generated in the livestock or food processing sectors is used. Biomethane is extracted from them, avoiding the release of this extremely harmful gas into the atmosphere. Biomethane gas is significantly more harmful than carbon dioxide; therefore, biogas power plants will also be relevant in the long term.

Due to its age, the biomass energy sector includes both traditional and modern technologies. New biomass technologies include more efficient energy extraction technologies from lower quality feedstock. However, traditional energy extraction by burning biomass still has a great influence today. Figure 3.1 shows that bioenergy includes different products and raw materials. Among the types of energy production presented, biofuel production is the least sustainable, as it often still uses food-grade raw materials. Second-generation biofuels help to solve this problem, but only partially. For this type of biofuel, palm oil is usually used, which is extracted in areas where valuable forests have been destroyed. Second-generation biofuels produced in EU countries are often labeled as palm oil-free. As technology advances, a syngas breakthrough is possible, further facilitating the decarbonization of the transportation sector.

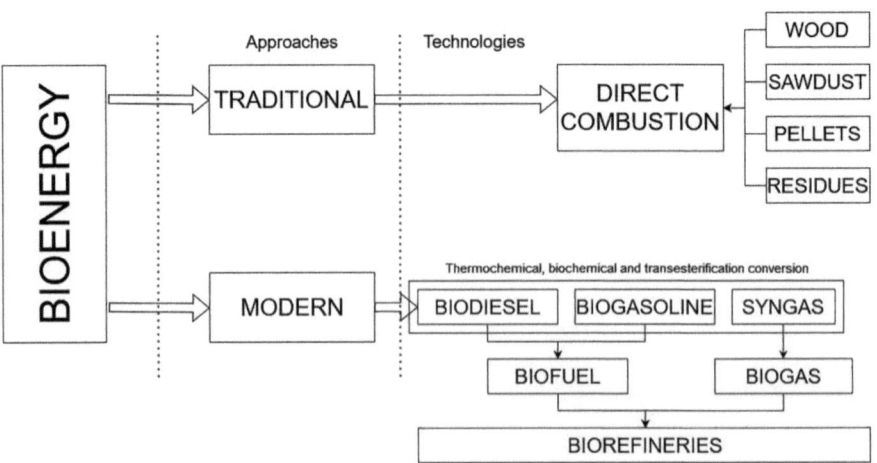

Fig. 3.1 Typical roadmap of bioenergy production [33]

Traditional biomass burning technologies are most efficiently used based on cogeneration technology. Because a large amount of heat is released during the production of electricity, biomass power plants are smaller than coal or gas power plants. This helps to decentralize the energy system—biomass cogeneration power plants are built near sources of heat consumption. In this way, the produced heat is used more efficiently and risks arising from power plant failures or external factors are reduced. By extracting two types of energy, available biofuels are used more efficiently, and consumer needs are met more widely. Biomass cogeneration systems typically use organic materials derived from plants, animals, or waste as fuel to produce both electricity and thermal energy. Cogeneration, or combined heat and power (CHP), represents a paradigm shift in energy production, aimed at optimizing resource utilization and minimizing environmental impact. The cogeneration process is grounded in the second law of thermodynamics, emphasizing the significance of harnessing waste heat to enhance overall energy conversion efficiency. Notable references supporting this thermodynamic foundation include works by Cengel and Boles, Gimelli and Luongo, Santos et al. [34–36]. Biomass cogeneration utilizes biomass feedstocks, such as wood, agricultural residues, or organic waste, to produce electricity through a power generation system (usually a steam turbine or internal combustion engine). The waste heat generated during electricity production is then captured and used for heating or other industrial processes, maximizing the overall energy efficiency of the system.

Biomass cogeneration systems can use various technologies, including steam turbines, internal combustion engines, and gasification systems. These technologies can be adapted to different scales, from small-scale decentralized systems to large-scale power plants. In addition, it is necessary to emphasize that in some cases biomass can be burned in coal-fired power plants. This would avoid major investments in the short term until the coal plant is fully depreciated [37]. Biomass cogeneration is considered a renewable and sustainable energy option with potential environmental benefits. It can contribute to reducing greenhouse gas emissions, provide a reliable source of energy, and support local economies by utilizing local biomass resources [38]. From the perspective of sustainability, the use of worn-out power plant foundations or changing the mode of operation of a worn-out power plant significantly contributes to improving the quality of the environment. In addition, coal or gas power plants converted to biofuel cogeneration power plants will reduce the burden of administrative design and obtain permits, save space for construction, and speed up project implementation.

The new type of cogeneration power plants is characterized by a high level of efficiency. Currently, technologies are already being developed that would allow the production of efficient cogeneration power plants of lower power. This would expand the application of technology in areas where electricity generation activities were not carried out before. As the need for balancing renewable energy grows, the importance of biomass cogeneration will continue to grow. The main technological progress of cogeneration includes:

- Prime mover: Various prime movers, including gas turbines, steam turbines, reciprocating engines, and fuel cells, form the backbone of cogeneration systems. Comprehensive studies were conducted by Heywood [39] on internal combustion engines.
- Heat recovery systems: Efficient heat recovery, a cornerstone of cogeneration, is facilitated by components such as heat exchangers and recuperators. Condensation economizers, which extract energy from hot smoke released into the atmosphere, are an integral part of cogeneration power plants [40].
- Control systems: Advanced control systems play a pivotal role in optimizing the performance of cogeneration plants. Notable references include the work by Åström and Murray [41] on feedback systems and control.

Technological progress in cogeneration creates clear operational advantages. Cogeneration technology has developed in the direction of using both biomass and biogas. In addition to the large amount of energy that can be produced, clean energy production that does not create a negative impact on the environment is ensured. The use of local organic resources prevents more harmful substances such as methane from entering the environment. The main advantages of biomass cogeneration are the following:

- High efficiency: Cogeneration systems are lauded for their high overall efficiency, as documented in studies such as the review by Karki et al. [42] on efficiency improvements in CHP systems.
- Energy cost savings: Economic benefits associated with cogeneration are supported by studies such as the analysis by Bauen [43] on the economic potential of CHP in the European Union.
- Environmental benefits: Cogeneration's positive environmental impact is corroborated by research, including the meta-analysis by Valente et al. [44] on the life cycle assessment of CHP technologies.

As evidenced by the referenced literature, cogeneration stands at the forefront of sustainable energy solutions. Biomass cogeneration provides a versatile and sustainable option for energy production, combining electricity generation with the utilization of waste heat for heating or industrial processes. It aligns with the principles of circular economy and renewable energy, offering a potential solution for decentralized and distributed energy systems. Another important characteristic of energy from biomass is the peculiar factors of the market structure, involving many local business and public entities.

3.4 Characteristics of Biomass Energy Sector

The impact of biomass utilization at different economic levels is significant. The development of the biomass energy business provides prerequisites for the use of local resources, the creation of new jobs, and the start of economic activity in rural areas. Due to the newness of the sector, it is not entirely clear what factors affect the performance of biomass utilization in cogeneration power plants. It is also not entirely clear what market relations unite the biomass processing and energy production markets. The entry of new business entities into the market and their ability to create added value significantly depends on the type of relationship. The scientific literature lacks information on how the value creation process takes place, which entities interact with each other to create a positive impact. It is from this interaction, based on local renewable biofuels, that potential directions of impact arise.

Another relevant shortcoming is that no attention is paid to the regional dimension. In the conducted theoretical or empirical studies emphasizing the benefits of using biomass in general, abstractness prevails, and directions of positive effects are presented without verifying them. When assessing effects at the country level, one is limited to looking for certain correlations. In this case, the assessment is carried out only for one country or a group of countries, but there is no uniform methodology that would allow comparing the countries with each other, considering the differences in their size, economic capacity, and opportunities to obtain fuel. Regional dynamics studies enable comparison of the regions of one country and individual countries. However, there is a notable lack of such studies evaluating the impact of biomass use. The main aspect, assessed from a regional perspective, is the conversion of some object (e.g., adaptation of a coal-burning power plant to biomass burning [45]). Synergistic effects are ignored in this case.

Finally, impact assessment is limited to economic factors and excludes impacts on social well-being and environmental improvement. There is a lack of generalized assessment of the impact of the use of local resources. Nor is there a criterion for assessing the impact of the use of biomass resources on the dynamics of changes in certain indicators. This is also related to the correlation between the use of local biomass and the change in social status. Research is conducted to assess the impacts created by energy production, but the impacts created by the fuel preparation sector are ignored. It is in the latter sector that the prerequisites for the reduction of social inequality and the sustainable use of resources arise. This creates a positive economic impact, but existing research does not address the question of how the economic, social, and environmental factors of renewable fuel production fit together and what impact they create together.

The systematization of the biomass energy sector is defined through the interaction of resource and product markets. The resource market includes biomass processing entities, biomass production owners, logistics, and transportation structures. The main goal of resource market participants is to supply biomass to power plants that use it and create value from biological raw materials that are considered waste [46]. Many market participants operate in the resource market, as the aim is to decentralize biomass supply directions. All entities possessing biomass resources can participate in the market. Solid biomass, solid and liquid agricultural waste, and by-products obtained during environmental management are sold in the resource market. They are properly processed and fed to the incinerators. Many low-skilled people are employed in market activities, and in this way, the regional employment problem is solved. The activities are carried out in regional rural areas with abundant renewable biomass resources. The main direction of supply of prepared biomass is urban areas and industrial companies that need thermal energy, electricity, or biogas. Market operation phases are related to weather conditions and continuous energy demand. During the heat supply season, the demand for biomass increases, and in the warm period, biomass is used to meet the needs of industrial companies and domestic electricity and gas consumers.

Within the structure of the biomass energy sector, there is also a product market, which is the actual reason for the emergence of the resource market. This is due to the emergence of infrastructure using renewable biomass. For that purpose, it is necessary to create a supply chain that allows supplying the power plant. In the activity of the product market, four types of energy are obtained—electricity, heat, steam, and biogas. It is these types of energy that are realized as products of the product market. The product market realizes the potential created in the resource market—local biomass resources that are considered waste. The main objective of the product market participants is to meet the needs of urban types of areas and the needs of industrial enterprises in the supply of energy [47]. In the market for biomass energy products, energy is obtained using fuel processed in the resource market. The product market has signs of decentralization—it is dominated by medium-power power plants located near energy consumption points, distribution networks, and entities responsible for system maintenance. The activity is carried out in those areas that have developed energy distribution networks and demand for energy consumption. The market consists mainly of highly qualified workers who can manage complex energy systems.

The use of biomass in energy is changing the structure of the entire economy. More efficiently used monetary funds are directed in different directions, enabling the positive impact to be multiplied in monetary terms. As fossil resource imports decline, cash remains in the country and helps create added value. It is created not only in an economy, but also in social and environmental spheres. Internal circulation of money begins with the use of hitherto unused biological resources, and their implementation requires both skilled and low-skilled workers. In the development of renewable, biomass-based energy, the progress of local production technologies is promoted, which helps to multiply the added value created within the country, as well as to expand the export of services [48]. Many new products are created using biomass—energy is extracted from biological waste, and organic fertilizers and ash are obtained in intermediate production processes, which significantly increase agricultural production. The resulting synergistic effects allow to state that the use of local biomass significantly boosts the country's economy in the regions and enables the creation of new business units in them, mobilizing human resources of various qualifications. By importing mineral resources from abroad, the flow of money is directed to foreign countries and the opportunity to create value domestically using available physical and human resources as well as scientific and technical potential is lost.

All the above statements define the structure of the biomass energy market as a general part of the energy system (Fig. 3.2). The figure presents the main product lines of the system, changes in the market structure and their conditions, and

3.4 Characteristics of Biomass Energy Sector

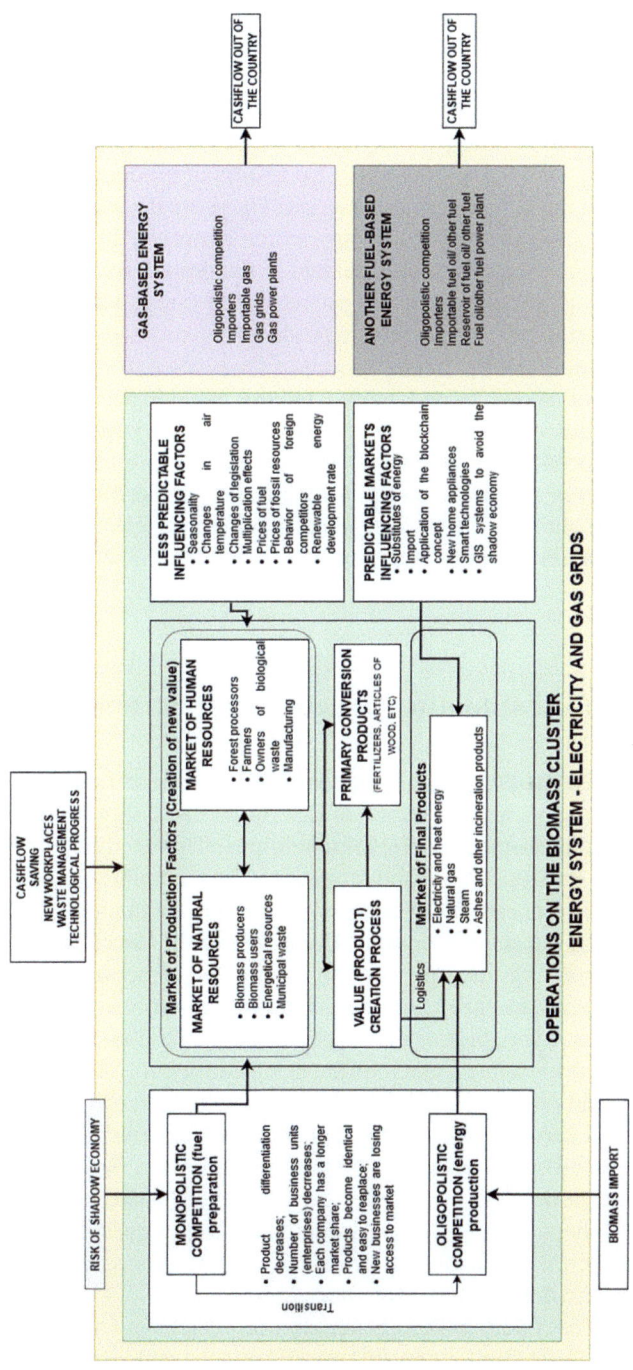

Fig. 3.2 Decentralized regional biomass market structure factor

influencing factors. The scheme highlights the complexity and multifaceted impact of the biomass sector on the economy. The primary products obtained in the factor market create product market products and final products such as fertilizers, wood products, and other products. The product market is dominated by energy products made using local waste. The products of this market include ash, which can be used for the formation of road relief, the laying of landfills, and other complementary activities. The figure shows that the market for factors of production consists of the resource market and the human resource market. These are the main ingredients that shape the performance of the biomass energy sector. However, there is another modification of production factors, which is related to the productive use of waste. This is how the main value (product) creation process takes place, where residual waste from the manufacturing process of end-use products is converted into energy. In this way, there is a transition to the derivative unit of the market structure—the product market. It consists of electricity and thermal energy, ash, biogas, and steam energy. Also included are other combustion products that may be extracted from the biomass processing process. It can be various resins and other by-products. In the product market, all energy products are quite identical, i.e., the form of their use or application differs, but the current energy needs of consumers are met. Later, the structure of the biomass energy sector is examined through the section of the market conjuncture.

3.5 Methods for Estimating Cogeneration Parameters

The research will use the Design of Experiment (DOE) research method. Based on this method, experiments are conducted to determine the ability of one or another production method to compete in market conditions. This method allows to combine relevant data groups into a single system, thus obtaining optimal results. Experimental designs are especially useful in addressing evaluation questions about the effectiveness and impact of programs. Emphasizing the use of comparative data as context for interpreting findings, experimental designs increase our confidence that observed outcomes are the result of a given program or innovation instead of a function of extraneous variables or events [49]. This method is suitable in the case where the aim is to discover new and relevant scientific results. The method can also be used when certain prevention before decision-making is aimed at, since with the help of the method certain optimal interactions of phenomena can be found. This method aims to identify and understand causal relationships between variables. It involves careful experimental design to control potential confounding factors and ensure that data collection effectively answers the research questions and hypotheses. Designing experiments involve selecting factors and procedures and collecting and analyzing data to draw meaningful conclusions.

The experiment uses data from cogeneration power plants located in the Baltic States and includes data from currently prevailing renewable energy technologies based on biomass. Two indicators are selected as processing values:

3.6 Investigation of Cogeneration Conditions in Rural Areas

- Thermal power of cogeneration biomass power plant
- Electric power of cogeneration biomass power plant

These indicators are interrelated and visible in the case of real biomass cogeneration plants. During the development of this type of power plant, heat and electricity must be balanced. The selection is based on the case of the Baltic countries; therefore, since biomass cogeneration practices are widely applied in these countries, the latest and most relevant cogeneration technologies are also used. In addition, a clear sample of data increases the reliability of data sampling. Careful design of experiments is necessary to minimize the number of experiments which need to be carried out in the overall space of variables and parameters (the design space) [50]. Experimental data must be clearly argued, supported either by real examples or previous research [51].

The electricity price indicator is chosen as the dependent variable (Y). The characteristics of the electricity price are the most important in promoting energy transformation in the short term. Since there is a lack of green electricity generation, biomass cogeneration would ensure stable electricity production. However, the cost of electricity production in power plants of different capacities is different. Electricity is considered a by-product of cogeneration, so cost-effective maximization of its production is considered a technological challenge. Balancing the cogeneration power plant allows to achieve the intended goals while obtaining profit from both heat and electricity production.

Response surface methodology (RSM) is used for the research, which allows studying the relationships between explanatory variables and one or more response variables [52]. RSM is suitable for fitting a quadratic surface, and it helps to optimize the process parameters with a minimum number of experiments, as well as to analyze the interaction between the parameters [53]. By combining mathematical and statistical instruments, RSM will provide an opportunity to obtain relevant results on the larger application possibilities of biomass cogeneration. This will lead to a better understanding of the phenomenon, as the study will use practical data.

After RSM-based analysis of biomass cogeneration factors, the optimal combination will be determined from the obtained data, which will allow to achieve the best biomass cogeneration solution. The optimal combination will be used to make investment decisions. Based on this, the optimal price of electricity will be determined, at which it would be possible to develop profitable biomass cogeneration capacities. The optimal combination is based on today's situation of power capacity and recorded energy sales prices.

3.6 Investigation of Cogeneration Conditions in Rural Areas

The initial stage of the research is related to the formation of a suitable data set for the experiment. Due to the specificity of the study, when it consists of two processing values (X1, X2) and one dependent variable (Y), 13 data lines are involved in the experiment. Table 3.4 provides detailed information about the initial phase of the experiment. The main parts of the experiment are heat power (TP) and electricity power (EP). Electricity price is determined based on concluded PPA contracts (average price of 2023), as well as long-term fixed electricity price transactions. Since there are two processing values in this experimental model, exactly 13 tests are performed according to the experimental methodology. The prices of electricity produced with the help of biomass stabilized in 2022, when electricity prices rose significantly in Eastern Europe. This made it possible to form a sustainable business model, where heat energy is sold to cities or factories, and heat energy is transmitted through state-run transmission networks. The transfer of heat to consumers has allowed to avoid the situation where excess heat is released into the environment in the name of electricity production. What's more, connected condensing economizers make it possible to further increase the efficiency of heat production. This justifies the expediency and neutral impact of electricity production on the environment.

Before performing analytical steps, it is necessary to study the main indicators of the model. Table 3.5 presents the main research coefficients, which show the basic diagnostics of the necessary coefficients. This will create conditions for validating the results of future studies.

One such is the coefficient of determination, which indicates the appropriateness of the model for further research. The information presented in Table 3.6 shows that both R-sq and adjusted R-sq indicators are extremely high. It allows making a preliminary conclusion that the model is built responsibly and will be based on the correct equation.

Table 3.4 Experimental design

Experiment number	Processing valuables		Electricity price, EURO ct./kWh
	TP, MW	EP, MW	
Low level (−1)	20	4	
Medium level (0)	30	8	
High level (+1)	40	12	
1	0	0	11.5
2	1	−1	12
3	0	0	10
4	−1	1	8.5
5	−1	0	9
6	0	0	10.1
7	0	0	10.5
8	0	−1	10.8
9	0	0	9.8
10	1	1	7.9
11	0	1	8.6
12	−1	−1	9.7
13	1	0	9.6

3.6 Investigation of Cogeneration Conditions in Rural Areas

Table 3.5 Research coefficients

Term	Coef	SE Coef	T-Value	P-Value	VIF
Constant	0.49	0.247	41.48	0.000	
Heat	0.569	0.243	1.58	0.039	1.00
Electricity	0.474	0.243	5.14	0.001	1.00
Heat*Heat	−0.00643	0.358	−1.80	0.016	1.17
Electricity*Electricity	−0.0152	0.358	−0.68	0.019	1.17
Heat*Electricity	−0.01813	0.298	−2.44	0.045	1.00

Table 3.6 Model summary

S	R-sq	R-sq (adj)	R-sq (pred)
0.595360	99.19%	98.61%	96.72%

The next stage of the research is related to checking the adequacy of the data analyzed. In this case, the value of the coefficient of determination, which evaluates possible changes in the dependent variable, is evaluated. In this model, the value of the coefficient of determination reaches 99.19%. Next, analysis of variance is carried out, which will allow the model equation to be formed. Table 3.7 presents the main results of the analysis. This analysis is important in that it provides the indicators necessary to construct the model equation. In the presence of inappropriate indicators, the equation may not be accurate and may not give the required results.

Table 2.5 shows that the analyzed model is appropriate—lack of fit >0.05. This means that there is an adequacy between the proposed model and the experimental data [54]. This situation makes it possible to form a second-level equation, which is optimal for performing similar calculations. The equation of the model includes the determination of the relationships between the price of electricity and the energy released during cogeneration. The regression equation in uncoded units is as follows:

$$Y = 0.49 + 0.569\,TP + 0.474\,EP - 0.00643\,TP^*TP - 0.0152\,EP^*EP - 0.01813\,TP^*EP \tag{3.1}$$

The specified equation is related to graphically presented three-dimensional response surface plots. Constant values are selected in Fig. 3.3.

The next stage of the study is related to the determination of optimal parameters. Optimal parameters will help answer the question of what combination of cogeneration power plants would ensure a competitive energy price. For this purpose, a contour plot is created, which includes thermal and electrical power, as well as the cost of electricity. The contour plot presented in Fig. 3.4 shows the distribution of the relevant indicators. This contour plot shows that the interaction between heat and electricity power has significant effect on electricity price. This is reflected in the shape of the ellipse visible in the graph. In this case, a clear influence of variables on the dependent variable can be seen when evaluating power differences. In future

Table 3.7 Analysis of variance

Source	DF	Adj SS	Adj MS	F-Value	P-Value
Model	5	14.2711	2.8542	8.05	0.008
Linear	2	10.2567	5.1283	14.47	0.003
Heat	1	0.8817	0.8817	2.49	0.159
Electricity	1	9.3750	9.3750	26.45	0.001
Square	2	1.9120	0.9560	2.70	0.135
Heat*Heat	1	1.1423	1.1423	3.22	0.116
Electricity*Electricity	1	0.1632	0.1632	0.46	0.419
2-Way Interaction	1	2.1025	2.1025	5.93	0.045
Heat*Electricity	1	2.1025	2.1025	5.93	0.045
Error	7	2.4812	0.3545		
Lack-of-Fit	3	0.6532	0.2177	0.48	0.716
Pure Error	4	1.8280	0.4570		
Total	12	16.7523			

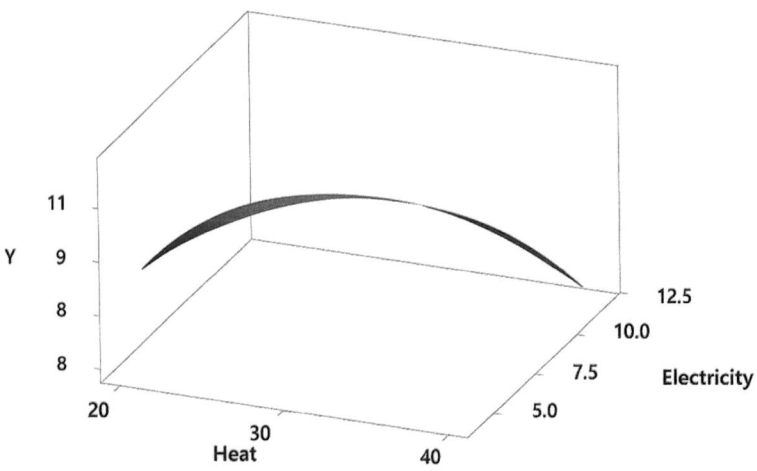

Fig. 3.3 Combined effect of electricity (EP) and heat (TP) on electricity price (Y)

research, if the supply policy changes, one more component—cooling—could be included. For now, these studies are more at the concept level [55], but in the future, it will be necessary to evaluate the potential of combined cooling, heating, and power in cities.

The data of the previously mentioned experiments are used to determine the optimal indicators. The results are presented in Fig. 3.5. When determining the optimal parameters, large thermal and electric power plants work most efficiently. Thus, 40 MW of thermal power was selected, combining it with 12 MW of electrical

3.6 Investigation of Cogeneration Conditions in Rural Areas

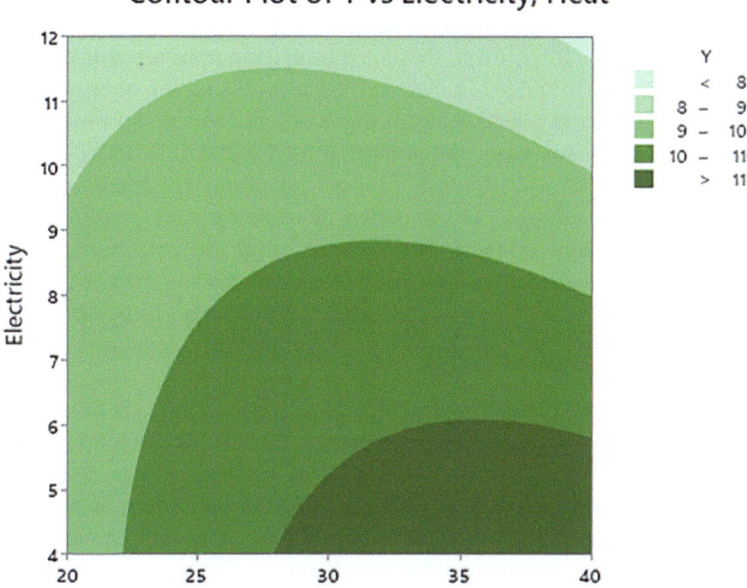

Fig. 3.4 Contour plot of electricity (EP) and heat (TP) on electricity price (Y)

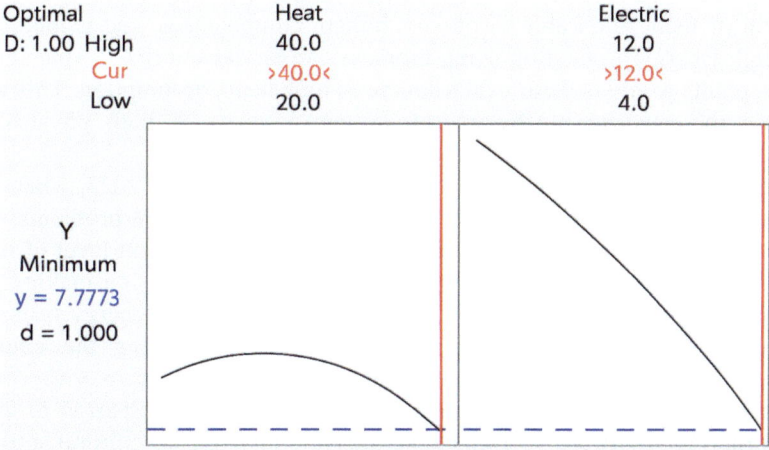

Fig. 3.5 Optimal parameters of electricity (EP), heat (TP), and electricity price (Y)

power. This power is suitable for cities with a population of around 40,000 or large factories. A combined option is also possible when such a power plant is developed by a factory, and the excess heat is transferred to the residents of a nearby city. This optimal combination results in 0.77773 EURO ct. price per kWh of electricity.

The application of cogeneration technology is a suitable solution for the energy transformation of the intermediate period. This allows achieving a multidirectional positive effect. First, there is a transition to renewable energy based on the use of local raw materials. Second, by reorienting the energy system, the problems of using local waste, employing workers, and using polluting power plants are solved. In this case, the conversion of waste into energy is ensured, and in some cases, the use of fossil fuel power plants for the consumption of renewable energy resources. Third, when developing new power plants, they can be built near major consumption centers, thus decentralizing production capacity. The performed analysis showed that current examples of cogeneration can provide opportunities to evaluate optimal production indicators, thus confirming the necessity and profitability of sustainable, decentralized energy solutions.

Decarbonization of the energy sector will require significant financial investment and infrastructure changes. These processes will take place for decades to come, but faster interim solutions are necessary to stop climate change. One of the intermediate solutions for electricity production and network balancing can be the use of biomass cogeneration. This would make it possible to use renewable local biofuel resources and old coal power plants and to prepare for a new era of hydrogen use.

The biomass cogeneration sector is characterized by distinctive market structure factors involving a wide range of stakeholders. Due to the abundance of products made from biomass, suitable conditions are created to adapt to market changes and ensure the decarbonization of the energy sector. This is done with the help of local renewable resources, human competences, and technological potential. Energy production using biomass can be decentralized, since cogeneration plants would be built near a source of high heat consumption. This would increase the security of the energy system in case of both physical and cyberattacks.

The need to deploy renewable energy became apparent in 2022, when fossil fuel prices were historically high. This highlighted the main problems, especially in Europe—dependence on fossil fuel prices, insufficient level of investment in renewable energy technologies, and slow decision-making. The production of green electricity ensures decentralization of the energy system and resistance to supply and price shocks, while strengthening the country's economy.

In addition to the use of biomass during the intermediate period of energy transformation, there are potential synergies arising from agricultural activities. Agricultural activities generate a wide variety of biomass suitable for energy production. In the context of increasing levels of agricultural pollution, energy transformation activities would help to reduce the negative aspects of agrarian activities. At the same time, it would contribute to the strengthening of communities and the possibility to further diversify the energy system.

References

1. Caineng, Z. O. U., Xiong, B., Huaqing, X. U. E., Zheng, D., Zhixin, G. E., Ying, W. A. N. G., et al. (2021). The role of new energy in carbon neutral. *Petroleum Exploration and Development, 48*(2), 480–491.
2. Lund, H., & Mathiesen, B. V. (2009). Energy system analysis of 100% renewable energy systems—The case of Denmark in years 2030 and 2050. *Energy, 34*(5), 524–531.
3. Farhangi, H. (2009). The path of the smart grid. *IEEE Power and Energy Magazine, 8*(1), 18–28.
4. Jing, H., Zhu, P., Zheng, X., Zhang, Z., Wang, D., & Li, Y. (2022). Theory-oriented screening and discovery of advanced energy transformation materials in electrocatalysis. *Advanced Powder Materials, 1*(1), 100013.
5. Chu, S., & Majumdar, A. (2012). Opportunities and challenges for a sustainable energy future. *Nature, 488*(7411), 294–303.
6. Harrison, K. W., Remick, R., & Martin, G. D. (2010). *Hydrogen production: Fundamentals and case study summaries*. National Renewable Energy Laboratory (NREL).
7. Yasmeen, R., Zhang, X., Tao, R., & Shah, W. U. H. (2023). The impact of green technology, environmental tax and natural resources on energy efficiency and productivity: Perspective of OECD rule of law. *Energy Reports, 9*, 1308–1319.
8. Igliński, B., Kiełkowska, U., Pietrzak, M. B., Skrzatek, M., Kumar, G., & Piechota, G. (2023). The regional energy transformation in the context of renewable energy sources potential. *Renewable Energy, 218*, 119246.
9. Güler, İ., Atan, M., & Adalı, Z. (2024). The effect of economic growth, investment, and unemployment on renewable energy transition: Evidence from OECD countries. *Environmental Science and Pollution Research, 31*(39), 52001–52016.
10. Bali Swain, R., Karimu, A., & Gråd, E. (2022). Sustainable development, renewable energy transformation and employment impact in the EU. *International Journal of Sustainable Development & World Ecology, 29*(8), 695–708.
11. Xu, Y., Liu, A., Li, Z., Li, J., Xiong, J., & Fan, P. (2023). Review of green supply-chain management diffusion in the context of energy transformation. *Energies, 16*(2), 686.
12. Chomać-Pierzecka, E., Sobczak, A., & Urbańczyk, E. (2022). RES market development and public awareness of the economic and environmental dimension of the energy transformation in Poland and Lithuania. *Energies, 15*(15), 5461.
13. Sánchez García, J., & Galdeano Gómez, E. (2023). What drives the preferences for cleaner energy? Parametrizing the elasticities of environmental quality demand for greenhouse gases. *Oeconomia Copernicana, 14*(2), 449–482.
14. Chudy-Laskowska, K., & Pisula, T. (2022). An analysis of the use of energy from conventional fossil fuels and green renewable energy in the context of the European Union's planned energy transformation. *Energies, 15*(19), 7369.
15. Mohamed, M., & El-Saber, N. (2023). Toward energy transformation: Intelligent decision-making model based on uncertainty neutrosophic theory. *Neutrosophic Systems with Applications, 9*, 13–23.
16. Pietrzak, M. B., Olczyk, M., & Kuc-Czarnecka, M. E. (2022). Assessment of the feasibility of energy transformation processes in European Union member states. *Energies, 15*(2), 661.
17. Kiciński, J. (2021). Green energy transformation in Poland. *Bulletin of the Polish Academy of Sciences. Technical Sciences, 69*(1), 136213.
18. He, L., Wang, B., Xu, W., Cui, Q., & Chen, H. (2022). Could China's long-term low-carbon energy transformation achieve the double dividend effect for the economy and environment? *Environmental Science and Pollution Research*, 1–17.
19. Hughes, T. P. (2011). *Networks of power: Electrification in Western Society, 1880-1930*. JHU Press.
20. International Atomic Energy Agency. (2022). *Advances in small modular reactor technology developments*. IAEA: Advanced Reactors Information System (ARIS).

21. Fearnside, P. M. (2014). Impacts of Brazil's Madeira River dams: Unlearned lessons for hydroelectric development in Amazonia. *Environmental Science & Policy, 38*, 164–172.
22. Jonek-Kowalska, I. (2022). Assessing the energy security of European countries in the resource and economic context. *Oeconomia Copernicana, 13*(2), 301–334.
23. U.S. Department of Energy. (2021). *Annual energy outlook*. U.S. Department of Energy.
24. Janssens-Maenhout, G., Crippa, M., Guizzardi, D., Muntean, M., Schaaf, E., Dentener, F., et al. (2019). EDGAR v4. 3.2 global atlas of the three major greenhouse gas emissions for the period 1970–2012. *Earth System Science Data, 11*(3), 959–1002.
25. Chovancová, J., & Tej, J. (2020). Decoupling economic growth from greenhouse gas emissions: The case of the energy sector in V4 countries. *Equilibrium. Quarterly Journal of Economics and Economic Policy, 15*(2), 235–251.
26. Pavlov, G. K., & Olesen, B. W. (2012). Thermal energy storage—A review of concepts and systems for heating and cooling applications in buildings: Part 1—Seasonal storage in the ground. *HVAC&R Research, 18*(3), 515–538.
27. Dincer, I., & Rosen, M. A. (2015). *Thermal energy storage: Systems and applications*. Wiley.
28. Speece, R. E. (1996). *Anaerobic biotechnology for industrial wastewaters*. Archae Press.
29. Demirel, B., & Scherer, P. (2008). The roles of acetotrophic and hydrogenotrophic methanogens during anaerobic conversion of biomass to methane: A review. *Reviews in Environmental Science and Bio/Technology, 7*, 173–190.
30. European Biogas Association (EBA). *EBA's vision for renewable gas in the green transition.* https://www.europeanbiogas.eu/wp-content/uploads/2018/09/EBA-Vision-for-Renewable-Gas.pdf
31. National Renewable Energy Laboratory (NREL). *Hydrogen production: Natural gas reforming*. https://www.nrel.gov/hydrogen/proj_production_nat_gas_reforming.html
32. U.S. Department of Energy (DOE). *Hydrogen basics*. https://www.energy.gov/eere/fuelcells/hydrogen-basics
33. Rashidi, N. A., Chai, Y. H., & Yusup, S. (2022). Biomass energy in Malaysia: Current scenario, policies, and implementation challenges. *Bioenergy Research, 15*(3), 1371–1386.
34. Cengel, Y. A., & Boles, M. A. (2014). *Thermodynamics: An engineering approach*. McGraw-Hill Education.
35. Gimelli, A., & Luongo, A. (2014). Thermodynamic and experimental analysis of a biomass steam power plant: Critical issues and their possible solutions with CCGT systems. *Energy Procedia, 45*, 227–236.
36. Santos, V. O., Queiroz, L. S., Araujo, R. O., Ribeiro, F. C., Guimarães, M. N., da Costa, C. E., et al. (2020). Pyrolysis of acai seed biomass: Kinetics and thermodynamic parameters using thermogravimetric analysis. *Bioresource Technology Reports, 12*, 100553.
37. Yang, W., Pudasainee, D., Gupta, R., Li, W., Wang, B., & Sun, L. (2021). An overview of inorganic particulate matter emission from coal/biomass/MSW combustion: Sampling and measurement, formation, distribution, inorganic composition and influencing factors. *Fuel Processing Technology, 213*, 106657.
38. Hiloidhari, M., Sharno, M. A., Baruah, D. C., & Bezbaruah, A. N. (2023). Green and sustainable biomass supply chain for environmental, social and economic benefits. *Biomass and Bioenergy, 175*, 106893.
39. Heywood, J. B. (2014). *Internal combustion engine fundamentals*. McGraw-Hill Education.
40. Xu, Q., Wu, J., Guo, Z., Xue, X., & Li, X. (2022). Analysis of optimal intermediate temperature and injection pressure for refrigerant injection heat pump systems with economiser. *Applied Thermal Engineering, 210*, 118361.
41. Åström, K. J., & Murray, R. M. (2010). *Feedback systems: An introduction for scientists and engineers*. Princeton University Press.
42. Karki, S., Kulkarni, M., Mann, M. D., & Salehfar, H. (2007). Efficiency improvements through combined heat and power for on-site distributed generation technologies. *Cogeneration and Distributed Generation Journal, 22*(3), 19–34.

References

43. Bauen, A. (2010). *The economic potential of CHP in the European Union*. International Energy Agency (IEA).
44. Valente, A., Iribarren, D., & Dufour, J. (2017). Life cycle assessment of hydrogen energy systems: A review of methodological choices. *The International Journal of Life Cycle Assessment, 22*, 346–363.
45. Toklu, E. (2017). Biomass energy potential and utilization in Turkey. *Renewable Energy, 107*, 235–244.
46. Popp, J., Kovács, S., Oláh, J., Divéki, Z., & Balázs, E. (2021). Bioeconomy: Biomass and biomass-based energy supply and demand. *New Biotechnology, 60*, 76–84.
47. Favero, A., Daigneault, A., Sohngen, B., & Baker, J. (2023). A system-wide assessment of forest biomass production, markets, and carbon. *GCB Bioenergy, 15*(2), 154–165.
48. Zetterholm, J., Bryngemark, E., Ahlström, J., Söderholm, P., Harvey, S., & Wetterlund, E. (2020). Economic evaluation of large-scale biorefinery deployment: A framework integrating dynamic biomass market and techno-economic models. *Sustainability, 12*(17), 7126.
49. Gribbons, B., & Herman, J. (2019). True and quasi-experimental designs. *Practical Assessment, Research, and Evaluation, 5*(1), 14.
50. Anderson, V. L., & McLean, R. A. (2018). *Design of experiments: A realistic approach*. CRC Press.
51. Wen, C., Zhang, Y., Wang, C., Xue, D., Bai, Y., Antonov, S., et al. (2019). Machine learning assisted design of high entropy alloys with desired property. *Acta Materialia, 170*, 109–117.
52. Karimifard, S., & Moghaddam, M. R. A. (2018). Application of response surface methodology in physicochemical removal of dyes from wastewater: A critical review. *Science of the Total Environment, 640*, 772–797.
53. Behera, S. K., Meena, H., Chakraborty, S., & Meikap, B. C. (2018). Application of response surface methodology (RSM) for optimization of leaching parameters for ash reduction from low-grade coal. *International Journal of Mining Science and Technology, 28*(4), 621–629.
54. Chelladurai, S. J. S., Murugan, K., Ray, A. P., Upadhyaya, M., Narasimharaj, V., & Gnanasekaran, S. (2021). Optimization of process parameters using response surface methodology: A review. *Materials Today: Proceedings, 37*, 1301–1304.
55. Tataraki, K., Giannini, E., Kavvadias, K., & Maroulis, Z. (2020). Cogeneration economics for greenhouses in Europe. *Energies, 13*(13), 3373.

Open Access This chapter is licensed under the terms of the Creative Commons Attribution-NonCommercial-NoDerivatives 4.0 International License (http://creativecommons.org/licenses/by-nc-nd/4.0/), which permits any noncommercial use, sharing, distribution and reproduction in any medium or format, as long as you give appropriate credit to the original author(s) and the source, provide a link to the Creative Commons license and indicate if you modified the licensed material. You do not have permission under this license to share adapted material derived from this chapter or parts of it.

The images or other third party material in this chapter are included in the chapter's Creative Commons license, unless indicated otherwise in a credit line to the material. If material is not included in the chapter's Creative Commons license and your intended use is not permitted by statutory regulation or exceeds the permitted use, you will need to obtain permission directly from the copyright holder.

Chapter 4
The Relation Between the Agricultural Sector and the Energy Transformation

4.1 Paradigm Shift in the Agricultural Sector from an Energy Perspective

As the energy system expands, more and more stakeholders are involved. The decentralization of the energy system is no longer a surprising factor, but synergies with agricultural activities are becoming more and more apparent. Farmers face the huge challenge of climate change. Livestock farming is increasingly recognized as environmentally damaging, but there is still a lack of technology to decarbonize this sector. Manure-to-energy conversion is already advanced and cost-effective, but daily emissions from livestock are still a problem. In addition, unsustainable tillage also leads to higher emissions instead of fixing carbon in the ground. Food waste is another major problem, both from the processing of the produce grown and from the non-consumption of the finished product. Manure treatment plants can also help solve this problem.

The synergy between renewable energy and agriculture involves integrating renewable energy systems into agricultural operations to create mutual benefits for both sectors. This relationship is crucial for advancing sustainable practices, enhancing energy security, and addressing the global challenge of climate change. Farms, especially those involved in the processing of produce, are becoming increasingly large energy consumers. There are different solutions that can help farms to decarbonize their operations while having a positive impact on the environment. Farms can host solar photovoltaic (PV) systems, either on the ground or integrated into buildings, such as on barn roofs. This not only provides a clean energy source for the farm's operations but can also generate additional income through the sale of excess electricity. Agrivoltaic systems, which combine solar energy production with crop cultivation, can enhance land use efficiency and reduce water evaporation from crops, improving agricultural productivity [1]. This solution requires the lowest time and financial costs, and with flexible planning, synergies can be achieved—solar cells can be the basis for new carports or used as roofs on new buildings. For existing buildings, additional measurements are required to maximize efficiency. The solutions analyzed below require more lead time and the initial investment is relatively higher than for solar power plants. Wind turbines can be installed on agricultural land with minimal disruption to farming activities. This allows farmers to diversify income through leasing land for wind energy production or owning turbines directly. The income from wind energy can help stabilize farm income, which is often subject to variability due to price fluctuations and weather conditions [2]. Wind energy is favorable to farms, as those farms that own the land can choose the most suitable area for a wind turbine project. However, the coordination of wind turbine projects takes a relatively long time. During this period, the cost-effectiveness and grid capacity characteristics of the wind farm may change substantially.

There are other alternatives that are not widely used because of their geographical characteristics. These solutions can be used to complement the technologies presented above. Geothermal energy can be used for heating greenhouses, enabling year-round cultivation in cooler climates. This use of renewable heat sources can reduce dependency on fossil fuels and lower greenhouse gas emissions, contributing to more sustainable agricultural practices [3]. An essential element of this technology is a stable electricity supply to support the geothermal water recovery process. This makes it necessary to pursue solar energy development alongside geothermal energy development. This aspect and the lack of practical application of geothermal energy have led to a reduction in the use of this type of energy production on farms. Another technology that can be used on farms is hydropower. Small-scale hydropower systems can be used to generate electricity or irrigate the land. Dams are an appropriate remedy to control floods and maintain or increase agricultural production in the farm. This can provide power for irrigation systems and other farm operations, improving energy access and efficiency in rural areas [4]. However, there are a couple of nuances to consider when looking at the use of hydropower in agriculture. Firstly, the ethical aspect of hydropower is increasingly being addressed, with its significant environmental and fish migration impacts. Secondly, the potential of hydropower is only available to a small proportion of farms that are located close to watery rivers. Thirdly, the development of new hydropower plants, particularly in the European Union and the USA, is highly regulated. The information presented suggests that the main trends in farm decarbonization relate to wind, solar, and biomass.

However, the clearest potential for synergies relates to the use of biomass and bioenergy. This is particularly true for the use of waste from agricultural activities. Agriculture is generally very wasteful and therefore also a source of greenhouse gases. The issue of methane production from livestock on farms should be viewed as a positive option to create green energy and help reduce greenhouse effects. The main challenge is to establish small- or medium-sized family farms that essentially lack biogas potential and large modern farms that can be targeted for biogas production [5]. Agriculture produces various by-products, such as crop residues, manure, and other organic waste, which can be converted into bioenergy. This process can provide a renewable energy source while reducing waste and greenhouse gas emissions. Anaerobic digestion of agricultural waste can produce biogas for heating, electricity, and fuel, contributing to farm sustainability and energy self-sufficiency. The possibilities that have a shining future are the large farms and industries that need to be actively stimulated. It includes not only existing farms with biological gas potential but also future farms to be built in the near future. Both legally and economically, those farms need to be incentivized as producers of biogas, not just based on whether they can produce energy, but because they will engage not only for the sake of communication but also due to the fact that biogas production effectively addresses both biological waste issues and waste management on farms [6]. One of the biggest challenges for the future is the treatment of food waste. The developed world is witnessing an increasing food waste dynamic. Consumer awareness can help reduce food waste, but it will not eliminate the problem of treating the waste that is already generated. Farms can make a significant contribution to converting food waste into energy or gas. A key element is biogas production capacity. New supply chains can be created alongside the use of on-farm waste to feed urban food waste into farm-managed biogas reactors. This would improve the possibility of producing high-quality biogas, thus allowing for increased farm income from energy sales. In addition, the material obtained from the recycling of waste would be suitable for fertilization of crops. Another challenge is the situation in less-developed countries. Previous research showed positive relationship between CO_2 emissions and real GDP, nonrenewable energy consumption, and agricultural value added in the long run [7]. A lack of cost-effective technologies is holding back the progress of decarbonization in agriculture. Other research shows that per capita output and RE have a negative relationship, related to carbon emissions, while per capita nonrenewable energy and agriculture exert positive effects on carbon emissions [8]. This research investigated the BRICS countries. The very slow progress in developing countries will make it difficult to decarbonize the sector. Even more, the growing agricultural production in these countries creates the assumption that the scale of environmental problems will only grow.

Previous research papers have only analyzed certain conceptual aspects of energy, with less consideration of the potential synergies between technologies. The studies recognize the key factor that renewable energy can help reduce CO_2 emissions from agriculture [9–11]. However, other key aspects are dealt with in a piecemeal manner. On the one hand, there are studies that look at the possible links between the two concepts [12,13]. Nevertheless, these studies deal with some generic aspects, and the climate impacts of decarbonization of agriculture have not yet been assessed in sufficient depth. There are studies that look at circular economy alternatives in agriculture using renewable energy [14]. However, the concept of renewable energy in agriculture has not yet been fully developed, as there is no clear strategic thinking to consistently direct resources toward decarbonizing the agricultural sector. This paper outlines the key synergies that would enable a coherent path toward decarbonization. The main problem is how to seamlessly integrate energy and climate change mitigation activities into the structure of different farm sizes. As small farms are one of the most vulnerable sectors of the economy, their integration into decarbonization activities must be carried out in a responsible manner, making the best use of the resources already available. The novelty of the paper is related to the clearly identified opportunities for farms to both comply with the principles of sustainable development and to generate additional income from energy activities without substantial material investment. The focus is on directions that would not only meet the energy impacts of farms but also enable them to sell energy on the market. In the case of livestock farms, a clear alternative to fossil fuels emerges in the form of biomethane produced in biogas reactors. It can be used to power specially adapted tractors or other implements that currently use diesel. The resulting double effect—reduced pollution on farms and in the use of machinery—would lead to significant reductions in harmful gas emissions in the short term.

4.2 The Necessity of Renewable Energy for the Decarbonization of Farms

As the impacts of climate change become more acute, there is a need to broaden the scope for decarbonization. There is a growing consensus that decarbonization of the agriculture sector is inevitable. This process can be pursued in several ways. It is necessary to manage the waste of animal origin generated in livestock farms considering environmental and economic aspects. However, there is another problem: the need to reduce daily emissions from livestock. This can be done by producing functional feed that is easier to digest. This would reduce the daily release of gases into the environment, while reducing the amount of feed wasted. On crop farms, the trend toward reducing emissions is more varied. The first step is to optimize fuel consumption by moving away from plowing and toward direct drilling technologies. Reducing pesticide use can also help reduce pollution. However, the production and use of renewable energy are key factors in decarbonization. Renewable energy systems can significantly reduce agricultural greenhouse gas (GHG) emissions through substitution of fossil fuel-based energy sources, energy efficiency, and agriculture using waste to generate energy. To maximize success, key synergies need to be identified.

The processing of agricultural by-products and waste in biogas reactors is necessary in order to reduce the negative impact on the environment. On the one hand, the use of these materials would reduce the use of coal and fossil fuels, while eliminating the possibility of biological materials simply rotting in the open, releasing energy [15]. On the other hand, biogas production must be carried out responsibly, without the inclusion of food-grade materials [16]. This challenge can be solved by cooperatives for several farmers or by creating separate cooperatives focused on biogas production. Another opportunity to decarbonize the environment is related to more active use of biomass. Currently, a large part of the biomass comes from forests, and it is often not possible to check whether waste or high added value wood is being burned. To avoid the burning of wood suitable for industry and better use of less productive areas, promotion of agroforestry is necessary. Such a solution would allow to increase the volume of carbon storage in the land, while providing

4.2 The Necessity of Renewable Energy for the Decarbonization of Farms

economic benefits to farmers [17]. This solution may be appropriate in Asia, where deforestation is a major problem. It is assumed that this will enable the achievement of climate change mitigation goals [18]. India, one of the largest countries in the region, uses agroforestry to achieve compact climate and farmers' economic viability goals [19]. Another important aspect is that it helps to promote biodiversity [20]. In any case, the most important thing on the path of decarbonization is to implement complex solutions. This will create the conditions to prevent the waste of resources and contribute more effectively to the goals of stopping climate change.

Different technologies, when combined, can enable the efficient use of waste from farms while reducing the need for fossil fuels. Energy production can be carried out on a large scale (to sell part of the energy) or in an optimal mode (to produce energy and hot water for the farm). In all cases, renewable energy contributes to the contribution of farms to reducing the level of climate change impacts. The choice of technology is a particularly important aspect for farms, as a significant proportion of farms are small family farms. Their resource constraints make it necessary to have clear investment priorities. Moreover, the direction of investment varies according to the structure of the farm. Key aspects of farm decarbonization are as follows:

- Solar photovoltaic (PV) panels and solar energy systems can power agricultural operations, irrigation systems, and factories. They can reduce the carbon footprint and reduce the environmental impact of agricultural operations [21]. The farms use different buildings, which allows synergies to be achieved simultaneously by using solar panels on the roof. When new buildings are built, they should be designed to maximize solar potential. With the development of the battery market, the energy produced by solar panels can be stored cost-effectively in on-farm energy storage facilities. Solar energy forms new alternatives for activities. One of these is aeroponics, the operation of which requires electricity. The advantage of solar energy is that it can be integrated into greenhouses [22,23]. It is argued that solar energy can make a particularly big impact in the global south, where there is a lack of stable sources of energy production [24].
- Wind farms located on or near farmland can provide a clean, renewable source of electricity for agricultural operations, thereby reducing the need for coal, natural gas, and oil-based electricity GHG emissions directly associated with on-farm energy use [25]. Developing wind energy capacity can create synergies with other developers: by cooperating, faster construction speeds can be achieved, with less impact on the soil. Storage batteries are essential. However, it is agreed that the synergy between wind energy and farm operations is problematic enough. This is because the state-of-the-art wind energy technologies available for a statistical farm are redundant [26]. These solutions are more suitable for agro-industry, and not for a medium-sized farm, because in the latter case, the necessary costs for the adaptation and efficient use of such a power plant are much higher. Greater synergy is possible when a certain part of the land managed by the farm is leased to wind power developers [27,28].

These two types of energy can be compared with each other, since they are suitable for development on land areas managed by farmers. Due to the already established practice of developing such power plants, it is possible to single out essential elements that are relevant both for the farm and the region. Table 4.1 presents a comparison of the main characteristics relevant to the farm. The table shows the complexity of the situation, when it is necessary to weigh both initial investments and subsequent costs.

Next to these types of energy production, there are already tested technologies whose interaction with the agricultural sector is relatively well studied. However, these solutions are constantly being improved to achieve better economic and environmental results. Using these energy resources together with the latest energy efficiency technologies, the farm can significantly reduce operating costs. The following renewable energy solutions suitable for farms are:

- Bioenergy production: The conversion of agricultural waste (e.g., crop residues, manure) into bioenergy (biogas, biofuel) through processes such as anaerobic digestion and biomass gasification helps manage waste and reduces emissions from decomposition. The potential of this bioenergy source replaces fossil fuels in heat, electricity generation, and transport [29]. The potential for bioenergy on farms is greatest in the short term—organic waste that is converted into energy can form the basis of energy production on farms. As the cost of more advanced technologies decreases, small farms will have the opportunity to install solar and wind energy capacity, as well as energy storage facilities, more cost-effectively.
- Carbon sequestration: Some energy crops can sequester carbon in their biomass and soil, further reducing GHG emissions. However, total life cycle emissions and land use changes resulting from bioenergy cropping need to be considered to ensure that it provides environmental benefits it is expected to provide [30]. Carbon retention in soil grows with fermented organic matter.
- Energy efficiency improvements: Renewable energy systems are often technological improvements that increase the energy efficiency of the farm. Energy efficiency means that less energy is required, further reducing the company's overall GHG emissions [31]. Energy efficiency can be developed in several ways. Firstly, an energy audit is needed to identify areas of energy waste. By identifying the sources of waste, investments are directed towards eliminating them. Once these objectives have been achieved, additional investments in energy production can be considered.
- In geothermal fields, this energy can be used for greenhouses and other agricultural areas. Geothermal energy produces carbon-free heat and energy, helping to reduce GHG emissions from agriculture [32]. The high cost of geothermal energy technology means that it is only suitable for large, high value-added

Table 4.1 Characteristics of wind and solar energy in farms

Type	Need of land	Need of capital	Efficiency, %	Usage for farm	Need of service
Wind	Little	High	>50	Complicated	Necessary
Solar	Great	Low	~28	Suitable	Annual

farms. The use of geothermal water inevitably requires the creation of electricity generation capacity; otherwise, the potential of green production will be only partially exploited.
- Small hydroelectric systems can be installed in agricultural water systems, such as irrigation systems and dams. These systems provide a renewable source of electricity with very low GHG emissions compared to fossil fuel energy production [33]. However, due to ethical concerns and the loss of land suitable for farming, small hydropower is increasingly underdeveloped in developed countries.

Looking at the situation of both small and large farms, it can be concluded that the use of renewable energy would help to solve the complex problems of pollution generated by farms. According to the structured information, two directions of change can be distinguished: long and short term. In the long term, it is necessary to focus on technologies that not only ensure high energy productivity but also maintain an appropriate level of energy efficiency. In order to achieve these goals, it is necessary to look for technologies on a large scale, thus creating conditions for the development of agriculture. The search for technologies can be promoted with one-time support focused on raising qualifications and identifying the need for technologies [34]. Energy system monitoring measures avoid situations where energy is wasted because of certain isolated problems. Energy power management will also help improve the efficiency of the farm's energy system. The development of energy storage technologies will bring about a fundamental change for farms by using the energy generated by surplus production to meet the needs of farms during the night. In the short term, the development of bioenergy initiatives is a key factor for farm success. The treatment of various animal and plant waste streams would generate large amounts of energy. This energy would enable the energy needs of the farm to be met, with the surplus being sold on the market. Bioenergy activities are characterized by stability of production: with sufficient waste potential, production can be continuous. The liquid material generated after production is used to fertilize fields. The potential for synergies between energy and agriculture activities using biomass is explored in more detail.

4.3 Bioenergy Potential in the Agriculture Sector

The potential of bioenergy essentially lies in the recycling of waste into other materials for energy recovery. Energy can be of three types—electricity, heat, or biomethane gas. Farms processing agricultural products may require all three types of energy. Biomethane is the most promising type of bioenergy as it can be used as fuel for tractors. The biomethane concept is best developed in the agricultural machinery sector. In principle, biomethane has no other environmentally friendly substitutes for tractors.

The main potential for bioenergy lies in biomethane. The extraction of this gas from organic waste has created a breakthrough in the energy sector, reducing the impact of natural gas and diesel on agriculture. Biomethane is a higher value-added product than electricity and heat, with fewer renewable substitutes. Although biomethane development technologies are more expensive, they are more marketable due to the uniqueness of the product. It is noted that the main market for biomethane development is Europe. Biomethane production is being strongly promoted through the EU Green Deal initiatives. Biomethane production in Europe has grown exponentially, driven by the industry's commitment to carbon emissions and energy security. In 2021, Europe reached a record number of biomethane plant demolitions, with a total of 1023 sites. This expansion represents a significant step toward decarbonization of the EU economy [35]. Biomethane can also be produced by industrial companies that process cereal products. The main factor for the development of biomethane is the possibility to connect to main gas pipelines. This allows for the sale of treated biomethane on the market, creating the conditions for a cross-border biomethane sales market. This is driving the rapid expansion of the biomethane industry on the continent. The European Biogas Association (EBA) and Gas Infrastructure Europe (GIE) revealed that the number of biomethane plants increased by almost 30% compared to the previous phase of their biomethane map. This increase helps to scale up to reach of the European Commission's target of 35 billion cubic meters by 2030. It emphasizes the promotion of sectoral efforts, as outlined in the REPowerEU framework. This objective aims to enhance the EU's energy security and to increase the uptake of biomethane [36]. If the forward-looking plans come to fruition, a large part of food waste will be recycled into energy, and the production of natural fertilizers will reach a level that can compete significantly with chemical fertilizers. Also, biomethane production in Europe increased from 31 terawatt-hours (TWh) or 2.9 billion cubic meters (bcm) in 2020 to 37 TWh or 3.5 bcm in 2021, marking a 20% increase. This reflects a broader trend emphasizing biomethane more than the biogas segment, a shift that is expected to continue over the next decade. Biomethane's versatility as an energy carrier makes it suitable for a variety of industries such as transportation, infrastructure, electricity, and heating [37]. For the European Union, much greater investment in biomethane promotion is foreseen in future periods to encourage more farms to join renewable energy activities. The influence of industries processing organic materials must also be emphasized. For these companies, incentive instruments are also being developed to accelerate the start-up of biomethane production. However, these activities are not yet available in all EU countries. This is due to the incomplete legal framework, which does not in all cases allow the direct supply of purified biogas to national gas pipelines. Projections suggest that the combined biogas and biomethane sector could more than double from 18.4 BCM by 2021 to around 35–45 BCM by 2030. By 2050, production should increase at least fivefold from the current level to 95–167 BCM. Such growth would represent a substantial portion of the EU's gas consumption, highlighting biomethane's potential to cover a significant part of the energy demand by 2050 [38]. This aspect shows that biomethane is an important part of the renewable energy agenda. Farmers extracting biomethane could become an important part of energy transformation, while at the same time providing them with the opportunity to generate additional income from spin-off activities. In the case of biogas, there is one significant challenge. To achieve sustainable biogas production, it is necessary to create a sustainable value chain that will allow the transformation of waste into energy. This is related to the failure to supply products suitable for food to biogas reactors, the delivery of waste to them, and the creation of the necessary legal acts [39].

Figure 4.1 shows the potential for energy recovery from biowaste. Bioenergy activities have an important impact on the climate by preventing the release of methane, which is extremely harmful to the environment, from the waste treated. The main bioenergy processes are related to biogas production. Biogas production is based on anaerobic digestion. In this case, it is possible to mix different organic wastes, thereby increasing the biogas production. Concentrated biogas production avoids the development of pollution hotspots, while providing the basis for positive economic impacts. The figure shows the potential for fertilizer generation. Organic fertilizers are an important advantage of biogas production, as the resulting concentrate is regarded as an environmentally friendly material. This allows farmers to improve their performance without damaging the environment. This fertilizer allows the soil to be enriched, thus returning useful nutrients to the soil. Decentralized gasification solutions are one of the potential technologies for the production of biomass and bioenergy using agricultural wastes (especially in the food industry). This provides a sustainable alternative to fertilizers for agro-ecosystems, and biogas production from anaerobic digestion is a win–win strategy where animals and crop producers can consume edible waste, support energy supply, and address issues such as groundwater contamination, odor, and greenhouse gas emissions [40]. These solutions would help solve a big problem of recent times—environmental pollution. In the case of the EU, agriculture generates about 50% of all energy costs, of which 31% consists of diesel [41]. There are several nuances to be resolved in the bioenergetics cycle above. Firstly, the delivery of waste and the removal of organic

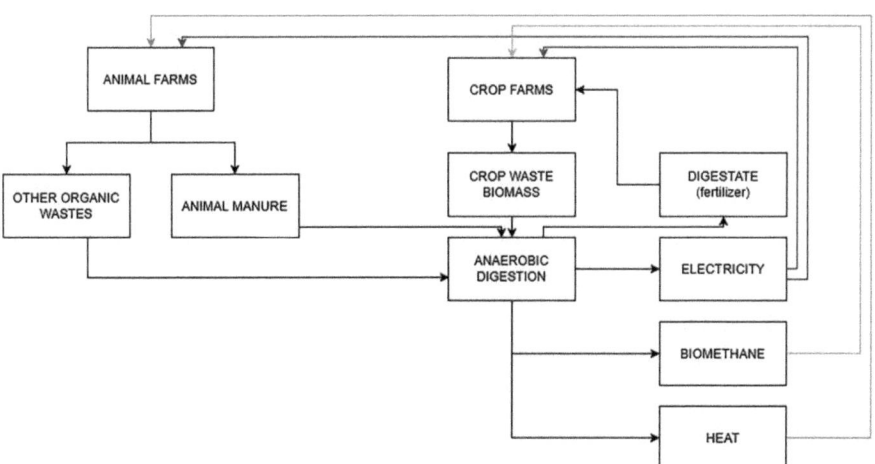

Fig. 4.1 Bioenergy circle—energy sources and end products

fertilizers are currently carried out on the basis of fossil-fueled vehicles. Tractors are also based on fossil fuels. Some of the biogas treated can be used to power tractors or trucks, but these technologies are relatively underdeveloped. These actions would help achieve a reduction of pollution of the sector. There are more synergies. The harvest residues can be used to make fuel briquettes, which in turn would reduce the need for wood for burning. This is relevant for poorer regions where deforestation is the only fuel alternative [42, 43].

The focus on bioenergy must go beyond environmental concerns. Recycling biowaste generates significant economic and social benefits. From an economic point of view, it offers farms the opportunity to generate more income and reduce energy costs. Socially, new jobs can be created in servicing biogas reactors. In addition, the quality of life of neighbors is improved as the environment is no longer polluted by biowaste, and the impact of unpleasant odors is reduced and concentrated. In addition, it is necessary to emphasize energy conservation initiatives. These can be organizational, technical, technological, energy-related, and activities should be selected and presented in the context of each direction [44].

Recycling organic waste has enormous synergy potential, transforming the agricultural and energy sectors, as well as people's daily lives. With sufficient infrastructure, the conditions are ripe for decarbonizing the transport, heating, ventilation, and electricity generation sectors. This is linked to several principles, the change of which would allow a significant expansion of agricultural activities:

- Manure management: Conventional and family farms produce a lot of by-products, which can cause environmental damage if not managed properly. Anaerobic digestion (AD) systems can treat these by-products; reduce odors, pathogens, and potential water damage; and produce biogas for on-farm use or sale. This combination can sustain the farm regularly and reduce greenhouse gas emissions [45]. Processing manure into gas and liquid fertilizer will allow better exploitation of animal waste. This will generate economic benefits and have a positive impact on the climate. Family farms could also benefit from this opportunity—cooperative manure processing capacity would create energy and fertilizer that would be returned to the farm in different fractions.
- Crop residue utilization: Agricultural residues, such as grass and corn stalks, can be difficult to manage and are often burned or left to decompose, releasing greenhouse gases. Using anaerobic digestion technologies to process these residues enables farms to convert them into energy, generating additional revenue and reducing carbon emissions [46]. In this case, the infrastructure used is similar to that used for manure processing. This creates further synergies as biogas plants can be developed by more than just livestock farms. Farm and crop waste can be mixed to produce energy.
- Integrated food and energy systems: Both of the above systems are combined in an integrated system that allows the farm to be self-sufficient in energy production. The main axis of integration is the on-farm consumption of the energy produced. Electricity can be used for day-to-day farm operations, heat can help dry crop production, and cleaned gas can be used for tractors, thus avoiding the use

of fossil fuels [47]. Such plants have a lower capacity than conventional plants because they are used to meet the needs of the farms. However, they allow farms to be decarbonized, as energy production would offset the pollution from livestock and some equipment. At the same time, this activity would protect farms from fluctuations in energy prices—the surplus of produced energy can be stored in batteries, and production operations can be carried out according to the dynamics of energy prices.

- Renewable energy production: If commercial energy production activities are carried out on the farm, there will be several options for energy outlets. This depends on the infrastructure development in the region where the farm is located [48]. In this case, the potential of biogas is highlighted. First, the latest technology, biomethane, must be mentioned. This type of energy can be used on a particularly large scale, as the gas is routed through trunk pipelines [49,50]. It can then be used by both domestic and business customers. In the absence of transmission or venting infrastructure, conventional electricity and heat production is possible. Biomethane production provides a solution to a pressing problem: as natural gas consumption declines, a large part of the trunk pipelines will be unsuitable for further operations. The potential for biomethane production would allow the infrastructure to be used in the interim period, to be replaced later by equipment suitable for hydrogen export.
- Community biogas projects: Community energy projects have significant untapped potential. Here, public and private actors, as well as farmers, can work in a cooperative way. This would make it possible to manage biowaste generated in cities and on farms [51]. This measure would create jobs in regions that are often economically vulnerable. This unlocks the social synergy potential of the agriculture and energy sector, which would benefit not only the region but also the country. In the latter case, the impact is seen through reduced spending on social benefits as well as the tax flow generated by new economic activities. Meanwhile, it is important to take into account the political context. Previous research shows that economic growth holds a long-run causality with financial development, total reserves, energy use, renewable energy use, and agriculture value addition on GDP per capita only in politically free countries [52]. Even earlier studies suggest that developing countries should not adopt energy-saving solutions at all [53]. This can make it difficult for community initiatives in that part of the world where processes are controlled centrally.

There is little mention of the social benefits of energy projects. Regions, especially those dominated by agriculture, are less economically developed than areas developing in the industrial or service sectors. Increasing energy efficiency is important now. Earlier studies revealed that a 1% increase in agricultural energy costs leads to a 0.008% increase in the level of environmental pollution [54]. Decentralization of the energy system would strengthen the regions, as a large amount of new energy generation capacity would create the preconditions for new economic activities. This would also help prevent power outages. In case of supply disruptions, the competitiveness of such farms may decline [55]. Decentralized systems can ensure continuous energy supply for such processes as freezing or cooling of production, incubation of young animals, drying of production, etc. For developing countries that are constantly faced with energy supply disruptions, renewable energy may be the only adequate alternative. Increasing the consumption of RE in agriculture is closely related to the farm parameters [56]. Different RE utilization solutions apply to farms of different sizes. However, this requires not only investments, but also a change in operational approach. It will not be enough without the consistent application of innovations. Synergies between different activities could also be represented graphically. It is agreed that reducing CO_2 emissions from farms should be the primary objective of decarbonization activities in rural areas. There are now visible trends showing that in the installation of, say, biogas production capacity, components such as artificial intelligence, remote monitoring, robots, and emissions management will inevitably appear. This will allow for better containment of harmful gases while creating economic value. At the same time, this creates conditions for the development of smart agriculture [57]. This would avoid a situation in the future where agriculture becomes one of the main emitters. Figure 4.2 presents the different agricultural alternatives, with a primary focus on smart solutions. Based on these alternatives, the integration of energy solutions would make a significant contribution to curbing the consequences of climate change.

The figure shows three pillars of sustainable agriculture. Their impact and area of operation depend on the area of operation, the size of the farm, the development concept chosen, and the receptivity to technology. Finding the right balance between all these technologies ensures the decarbonization of farms. However, the figure does not sufficiently illustrate the positive impact of energy solutions on decarbonization. Moreover, there is no mention of the fact that global change can help farms substantially increase their competitiveness while diversifying their sources of income. The application of the principles of sustainable agriculture would ensure the controlled production of biogas when non-food materials are used for its production. The application of innovations makes sense not only for organic, but also for conventional farms—this would allow reduced energy and fertilizer costs (precision agriculture, electric aerodrones, crop analysis using AI). This would reduce the need for fossil fuels and increase the possibilities for the farm to supply itself with the produced biogas. This paper highlights the fact that the development of on-farm energy solutions is essential for the implementation of the principles of sustainable development, which will have positive spillover effects such as the qualitative growth of family farms, the development of local supply chains, and the strengthening of regions.

Summarizing the information provided about the use of biogas in farms, it is necessary to compare the different advantages and disadvantages of using biogas in farms. Before farms make investment decisions, it is necessary to clearly know the quantities and directions of use of the produced energy. The comparative information presented in Table 4.2 identifies the main risks that may arise if the farm makes an incorrect investment decision.

The increased focus on biomethane production in Europe reflects the region's broader strategy for transitioning to a more sustainable and resilient energy system.

4.3 Bioenergy Potential in the Agriculture Sector

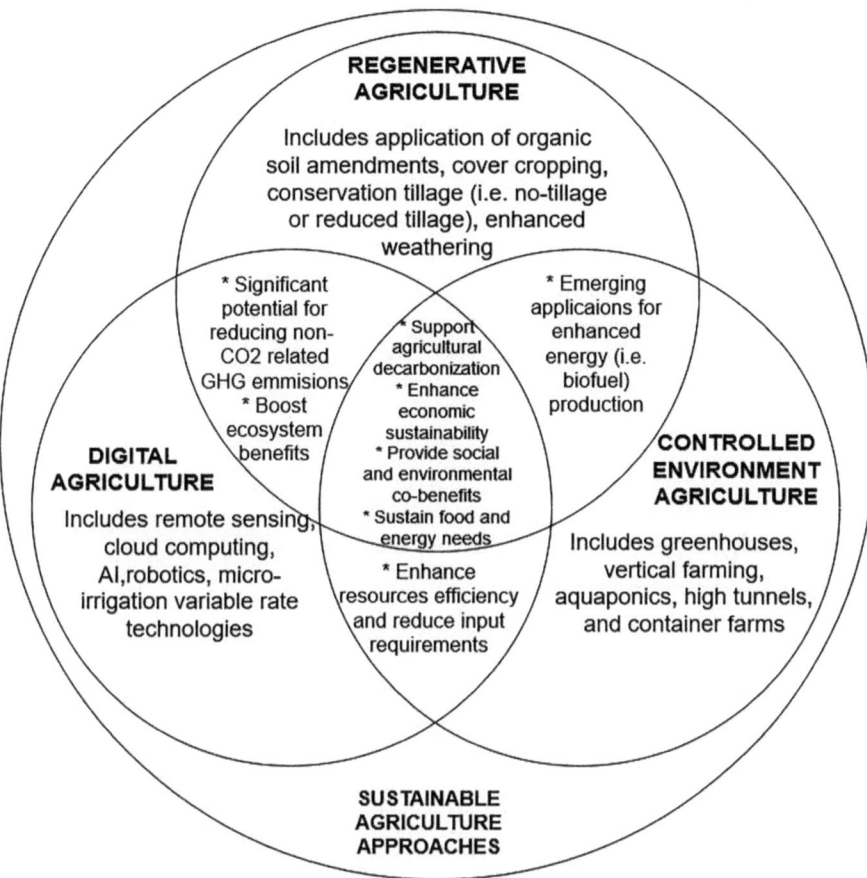

Fig. 4.2 Shared principles of climate-smart agriculture among digital agriculture, regenerative agriculture, and controlled environment agriculture approaches [58]

This shift not only supports environmental goals but also creates local workplaces and promotes energy independence by reducing reliance on imported fossil fuels. In the case of agriculture, it is necessary to develop clear operating principles that will allow a smooth transition to the energy production sector using the biowaste generated. Clear models that focus on exploiting synergies between agriculture and energy for decarbonization can help achieve this objective.

Table 4.2 Possibilities of different biogas technologies in farms

	Advantages	Disadvantages	Source
Biogas for energy	Non-polluting production preparation for the market is ensured The ability to meet the farm's energy needs Emergence of new branches of business Forming natural fertilizers The possibility of processing by-products and natural wastes	Energy production is almost uncompetitive compared to wind and solar Lack of innovation in the sector Small farm risks using food-grade products	[59–63]
Biomethane production	A more demanded product in the market Option to replace fossil fuels in tractors Forming natural fertilizers The possibility of processing by-products and natural wastes	Necessity of development of grids Significantly more expensive infrastructure It is necessary to build the filters for gas; tanks are required to store gas More expensive equipment maintenance A large, regional scale of activity is necessary	[64–68]

4.4 Agriculture and Energy Sector Synergy Model

To achieve universal synergy modeling, it is necessary to distinguish a typical farm model in which renewable energy solutions will be applied. Several studies have established positive causal relationships and the competitiveness of RE compared to nonrenewable resources [69]. Meanwhile there is a clear lack of RE progress in the world. The main challenge is how to find legal and investment regulations that would allow the development of RE faster and without subsidies. A farm can combine several different technologies, but the analysis of scientific literature has clearly shown that biogas reactors are the essential axis of agricultural decarbonization. They can either contain recycled animal waste or use certain other raw materials (grass not suitable for signature, food waste, etc.). Small farms can take advantage of the cooperation option and manage one biogas reactor. In the latter case, the economic benefit would be generated by selling the energy, as dividing it between owners can be difficult from an infrastructure point of view. Additional sales income would especially help in this matter, if the main activity of the farm was unprofitable in the current year. The use of biogas in farms is particularly extensive. They can be used for electricity production, heat for greenhouses in the cold season, grain drying, and industrial needs—product processing and signature preparation for self or commercial purposes. Since heat is a by-product of biogas in the case of electricity production, its responsible use can create significant added value for farms. There is also the opposite option—farms that do not have the ability to use a lot of heat can make a pointless investment from an economic point of view. In this case, it is necessary to look for directions for heat consumption both inside and outside.

4.4 Agriculture and Energy Sector Synergy Model

In the case of using a biogas reactor, it is desirable that the farm develops animal husbandry activities. This would make it possible to obtain by-products, which would later be used as fertilizer. The use of crop production waste alone would be pointless, as there is a risk that raw materials suitable for food would have to be used for biogas production. In this case, it is understood that owning a biogas power plant would be profitable for farms that have at least 1 MW energy power [70]. Otherwise, cooperation between different farmers is necessary. A fundamental decision is which technology to choose to achieve the goals of the farm or cooperation. If the farm is located near gas mains, it can produce biomethane [71, 72]. However, in this case, it would become difficult to use the gas independently, since the introduction of two technologies would be unprofitable. Another technology allows the production of electricity and heat based on cogeneration. This technology could be used not only in the farms directly, but also in the grain or animal food processing factories [73–75]. The main nuance is that it is not possible to produce one type of energy if the farm only needs its own electricity. Thus, the need to have a source of heat consumption arises. Not every farm could consume heat independently, so this creates an opportunity to inefficiently use the created energy production infrastructure. A broader interpretation is presented in Fig. 4.3. The basis of biogas activity is related to anaerobic digestion. It is a natural process that uses microorganisms to degrade four-phase (hydrolytic, fermentative, acetogenic, and methanogenic) compounds in the absence of oxygen, producing a high-CH_4 gas known as biogas. Benefits include reduced odors, pathogenicity, and greenhouse gas (GHG) emissions from agriculture [76]. The associated risks of air and water pollution can be reduced by better systems such as sealed digester storage and outer shoes, which may require planning, but crop digestion to produce biogas in dairy products is harmful to the environment, and in any case, it represents an inefficient strategy for GHG mitigation compared to other crop-based bioenergy options such as miscanthus heating sphere. In addition, bioenergy crops produced on dairy farms displace inputs such as wheat, soybean, flour, and their extracts. There is a high risk that

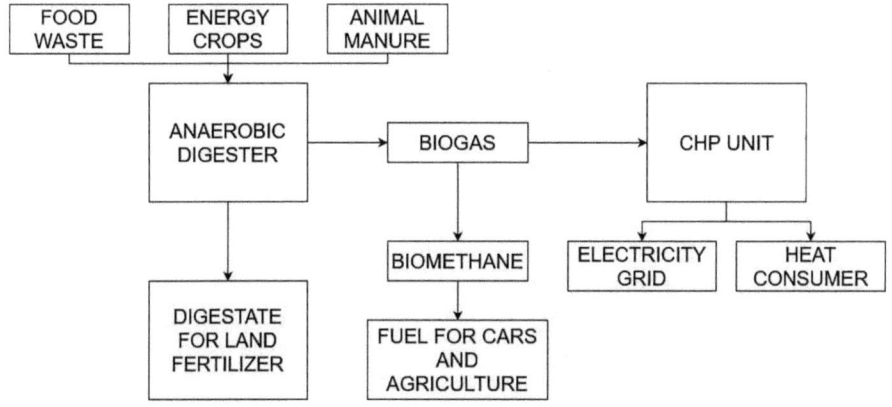

Fig. 4.3 Schematic of farm-scale anaerobic digestion plants [56]

increased demand for food will lead to land-use changes, potentially leading to significant increases in GHG emissions [77]. In addition, the component of energy security appears—biogas production allows decentralization of production, thus not only replacing fossil fuels, but also avoiding imports from politically hostile countries [78]. These systems in agricultural waste management reduce waste loads, generate bioenergy, and provide nutrients for vehicles and production, among others.

In modeling the use of biogas, there are also other examples. The main advantage of these solutions is the possibility of using them in regions that are economically less developed. There are a couple of alternatives to this. The first solution considers the microturbine as the primary drive, and the second considers the internal combustion engine. Both are combined with an absorption cooling system and a bio-slurry dryer. The energy source is based on the use of cattle dung for central biogas production. The final services provided to the plants are biogas, electricity, refrigeration (for preserving milk), and fertilizers [79]. The refrigeration alternative is relatively less used, but its adoption can increase a wide range of synergies in biogas production. In any case, the palette of final products is completed by biological fertilizers, which are applied for a new crop. According to the results of the aforementioned study, the polygeneration plant which implies the use of an internal combustion engine was found to be the most promising option as it has the lowest economic cost, is electricity efficient, and needs little support to compete in the market [80]. Economies of scale are an important factor in the biogas production business. Farms planning to make investment decisions must clearly assess the possibilities of developing the project profitably. In this case, a problem is encountered—not all farms have clear operational or development plans, so the development of the biogas project may be of poor quality. Larger farms have more opportunities to profitably develop energy production activities. The analysis has shown there are relatively high initial investment costs, especially for small biogas installations. The smaller the installation, the higher the investment cost per unit of capacity [81]. For small farms, it is necessary to work cooperatively, and for this, it requires a lot of attention from the state [82,83]. Otherwise, there is a risk of preserving sources of pollution that would be associated with small- and medium-sized farms. The state can help these farms in two ways. In the first case, subsidies may be provided for the energy sold. This is no longer an acceptable option due to cheaper renewable energy technologies. Another alternative is the procedure for issuing a simplified and prioritized construction permit for a biogas power plant. This would reduce the initial costs of small farms or their cooperatives and accelerate energy transformation in the agricultural sector.

The benefits of biogas development would have the greatest impact on climate change mitigation in agriculture. Different energy production solutions can be combined on the basis of biogas. If biogas is used to produce biomethane, the power plant can use solar or wind energy. When using these types of energy, it is recommended to combine them with energy storage solutions. The use of solar energy is fully compatible with the principles of sustainable development. If the gaps between the solar modules are large, there is a possibility of extracting production from the land areas (grass, berries, etc.) [84,85]. If the gaps are smaller, this area of land is suitable for small animal husbandry [86]. Raising animals such as sheep or goats is beneficial due to the possibility of producing higher value-added products, while providing the animals with the opportunity to eat grass and shelter from the sun [87]. Some farms that will only develop solar energy may have to partially change the way they farm by starting to raise other types of animals. Co-land for agriculture and PV agrivoltaics is an increasingly popular alternative to solar energy production. This intentional integration of agriculture and PV is aimed at reducing competition for land use and to increase the income of the landowners along with other benefits [13]. Solar energy can reduce the costs for farm electricity and heating. Solar energy collected can be used to dry crops and heat homes, stables, and home heaters. Solar water heaters can provide hot water for running daily needs. Photovoltaics (solar panels) can power agricultural operations, remote water pumps, lighting, and electric fences. Rooms and barns can be set up to capture natural daylight, and instead of using electric lamps, solar power is generally less expensive than broadband power lines, making the farm more cost-effective [88]. Thus, solar energy in agriculture can solve problems associated with an increasing population and limited land by increasing farmers' economic returns and promoting environmentally sustainable agriculture through controlled enhancements that reduce CO_2 emissions [89]. In the case of wind farms, crop production can be carried out essentially without restrictions. If power plants and access roads are designed compactly, this takes up a relatively small area of cultivated land [90]. Moreover, modern wind power plants can meet not only the needs of the farm, but also those of the wider community. Surplus energy can be realized in the market, especially at this moment when there are no developed cost-effective and efficient energy storage technologies in batteries. The construction of the wind power plant can be carried out independently, with partners (potential energy users) or by operating in a cooperative of farmers. However, on-farm wind energy initiatives are still quite rare. Due to huge investments in wind, policymakers and investors are continuously developing new ways to narrow the cost-benefit gap. Today, the importance of wind in agriculture has decreased [91]. In addition to the already mentioned technologies, there are opportunities to develop combined wind and solar energy activities. For this, a certain area of land would have to be donated, where only energy activities or small animal husbandry would be developed. However, Western Europe faces an ethical dilemma—how to enable farmers to participate in the energy sector in the interests of society [92–94]. The main interest of the public is the possibility of self-sufficiency in locally produced food at a competitive price. Unmeasured expansion of solar and wind farms on farmer-owned land can occur when large investment funds, state-owned companies, or entrepreneurs invest in it. In this case, it is necessary to ensure that it will be possible to engage in animal husbandry activities in these areas. However, growing grain in areas with abundant solar cells is no longer possible. In order to ensure the interests of decarbonization in agriculture and the strengthening of farms, it is necessary to establish clear conditions when solar energy can be developed industrially. This may involve the use of less productive or abandoned land from which it would be difficult to obtain a competitive economic result.

There are constraints to achieving a positive effect from farm activities. Often these are financial or economic in nature. There are a limited number of farms that can develop energy activities on their own. In other cases, financial or administrative resources may not be sufficient. However, project management has a major impact in all cases, regardless of the size of the farm. The main challenges for the deployment of renewable energy systems on farms relate to the integration of such systems into the farm structure. Synchronization of production and consumption processes is essential for the use of energy produced on the farm [95]. This will entail additional costs for farmers. There may also be infrastructure barriers. Since the development of renewable energy involves partial decentralization of the grid, ensuring smart grid management may pose challenges, at least in the short term [96]. Institutional and social interactions to involve local communities and farmers are important here [97]. In an effort to reduce farmers' skepticism about energy sector development, the involvement and encouragement of the government and municipalities will shape a substantial impact. Financial support does not constitute a major influence, but rather administrative assistance in obtaining permits and preparing business plans [98]. When introducing new technologies in the agriculture sector, it makes sense to target those on lower incomes. This is being done in developing countries to reduce regional exclusion. It would make sense to apply this model to the rest of the world [99]. In general, the absence of a long-term and clear policy on the deployment of RES deprives countries of the opportunity to achieve competitive advantage. It is not enough to develop infrastructure, but to balance consumption, to have a clear roadmap for development and to promote regional initiative [100]. Farmers can make a significant contribution to a country's energy goals, but it is necessary to have a clear framework for how this initiative will be developed.

Figure 4.4 presents a typical energy development framework of medium and large farm units. It can also be applied to small farm cooperatives. The model emphasizes the energy products created and the possibilities of cooperation with external entities. It is necessary to emphasize the fact that in order to avoid the use of food waste, cooperation between farmers and local communities is necessary. The latter can supply biogas reactors with food waste from schools, public catering facilities, etc. This would make it possible to comprehensively solve the problems of managing both food waste and organic waste generated on farms [101]. The directions of energy consumption are chosen considering the activities that can be developed in the farms and their energy needs. A particularly important factor is the possibility of using the heat generated in biogas reactors for grain drying. This is still a rarely used solution, but it allows to immediately replace diesel fuel or coal, which is usually used for such cases [102]. If the biogas power plant is built closer to the source of heat consumption, it can be realized on the market. The scheme also assesses potential synergies between different types of renewable energy, thereby complementing the farm's energy system. The main principle of drawing up the scheme is profitability. The aim is for farmers to use technologies that have real payback. The impact on the environment is also assessed—minimal interventions, essentially without changing the relief and landscape of the area. Primary

4.4 Agriculture and Energy Sector Synergy Model

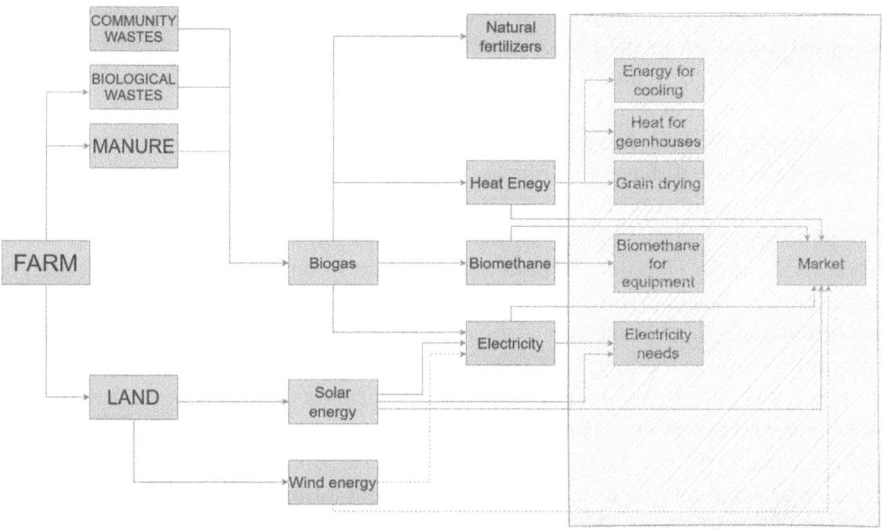

Fig. 4.4 A framework for mitigating the consequences of the agricultural sector's contribution to energy sector change

preference is given to energy consumption inside the farm, selling excess energy. If there is no such possibility, biomethane production on the farm and its delivery to centralized biomethane injection points are evaluated. On the right side of the picture, the activity of using the obtained organic fuel is marked. They directly reduce the need for fossil fuels both in the farms and in the market.

The model is based on the use of synergy. They are formed both in energy production and in energy consumption goals. The greatest areas of synergy are related to electricity production. If a farm has, say, solar and biogas capacity, it can have balanced energy production. During the day, solar energy can be used, while at night or during cold weather, the electricity produced in the biogas reactor would be used in time. The farm manages the main resources needed for energy—land (solar and wind energy), as well as biological waste (biogas power plant). Conditions for cooperation emerge from both sides. In the case of waste utilization, it can be delivered to the biogas reactor not only by the farmer or members of the cooperative, but also by local communities. In the case of land, agriculture can develop power plants independently or accept business partners. According to this scheme, the benefits of biogas development for the farm are the greatest. By consistently investing in biogas extraction and utilization capacities, the farm will not only be able to develop decarbonized activities but also become more financially stable. The model assesses the situation when the surplus energy produced on the farm can be sold on the market, thereby generating additional income.

Soon, it will be necessary to evaluate not only the decarbonization of farms in terms of energy resources, but also the reduction of pollution in daily farm processes. It will be possible to achieve this by creating fodder, the digestion of which emits less pollution, by improving no-till technologies, but the most important factor is the reduction of the use of mineral fertilizers and chemical products. In the latter case, products of biological origin are already distributed on the market, which can replace some chemical products. They are associated with better absorption of minerals from the soil. Meanwhile, in the case of fertilizers, the substances formed in biogas plants will have a significant influence. These aspects also have synergy with the daily activities of the farm. This allows us to say that farming activities in the future will have particularly serious challenges in the decarbonization process, since all the main elements of farm activities are in one way or another related to pollution. This leads to the need to invest in technologies suitable for farms, as failure to do so may lead to the risk of the agricultural sector becoming one of the most polluting sectors in the long run. This requires the concentration of the state, private business, technology developers, venture capital funds, and, of course, farmers. The slow development of new technologies increases the payback period of investments and may make farms less competitive in the future. Moreover, external assistance is necessary because in the future advanced farms investing from their own funds may be outcompeted by farms located in continents other than Europe, North America, or Australia, which have more liberal pollution regimes and lower levels of control. These challenges, if left unchecked, could mean even greater ecological, social, and economic problems both regionally and nationally.

The waste generated in the farms, available land areas, and consumption points opens opportunities to decarbonize this sector. Due to the lack of adapted technology, suitable for the agricultural sector, decarbonization may be slower than in other sectors. However, agriculture can contribute to a positive breakthrough in the energy sector by realizing surplus energy produced on farms. In order to achieve positive results, it is necessary to enable farms, especially medium-sized ones, to engage in this activity—to give priority when connecting to networks and to encourage recycling of community waste.

References

1. Barron-Gafford, G. A., Pavao-Zuckerman, M. A., Minor, R. L., Sutter, L. F., Barnett-Moreno, I., Blackett, D. T., et al. (2019). Agrivoltaics provide mutual benefits across the food–energy–water nexus in drylands. *Nature Sustainability, 2*(9), 848–855.
2. Sampson, G. S., Perry, E. D., & Taylor, M. R. (2020). The on-farm and near-farm effects of wind turbines on agricultural land values. *Journal of Agricultural and Resource Economics, 45*(3), 410–427.
3. Taibi, E., Gielen, D., & Bazilian, M. (2012). The potential for renewable energy in industrial applications. *Renewable and Sustainable Energy Reviews, 16*(1), 735–744.
4. Kougias, I., Szabo, S., Monforti-Ferrario, F., Huld, T., & Bódis, K. (2016). A methodology for optimization of the complementarity between small-hydropower plants and solar PV systems. *Renewable Energy, 87*, 1023–1030.
5. Pukšec, T., & Duić, N. (2010). Biogas potential in Croatian farming sector. *Strojarstvo, 52*(4), 441–448.

References

6. Scarlat, N., Dallemand, J. F., Monforti-Ferrario, F., & Nita, V. (2015). The role of biomass and bioenergy in a future bioeconomy: Policies and facts. *Environmental Development, 15*, 3–34.
7. Aydoğan, B., & Vardar, G. (2020). Evaluating the role of renewable energy, economic growth and agriculture on CO2 emission in E7 countries. *International Journal of Sustainable Energy, 39*(4), 335–348.
8. Liu, X., Zhang, S., & Bae, J. (2017). The nexus of renewable energy-agriculture-environment in BRICS. *Applied Energy, 204*, 489–496.
9. Jebli, M. B., & Youssef, S. B. (2017). The role of renewable energy and agriculture in reducing CO2 emissions: Evidence for North Africa countries. *Ecological Indicators, 74*, 295–301.
10. Chel, A., & Kaushik, G. (2011). Renewable energy for sustainable agriculture. *Agronomy for Sustainable Development, 31*, 91–118.
11. Park, J., & Kim, Y. (2019). The effects of renewable energy in agricultural sector. *Journal of the Korea Academia-Industrial Cooperation Society, 20*(1), 224–235.
12. Martinho, V. J. P. D. (2018). Interrelationships between renewable energy and agricultural economics: An overview. *Energy Strategy Reviews, 22*, 396–409.
13. Rahman, M. M., Khan, I., Field, D. L., Techato, K., & Alameh, K. (2022). Powering agriculture: Present status, future potential, and challenges of renewable energy applications. *Renewable Energy, 188*, 731–749.
14. Bardi, U., El Asmar, T., & Lavacchi, A. (2013). Turning electricity into food: The role of renewable energy in the future of agriculture. *Journal of Cleaner Production, 53*, 224–231.
15. Singh, A. K., Pal, P., Rathore, S. S., Sahoo, U. K., Sarangi, P. K., Prus, P., & Dziekański, P. (2023). Sustainable utilization of biowaste resources for biogas production to meet rural bioenergy requirements. *Energies, 16*(14), 5409.
16. Olatunji, O. O., Adedeji, P. A., Madushele, N., Rasmeni, Z. Z., & van Rensburg, N. J. (2024). Evolutionary optimization of biogas production from food, fruit, and vegetable (FFV) waste. *Biomass Conversion and Biorefinery, 14*(11), 12113–12125.
17. Jara-Rojas, R., Russy, S., Roco, L., Fleming-Muñoz, D., & Engler, A. (2020). Factors affecting the adoption of agroforestry practices: Insights from silvopastoral systems of Colombia. *Forests, 11*(6), 648.
18. Raihan, A. (2024). The potential of agroforestry in south Asian countries towards achieving the climate goals. *Asian Journal of Forestry, 8*(1).
19. Datta, P., & Behera, B. (2024). India's approach to agroforestry as an effective strategy in the context of climate change: An evaluation of 28 state climate change action plans. *Agricultural Systems, 214*, 103840.
20. Montagnini, F., & del Fierro, S. (2024). Agroforestry systems as biodiversity islands in productive landscapes. In *Integrating landscapes: Agroforestry for biodiversity conservation and food sovereignty* (pp. 551–588). Springer.
21. Pascaris, A. S., Schelly, C., Burnham, L., & Pearce, J. M. (2021). Integrating solar energy with agriculture: Industry perspectives on the market, community, and socio-political dimensions of agrivoltaics. *Energy Research & Social Science, 75*, 102023.
22. Ramalingannanavar, N., Nemichandrappa, M., Srinivasa Reddy, G. V., Dandekar, A. T., Kamble, J. B., & Dhanoji, M. M. (2020). Design, development and evaluation of solar powered Aeroponic system—A case study. *International Journal of Current Microbiology and Applied Sciences, 9*, 3102–3112.
23. Al-Omair, A., Djavanroodi, F., Yahya, E., Yahya, G., Yahya, O., & Jassim, E. (2023). Aeroponic tower garden solar powered vertical farm. *Materials Research Proceedings, 31*, 287–298.
24. Ukoba, K., Yoro, K. O., Eterigho-Ikelegbe, O., Ibegbulam, C., & Jen, T. C. (2024). Adaptation of solar power in the global south: Prospects, challenges and opportunities. *Heliyon, 10*, e28009.
25. Li, X., Cao, Y., Yu, X., Xu, Y., Yang, Y., Liu, S., et al. (2022). Breeze-driven triboelectric nanogenerator for wind energy harvesting and application in smart agriculture. *Applied Energy, 306*, 117977.

26. Winikoff, J. B., & Parker, D. P. (2024). Farm size, spatial externalities, and wind energy development. *American Journal of Agricultural Economics, 106*(4), 1518–1543.
27. Mu, Q., He, W., Shan, C., Fu, S., Du, S., Wang, J., et al. (2024). Achieving high-efficiency wind energy harvesting triboelectric nanogenerator by coupling soft contact, charge space accumulation, and charge dissipation design. *Advanced Functional Materials, 34*(2), 2309421.
28. Glasberg, D., Stratila, S., & Malael, I. (2024). A numerical analysis on the performance and optimization of the Savonius wind turbine for agricultural use. *Engineering, Technology & Applied Science Research, 14*(1), 12621–12627.
29. Gutiérrez, A. S., Eras, J. J. C., Hens, L., & Vandecasteele, C. (2020). The energy potential of agriculture, agroindustrial, livestock, and slaughterhouse biomass wastes through direct combustion and anaerobic digestion. The case of Colombia. *Journal of Cleaner Production, 269*, 122317.
30. Bell, S. M., Barriocanal, C., Terrer, C., & Rosell-Melé, A. (2020). Management opportunities for soil carbon sequestration following agricultural land abandonment. *Environmental Science & Policy, 108*, 104–111.
31. Wysokiński, M., Domagała, J., Gromada, A., Golonko, M., & Trębska, P. (2020). Economic and energy efficiency of agriculture. *Agricultural Economics/Zemedelska Ekonomika, 66*(8), 355.
32. Ramzan, M., Razi, U., Usman, M., Sarwar, S., Talan, A., & Mundi, H. S. (2024). Role of nuclear energy, geothermal energy, agriculture, and urbanization in environmental stewardship. *Gondwana Research, 125*, 150–167.
33. Alexander, S., Yang, G., Addisu, G., & Block, P. (2021). Forecast-informed reservoir operations to guide hydropower and agriculture allocations in the Blue Nile basin, Ethiopia. *International Journal of Water Resources Development, 37*(2), 208–233.
34. Wang, J. (2014). Decentralized biogas technology of anaerobic digestion and farm ecosystem: Opportunities and challenges. *Frontiers in Energy Research, 2*, 10.
35. Holm-Nielsen, J. B., Al Seadi, T., & Oleskowicz-Popiel, P. (2009). The future of anaerobic digestion and biogas utilization. *Bioresource Technology, 100*(22), 5478–5484.
36. Gas Infrastructure Europe (GIE). https://www.gie.eu/press/record-breaking-year-for-biomethane-production-shows-eba-gie-biomethane-map-2021/
37. Gas Infrastructure Europe (GIE). https://www.gie.eu/press/new-record-for-biomethane-production-in-europe-shows-eba-gie-biomethane-map-2022-2023/
38. Kuzmina, J., Atstaja, D., Purvins, M., Baakashvili, G., & Chkareuli, V. (2023). In search of sustainability and financial returns: The case of ESG energy funds. *Sustainability, 15*(3), 2716.
39. Thrän, D., Schaubach, K., Majer, S., & Horschig, T. (2020). Governance of sustainability in the German biogas sector—Adaptive management of the renewable energy act between agriculture and the energy sector. *Energy, Sustainability and Society, 10*, 1–18.
40. Ben Jebli, M., & Ben Youssef, S. (2017). Renewable energy consumption and agriculture: Evidence for cointegration and granger causality for Tunisian economy. *International Journal of Sustainable Development & World Ecology, 24*(2), 149–158.
41. Paris, B., Vandorou, F., Balafoutis, A. T., Vaiopoulos, K., Kyriakarakos, G., Manolakos, D., & Papadakis, G. (2022). Energy use in open-field agriculture in the EU: A critical review recommending energy efficiency measures and renewable energy sources adoption. *Renewable and Sustainable Energy Reviews, 158*, 112098.
42. Ali, S. M., Dash, N., & Pradhan, A. (2012). Role of renewable energy on agriculture. *International Journal of Engineering Sciences & Emerging Technologies, 4*(1), 51–57.
43. Panwar, N. L., Kaushik, S. C., & Kothari, S. (2011). Role of renewable energy sources in environmental protection: A review. *Renewable and Sustainable Energy Reviews, 15*(3), 1513–1524.
44. Boltianska, N. I., Manita, I. Y., & Komar, A. S. (2021). Justification of the energy saving mechanism in the agricultural sector. *Engineering of Nature Management, 1*(19), 7–12.

References

45. Sreekrishnan, T. R., Kohli, S., & Rana, V. (2004). Enhancement of biogas production from solid substrates using different techniques—A review. *Bioresource Technology, 95*(1), 1–10.
46. Gorjian, S., Kamrani, F., Ebadi, H., Samanta, S., & Savoldi, L. (2022). Applications of renewable energy sources in agriculture from a complementarity perspective. In *Complementarity of variable renewable energy sources* (pp. 615–647). Academic Press.
47. Nordberg, E. J., Caley, M. J., & Schwarzkopf, L. (2021). Designing solar farms for synergistic commercial and conservation outcomes. *Solar Energy, 228*, 586–593.
48. Pavičić, J., Novak Mavar, K., Brkić, V., & Simon, K. (2022). Biogas and biomethane production and usage: Technology development, advantages and challenges in Europe. *Energies, 15*(8), 2940.
49. Dale, B. E., Bozzetto, S., Couturier, C., Fabbri, C., Hilbert, J. A., Ong, R., et al. (2020). The potential for expanding sustainable biogas production and some possible impacts in specific countries. *Biofuels, Bioproducts and Biorefining, 14*(6), 1335–1347.
50. Sinsuw, A. A. E., Wuisang, C. E., & Chu, C. Y. (2021). Assessment of environmental and social impacts on rural community by two-stage biogas production pilot plant from slaughterhouse wastewater. *Journal of Water Process Engineering, 40*, 101796.
51. Ali, Q., Raza, A., Narjis, S., Saeed, S., & Khan, M. T. I. (2020). Potential of renewable energy, agriculture, and financial sector for the economic growth: Evidence from politically free, partly free and not free countries. *Renewable Energy, 162*, 934–947.
52. Rehman, H., & Bashir, D. F. (2015). Energy consumption and agriculture sector in middle income developing countries: A panel data analysis. *Pakistan Journal of Social Sciences (PJSS), 35*(1), 479–496.
53. Chandio, A. A., Jiang, Y., Rauf, A., Mirani, A. A., Shar, R. U., Ahmad, F., & Shehzad, K. (2019). Does energy-growth and environment quality matter for agriculture sector in Pakistan or not? An application of cointegration approach. *Energies, 12*(10), 1879.
54. Sebri, M., & Abid, M. (2012). Energy use for economic growth: A trivariate analysis from Tunisian agriculture sector. *Energy Policy, 48*, 711–716.
55. Rokicki, T., Perkowska, A., Klepacki, B., Bórawski, P., Bełdycka-Bórawska, A., & Michalski, K. (2021). Changes in energy consumption in agriculture in the EU countries. *Energies, 14*(6), 1570.
56. Paramati, S. R., Apergis, N., & Ummalla, M. (2018). Dynamics of renewable energy consumption and economic activities across the agriculture, industry, and service sectors: Evidence in the perspective of sustainable development. *Environmental Science and Pollution Research, 25*, 1375–1387.
57. Ragazou, K., Garefalakis, A., Zafeiriou, E., & Passas, I. (2022). Agriculture 5.0: A new strategic management mode for a cut cost and an energy efficient agriculture sector. *Energies, 15*(9), 3113.
58. Kazimierczuk, K., Barrows, S. E., Olarte, M. V., & Qafoku, N. P. (2023). Decarbonization of agriculture: The greenhouse gas impacts and economics of existing and emerging climate-smart practices. *ACS Engineering Au, 3*(6), 426–442.
59. Saha, C. K., Nandi, R., Rahman, M. A., Alam, M. M., & Møller, H. B. (2024). Biogas technology in commercial poultry and dairy farms of Bangladesh: Present scenario and future prospect. *Biomass Conversion and Biorefinery, 14*(7), 8407–8418.
60. Kusz, D., Kusz, B., Wicki, L., Nowakowski, T., Kata, R., Brejta, W., et al. (2024). The economic efficiencies of investment in biogas plants—A case study of a biogas plant using waste from a dairy farm in Poland. *Energies, 17*(15), 3760.
61. Gadirli, G., Pilarska, A. A., Dach, J., Pilarski, K., Kolasa-Więcek, A., & Borowiak, K. (2024). Fundamentals, operation and global prospects for the development of biogas plants—A review. *Energies, 17*(3), 568.
62. Brahmi, M., Bruno, B., Dhayal, K. S., Esposito, L., & Parziale, A. (2024). From manure to megawatts: Navigating the sustainable innovation solution through biogas production from livestock waste for harnessing green energy for green economy. *Heliyon, 10*(14), e34504.

63. Borusiewicz, A., Skibko, Z., Romaniuk, W., Pietruszynska, M., Milewska, A., & Marczuk, A. (2024). Agricultural micro biogas plants as a factor in farm development—A case study.
64. Catalano, G., D'Adamo, I., Gastaldi, M., Nizami, A. S., & Ribichini, M. (2024). Incentive policies in biomethane production toward circular economy. *Renewable and Sustainable Energy Reviews, 202*, 114710.
65. Dal Magro, A., Lovarelli, D., Bacenetti, J., & Guarino, M. (2024). The potential of insect frass for sustainable biogas and biomethane production: A review. *Bioresource Technology, 131384*, 131384.
66. Panda, S., & Jain, M. S. (2024). Assessment of the biomethane potential of commingled farm residues with sewage sludge and its techno-economic viability for rural application. *Biomass Conversion and Biorefinery*, 1–14.
67. Muñoz, P., González-Menorca, C., Sánchez-Vázquez, R., Sanchez-Prieto, J., & Del Pozo, A. F. (2024). Determining biomethane potential from animal-source industry wastes by anaerobic digestion: A case study from La rioja, Spain. *Renewable Energy, 235*, 121175.
68. Oliveira, H. R., Kozlowsky-Suzuki, B., Björn, A., Yekta, S. S., Caetano, C. F., Pinheiro, É. F. M., et al. (2024). Biogas potential of biowaste: A case study in the state of Rio de Janeiro, Brazil. *Renewable Energy, 221*, 119751.
69. Klimek, K., Kapłan, M., Syrotyuk, S., Bakach, N., Kapustin, N., Konieczny, R., et al. (2021). Investment model of agricultural biogas plants for individual farms in Poland. *Energies, 14*(21), 7375.
70. Pappalardo, G., Selvaggi, R., & Pecorino, B. (2022). Biomethane production potential in southern Italy: An empirical approach. *Renewable and Sustainable Energy Reviews, 158*, 112190.
71. Koonaphapdeelert, S., Aggarangsi, P., & Moran, J. (2019). *Biomethane: Production and applications*. Springer Nature.
72. Fan, W., Huang, L., Tan, Z., Xue, F., De, G., Song, X., & Cong, B. (2021). Multi-objective optimal model of rural multi-energy complementary system with biogas cogeneration and electric vehicle considering carbon emission and satisfaction. *Sustainable Cities and Society, 74*, 103225.
73. Dalpaz, R., Konrad, O., da Silva Cyrne, C. C., Barzotto, H. P., Hasan, C., & Guerini Filho, M. (2020). Using biogas for energy cogeneration: An analysis of electric and thermal energy generation from agro-industrial waste. *Sustainable Energy Technologies and Assessments, 40*, 100774.
74. Manganelli, B. (2014). Economic feasibility of a biogas cogeneration plant fueled with biogas from animal waste. *Advanced Materials Research, 864*, 451–455.
75. European Biogas Association. (2022). *Gas sector situation*. https://www.europeanbiogas.eu/SR-2022/EBA/
76. O'Connor, S., Ehimen, E., Pillai, S. C., Black, A., Tormey, D., & Bartlett, J. (2021). Biogas production from small-scale anaerobic digestion plants on European farms. *Renewable and Sustainable Energy Reviews, 139*, 110580.
77. Bielski, S., Marks-Bielska, R., Zielińska-Chmielewska, A., Romaneckas, K., & Šarauskis, E. (2021). Importance of agriculture in creating energy security—A case study of Poland. *Energies, 14*(9), 2465.
78. Styles, D., Gibbons, J., Williams, A. P., Stichnothe, H., Chadwick, D. R., & Healey, J. R. (2015). Cattle feed or bioenergy? Consequential life cycle assessment of biogas feedstock options on dairy farms. *GCB Bioenergy, 7*(5), 1034–1049.
79. Villarroel-Schneider, J., Mainali, B., Martí-Herrero, J., Malmquist, A., Martin, A., & Alejo, L. (2020). Biogas based polygeneration plant options utilizing dairy farms waste: A Bolivian case. *Sustainable Energy Technologies and Assessments, 37*, 100571.
80. Trypolska, G., Kyryziuk, S., Krupin, V., Wąs, A., & Podolets, R. (2021). Economic feasibility of agricultural biogas production by farms in Ukraine. *Energies, 15*(1), 87.
81. Yazan, D. M., Fraccascia, L., Mes, M., & Zijm, H. (2018). Cooperation in manure-based biogas production networks: An agent-based modeling approach. *Applied Energy, 212*, 820–833.

82. Porto, B. H. C., Soares, J. P. G., Rodrigues, G. S., Junqueira, A. M. R., de Azevedo Caldeira-Pires, A., Martinez, D. G., & Kunz, A. (2021). Socioenvironmental impacts of biogas production in a cooperative agroenergy condominium. *Biomass and Bioenergy, 151*, 106158.
83. Valle, B., Simonneau, T., Sourd, F., Pechier, P., Hamard, P., Frisson, T., et al. (2017). Increasing the total productivity of a land by combining mobile photovoltaic panels and food crops. *Applied Energy, 206*, 1495–1507.
84. Walston, L. J., Barley, T., Bhandari, I., Campbell, B., McCall, J., Hartmann, H. M., & Dolezal, A. G. (2022). Opportunities for agrivoltaic systems to achieve synergistic food-energy-environmental needs and address sustainability goals. *Frontiers in Sustainable Food Systems, 6*, 932018.
85. Okoroigwe, F. C., Okoroigwe, E. C., Ajayi, O. O., Agbo, S. N., & Chukwuma, J. N. (2020). Photovoltaic modules waste management: Ethical issues for developing nations. *Energy Technology, 8*(11), 2000543.
86. Levin, M. O., Kalies, E. L., Forester, E., Jackson, E. L., Levin, A. H., Markus, C., et al. (2023). Solar energy-driven land-cover change could alter landscapes critical to animal movement in the continental United States. *Environmental Science & Technology, 57*(31), 11499–11509.
87. Chikaire, J., Nnadi, F. N., Nwakwasi, R. N., Anyoha, N. O., Aja, O. O., Onoh, P. A., & Nwachukwu, C. A. (2010). Solar energy applications for agriculture. *Journal of Agricultural and Veterinary Sciences, 2*, 58–62.
88. Aroonsrimorakot, S., Laiphrakpam, M., & Paisantanakij, W. (2020). Solar panel energy technology for sustainable agriculture farming: A review. *International Journal of Agricultural Technology, 16*(3), 553–562.
89. Hajto, M., Cichocki, Z., Bidłasik, M., Borzyszkowski, J., & Kuśmierz, A. (2017). Constraints on development of wind energy in Poland due to environmental objectives. Is there space in Poland for wind farm siting? *Environmental Management, 59*, 204–217.
90. Majeed, Y., Khan, M. U., Waseem, M., Zahid, U., Mahmood, F., Majeed, F., et al. (2023). Renewable energy as an alternative source for energy management in agriculture. *Energy Reports, 10*, 344–359.
91. Campos, I., & Marín-González, E. (2020). People in transitions: Energy citizenship, prosumerism and social movements in Europe. *Energy Research & Social Science, 69*, 101718.
92. Baiano, A. (2020). Edible insects: An overview on nutritional characteristics, safety, farming, production technologies, regulatory framework, and socio-economic and ethical implications. *Trends in Food Science & Technology, 100*, 35–50.
93. Parajuly, K., Fitzpatrick, C., Muldoon, O., & Kuehr, R. (2020). Behavioral change for the circular economy: A review with focus on electronic waste management in the EU. *Resources, Conservation & Recycling: X, 6*, 100035.
94. Gorjian, S., Ebadi, H., Jathar, L. D., & Savoldi, L. (2022). Solar energy for sustainable food and agriculture: Developments, barriers, and policies. In *Solar energy advancements in agriculture and food production systems 2022* (pp. 1–28). Academic Press.
95. Salkuti, S. R. (2020). Challenges, issues and opportunities for the development of smart grid. *International Journal of Electrical and Computer Engineering (IJECE), 10*(2), 1179–1186.
96. Kulkarni, V., & Kulkarni, K. (2020, June). A blockchain-based smart grid model for rural electrification in India. In *2020 8th international conference on smart grid (icSmartGrid)* (pp. 133–139). IEEE.
97. Streimikiene, D., Baležentis, T., Volkov, A., Morkūnas, M., Žičkienė, A., & Streimikis, J. (2021). Barriers and drivers of renewable energy penetration in rural areas. *Energies, 14*(20), 6452.
98. Sen, S., & Ganguly, S. (2017). Opportunities, barriers and issues with renewable energy development–A discussion. *Renewable and Sustainable Energy Reviews, 69*, 1170–1181.
99. Weiss, C., & Bonvillian, W. B. (2013). Legacy sectors: Barriers to global innovation in agriculture and energy. *Technology Analysis & Strategic Management, 25*(10), 1189–1208.

100. Fashina, A., Mundu, M., Akiyode, O., Abdullah, L., Sanni, D., & Ounyesiga, L. (2018). The drivers and barriers of renewable energy applications and development in Uganda: A review. *Clean Technologies, 1*(1), 9–39.
101. Jan, I., & Akram, W. (2018). Willingness of rural communities to adopt biogas systems in Pakistan: Critical factors and policy implications. *Renewable and Sustainable Energy Reviews, 81*, 3178–3185.
102. Abd-Allah, Y. S., Ahmed, T. H., & Metwally, K. A. (2023). Evaluation of the drying process of paddy rice with a biogas continuous rotary dryer. *Misr Journal of Agricultural Engineering, 40*(1), 59–74.

Open Access This chapter is licensed under the terms of the Creative Commons Attribution-NonCommercial-NoDerivatives 4.0 International License (http://creativecommons.org/licenses/by-nc-nd/4.0/), which permits any noncommercial use, sharing, distribution and reproduction in any medium or format, as long as you give appropriate credit to the original author(s) and the source, provide a link to the Creative Commons license and indicate if you modified the licensed material. You do not have permission under this license to share adapted material derived from this chapter or parts of it.

The images or other third party material in this chapter are included in the chapter's Creative Commons license, unless indicated otherwise in a credit line to the material. If material is not included in the chapter's Creative Commons license and your intended use is not permitted by statutory regulation or exceeds the permitted use, you will need to obtain permission directly from the copyright holder.

Chapter 5
Modeling of the Energy Transformation Process

5.1 The Main Risks of Energy Transformation

The main challenges of energy transformation are related to the development of the grid. Unlike the development of power generation plants, grid infrastructure is often the responsibility of public entities. This creates a risk that grid development projects will not be implemented in a timely manner and with greater financial resources. Without adequate grid capacity, the development of renewable energy may stall. Today, there is a lack of methodological solutions to assess the impact of grid development on the success of decarbonization. Often, only investments in generation are assessed, taking the grid situation for granted from an investment perspective. However, investments in networks raise several issues. They include capital costs, insufficient funding mechanisms, and construction and maintenance market development barriers [1]. In terms of the regional dimension, several solutions are possible in relation to the use of networks. These can be expressed through a temporal prism. The main groups of network development decisions are as follows:

- Structural solutions such as reinforcement of the grid by adding new equipment
- Operational solutions such as adequate operator preparation and material verification to allow a successful implementation of real time reactions [2]

In this case, it is proposed that the alternative of developing decentralized networks be rejected, as this could create regional imbalances. New, secure and integrated energy systems should be developed underground to protect them from changes in weather conditions and internal or external interventions.

The need to balance the network will also pose challenges. Unstable renewable energy production will lead to increasingly large production spikes. Analogue solutions are needed to smooth them out. This is also a major investment target. Large-scale, cost-effective balancing technologies have not yet been developed [3–5]. Hydrogen production and battery farms are still in the development phase. Different solutions are being used to address this situation. One of them is hybrid technology, combining different energy production solutions. In one case, a study carried out by researchers has shown that two elements are necessary for the successful development of hybrid technologies: public support in the form of building permits and community mobilization to implement them [6]. The compatibility of different energy generation technologies is at the heart of this solution. Factors to be considered include what to do in the event of insufficient solar and wind generation [7]. Households that are actively installing solar capacity can assist here. They could contribute to balancing the energy system by installing energy storage systems. The use of the latest algorithmic technologies is particularly favorable for balancing activities. They are able to adapt to changes in electricity prices and demand, thus balancing the energy system in a way that works for everyone. The algorithm facilitates fast consumption of renewable resources and offers a way to fair trade [8]. This combines both physical infrastructure and programming algorithms. This will achieve the desired results and make more efficient use of the energy produced in households. At the same time, it will at least partially resolve the imbalances in the balancing market that exist today. In the past, balancing technologies were based on biomass energy and cogeneration. Biomass is virtually the only suitable resource that can be used continuously for balancing the energy system. The main prerequisite is a large source of heat consumption. Electricity is needed for the primary process—to charge the core unit to high temperatures when electricity is cheap. The cheapest period for electricity is nighttime or weekends. Meanwhile, heat is either stored or put on the market [9]. It is precisely the gaps in the balancing system that are the main argument for refusing to develop renewable energy capacity. In order to reduce the importance of balancing, it is necessary to change the way energy is consumed, adapting it to the dynamics of production.

In developing countries, there is another risk component—political risk. This relates to inappropriate lobbying by incumbent businesses trying to defend their positions. This can lead to a situation where a renewable energy investment project in the development phase may be abandoned for subjective reasons. Renewable energy projects may be delayed or canceled due to lack of legal framework, lack of specialists, and lack of competence [10]. Political risk is probably the main insurance risk in the renewable energy sector in developing countries. Particularly in highly unstable developing countries, there is a risk of nationalization of new power plants, as the energy sector is often considered strategically important. Political risk is also frequently mentioned as a major or one of the main risks in the work of other researchers. Egli [11] identifies the following key risks associated with the development of renewable energy technologies: curtailment, policy, price, resource, and technology. Another study highlights the need for political stability for green investments [12]. High levels of political risk can hinder economic growth even when renewable energy investments are allowed. This is because investments in such cases are selectively chosen without considering economic and social fundamentals [13]. In this case, the narrow interest of a particular interest group may be relevant. This is not conducive to improvement and sustainable growth, and in some cases, it can even lead to regressive actions. This may be the case if the state engages in excessive subsidies.

In the case of this paper, where the regional structure is concerned, the position taken by the State is a major influence. If the state engages in incentive policies, this loosens national legislation. This makes it easier for regions to attract investors in the renewable energy sector or to invest themselves through the utilities they manage. In the absence of a national policy to promote renewable energy, proactive regions can engage in these activities and thus broaden the range of revenues. The absence of a state approach does not affect the actions of municipalities when it comes to increasing energy efficiency, making better use of biowaste, generating their own electricity, etc. Thus, in this case, a large part of the development process depends on the initiative shown by the region.

5.2 Solutions to Promote Energy Transformation

Current energy transformation initiatives are rather one-sided. There are currently three main actors in the energy transition: the state, energy companies, and investment funds. It is these actors that are responsible for progress in the energy sector. However, it can be argued that the development by these actors is selective, with a high degree of cherry-picking of investment projects, targeting only a few of the most productive areas. This situation calls for comprehensive solutions to promote a broader geographic breakthrough. It is the empowerment of the regions and the exploitation of the opportunities that exist in them that would create a breakthrough in the energy mix that would reach a wide range of people. The ways of promoting action are varied, but they have one common element: the broad involvement of stakeholders and the decentralization of electricity production.

One of the most productive opportunities for an energy breakthrough, especially among retail consumers, is the creation of energy communities. These communities could allow households to exchange energy, thus avoiding the energy price spikes of recent years. In many cases, communities bring households together, facilitating the balancing of the electricity they generate [14]. It is the balancing aspect that distinguishes partnerships from other energy generators. As energy is produced and exchanged by retail entities, they are essentially not involved in balancing activities [15]. Until battery technology is sufficiently developed, the State will have to come up with solutions to balance the energy produced by generating consumers. The scheme in Fig. 5.1 shows a community model where the generating consumers are accounted for in a single legal structure. This is a transparent model that allows a clear calculation of the benefits generated by the community for its members and the possibility of realizing surplus electricity on the market.

There are several challenges in developing energy communities in the regions. In addition to balancing the energy produced by such consumers, there are legal aspects. In particular, imperfections in the legal framework can hinder the rapid implementation of strategic alternatives. In archaic legal and energy systems, the status of generating consumers or energy communities is not yet fully understood on a broad scale [17]. It is the improvement of the legal framework that would pave

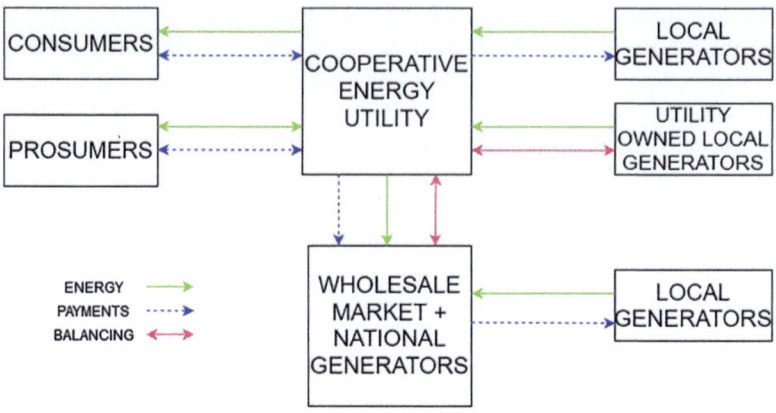

Fig. 5.1 The cooperative energy utility business model [16]

the way for new energy initiatives that strengthen regions and, more importantly, local communities [18]. Changes in the legal framework are needed to create the conditions for the development of a decentralized energy system, such as the promotion of complementary renewable energy sources, the development of energy communities in urban areas, and the development of experimental sandboxes alongside regional or national energy companies [14]. The identification of the legal aspects is inseparable from the overall national or regional renewable energy policy. With a proper project development policy, the legal aspects can be set up more smoothly and adequately. This reduces the likelihood that projects will be delayed or stalled due to gaps in the legal framework. In terms of the development of RE policy, five common criteria were identified to judge whether it is successful or not:

- Effectiveness (extent to which the objectives are met)
- Efficiency (innovation with decrease in costs)
- Equity (fair distribution of the rents between RE developer and government)
- Institutional feasibility (extent political support is provided to the policy)
- Replicability (extent to which the policy can be adopted in other countries [19]

Preventive action, linked to the right legislation, would provide a short-term breakthrough and lay the foundations for successful community building. It must be appreciated that the creation of communities in the regions would not create major grid congestion problems, as the energy intensity of regions is lower than that of cities. In addition, the dynamics of life in developed countries are leading to a decline in the regional population. This further frees up the networks, so that the development of energy communities allows for a better use of them.

The shift towards renewable energy must be coherent, measured, and not impact on established social life. Since the fundamental need for renewable energy solutions is relatively recent, the process can be fully digitized now. This will ensure full accountability of stakeholders, traceability of fuels and components, and the ultimate beneficiaries of new plants. Standardization of processes contributes

5.2 Solutions to Promote Energy Transformation

significantly both to the development of renewable energies and to the continuous monitoring of the sector [20–22]. The scheme in Fig. 5.2 clearly outlines the steps involved in the circular economic process in the energy sector. In the case of raw materials, it refers to biomass. Adequate traceability avoids situations where valuable wood suitable for industrial use is used for energy production [24]. However, the planning and policy component plays a key role in the scheme. It seeks to identify the social groups that will be most affected by renewable energy development. It is by working with them that significant savings in time and money can be made, which will be used to deploy solutions to the next generation.

Another development opportunity is to make better use of municipal enterprises for energy production. At present, it is still quite rare to see smaller regional cities operating electricity generation activities. However, with the price of renewable energy technologies on the rise, this situation may change. Initiatives are already being seen where a local utility is starting a new activity, electricity generation, which is then sold to municipally maintained institutions. This creates a clear economic effect. The high labor intensity of renewable energy-related jobs stimulated by the robust market results in positive multipliers promoting increased demand and consumption [25]. It is the short-term solutions that are needed here, as some renewable energy projects (green hydrogen development, offshore wind, etc.) can only be implemented over a very long period. Efficiency projects that reduce energy consumption and make use of the region's existing resources would help to achieve the short-term energy transition objectives. It is the empowerment of public utilities that would create positive effects and speed up the implementation of regional projects [26]. In the case of new or green energies, regional influence in their production or extraction is inevitable. The location of the grids creates a situation where non-urbanized regions are used as interconnection points for important electricity transmission networks. It is at these points that new hydrogen generation capacity can emerge. In general, the development of green energy scenarios has consistently emphasized several types of energy products—power-to-X (PtX) technologies, in

RAW MATERIALS	PLANNING AND POLICY	CONSUMPTION AND USE	WASTE MANAGEMENT
• Transparency and traceability about supply chains and sources. • Adherence to OECD principles. • Enforcement of occupational and community health guidelines.	• Inclusion of diverse groups. • Adherence to meaningful Free Prior Informed Consent. • Stronger Social and Environmental Impact Assessments or Impact Benefit Agreements.	• Promote shared ownership and new business models. • Compensation or retraining for disrupted sectors. • Strenghten consumer protections.	• Transparency and traceability about supply chains and sources. • Expansion of Extended Producer Responsibility. • Expanded legal sactions, fines and compliance.

Fig. 5.2 Renewable energy transition ways and policy mechanisms [23]

particular, power-to-heat and power-to-hydrogen. Where direct hydrogen cannot yet be used, it can be further converted to synthetic electricity-based fuels (e-fuels) as chemically bound RE, such as e-methane, Fischer-Tropsch fuels, e-ammonia, and e-methanol [27]. The development of these technologies needs to be adapted to regional contexts. Energy produced in the regions can be used not only for export but also to meet local needs. This is particularly true in the transport and agricultural sectors, which currently lack alternatives to fossil fuels. Regional energy systems will face a number of challenges in expanding renewable energy capacity. Preventing them would help to achieve the objectives of sustainable energy development [28, 29]. Significant challenges are the accurate output power prediction, voltage, frequency, angular stabilities, injection of harmonics, and system fault ride-through capability [29]. These challenges, which are technical in nature, can be addressed not only through additional investment in electricity-balancing solutions. Complex alternatives can be deployed to take better advantage of energy market developments in the short term. Intelligent grid applications such as demand-side integration and energy storage systems could alleviate voltage fluctuations with minimum grid support [30]. The example of India is particularly relevant here. The country is implementing an increasing number of renewable energy projects to reduce its use of fossil fuels. Due to the specific nature of the country, regions are home to large populations. In order to improve their quality of life, incentives are being created to encourage the creation of new businesses. At the same time, however, there is another problem: unstable energy supply. Regional energy development would help to solve both employment and electricity supply problems. India has ample, untapped RE resources which include the following:

- The vast land area has the potential for solar energy generation. Moreover, solar exposure is also high in most of the areas of India.
- There are many zones and areas where wind velocities are high, which can lead to a significant amount of wind energy generation by both offshore and land-based wind farms.
- The decent amount of yearly biomass production.
- Numerous rivers and waterways capable of a small hydro generation [31].

This example can be applied in a similar way to regions in developed countries, partially excluding hydropower development. The latter technology has certain negative environmental impacts due to landscape change. At the same time, however, there is another ethical dilemma. The further development of nuclear energy is not ruled out in order to solve the problems of balancing the energy system [32, 33]. While some countries have already moved away from nuclear power (most notably Germany), there is still a lack of progress in moving away from fossil fuels. Future projections show two alternatives, with or without nuclear power. Energy transitions also emphasize the use of water and land resources, which must overcome the social context [34]. As long as there are no clear balancing solutions, the prospect of nuclear power can continue to be developed. At the moment, concepts for low-power nuclear reactors are being developed at a theoretical level, but this does not eliminate the fundamental problem of storing spent fuel and dismantling the plant. In the event of an accident, entire regions will be uninhabitable.

The speed of transformation can be achieved through technology and by balancing the production and consumption sides. In the context of the Fourth Industrial Revolution (4IR), the transformation of the energy sector is one of the most important components. In order to optimize production costs and increase production volumes, a stable and cheap energy supply will play a crucial role. Existing studies confirm the potential of 4IR in the regions [35,36]. However, there is still a lack of solutions that fit the regions. By properly adapting currently available energy technologies and combining them with balancing opportunities, significant energy, economic, and social results can be achieved. The previous analysis shows that the impacts of 4IR technologies could be just as important in rural areas as in urban places [37]. Adapting technological and digital solutions and tailoring them to regions can significantly accelerate and cheapen the energy transformation process. In addition, the latest technologies could significantly strengthen the energy sector, which is currently particularly dependent on outdated management solutions and intermittent grid operation.

The study systematically presents the main gaps that prevented the catalysis of renewable energy development in the short term. The current pace of renewable energy development is insufficient both in terms of investment and mass. This study proposes to catalyze the energy transformation through actions that promote the development of new energy activities in the regions. This would solve the problems mentioned in the work of other scientists, while creating obvious economic benefits. The main problem identified during the analysis of scientific literature is how to encourage regions to carry out energy activities more widely and in which directions to do so.

The research shows that a responsible selection of indicators and their processing methods can help to identify areas that need special attention in energy transformation. The information obtained showed that there are municipalities that need to initiate energy transformation activities immediately. On the positive side, they will be able to do most of the activities without external investment. The main actions relate to the efficiency of processes and assets within the municipality.

Other studies have shown different solutions for energy transformation processes. However, previous studies have tended to focus more on the issues at stake but have not offered clear solutions to accelerate the transformation of the energy system. While the influence of regions on the transformation is discussed, it is not seen as a fundamental opportunity for the whole country. In one case, it is stated that the development of regional economies through energy transformation activities faces both administrative and financial challenges. First, there is a lack of competence to properly implement conversion processes in line with the project's projected budget. The complexity of the processes leads to risks related to project delays and inadequate implementation [38]. However, there is no mention in this case of what needs to be done differently to change the situation. Second, it is acknowledged that this type of project requires significant financial resources. Due to the lack of knowledge, debt options are the first to be sought. However, the issue of converting the existing asset structure is marginalized [39]. An objective review of existing assets and identifying idle assets would reduce the pressure on regional and national budgets, while securing initial funding for projects. Recruitment of competent professionals and better cooperation between science and business can help to address these issues. It has been suggested that private providers will benefit from targeted research inputs to strengthen knowledge gaps [40]. However, there is a lack of quantitative justification.

The scientific literature also suggests other ways of working together to accelerate the energy transformation. In one case, cooperation can be between companies developing renewable energy solutions. This type of collaboration is catalyzed by innovative companies that have a particular interest in renewable energy development [41]. Similar patterns of cooperation can prevail when it comes to cooperation between large and SME companies. The particular benefits of joint actions are seen if SME companies can offer innovative and significant solutions to increase the level of RES deployment [42]. In both cases, there is a lack of concrete assessments on how to realize these plans—no clear time horizon, investment orientations, and benefit assessment. Cross-border cooperation is another option often considered. Bringing together administrative, scientific, and legal potential can deliver significant results. Renewable energy development is no exception, with clear technological cooperation between the US, the EU, and China for many years [43]. These forms of cooperation can also affect regional prosperity to varying degrees. But it is not clear whether this will be the case, as further scientific and practical evaluations have not been carried out. It is generally agreed that opportunities for cooperation are particularly necessary for publicly owned enterprises run by municipalities. Academics can bring a new technological vision and business professionals, or industry representatives can become independent members of company boards. This form of cooperation would help to bring about the necessary changes more quickly. However, in the absence of a clear roadmap, these plans risk remaining theoretical insights.

The synergy component is also assessed by comparing the results obtained during the preparation of the paper with those of other studies. Exploiting synergies creates a situation where regional energy activities are directly linked to wider regional development. In both developed and developing countries, there is significant urbanization. This is mainly due to the fact that a large proportion of jobs are concentrated in the service sector in urban areas. The restructuring of the energy system and the decentralization of production will inevitably lead to an increase in regional activity. However, the challenge is how to carry out these structural transformations based on sustainable development principles [44]. The scale of this challenge is particularly evident in regions dependent on coal resources. The coal mining sector employs a large number of workers. As the energy system changes, the knowledge conversion of these workers is essential [45]. In some cases, this does not happen smoothly, so some social problems are possible in the tactical period. To mitigate these, coherent and long-term planning is needed to reduce coal extraction and to change the competencies of the workforce in parallel. This paper proposes clear solutions to address these issues and the challenges they pose.

5.2 Solutions to Promote Energy Transformation

The energy transformation model cannot be achieved without first improving the efficiency of energy consumption and production. This must be done in parallel with other transformation activities, as this will allow the greening of the energy system to be achieved faster. Efficiency touches all areas, both production and consumption activities. It is from efficiency plans that it becomes possible to see where investments are needed, how much investment is needed, and which capacities or assets are not being used properly. With the efficiency roadmap in place, it is then on to the real transformation actions.

The transformation of municipal companies is at the heart of the transformation efforts. Previous studies have highlighted the transformation axes—the use of existing resources in the region, synergies between municipal companies, and the production of energy from local renewable resources. Biological and municipal waste is a major influence, with the scale of its generation being directly proportional to the amount of energy produced. The model assumes that municipal enterprises will not be able to use all waste. This is particularly true for biowaste, as centralized logistics may not be cost-effective and sustainable. Farmers with their own biogas reactors could help to address this situation. This would have an impact on one of the most polluting business sectors. Biowaste from local communities is mixed with waste from livestock and crop farms. Municipal enterprises are unique in that they can not only produce energy but also consume it. Energy produced in biogas reactors can fuel city buses, while solar modules installed at water points generate electricity for public institutions. These synergies open huge potential for the qualitative development of municipal enterprises.

Energy communities are being promoted to empower not only businesses but also citizens. Several families or other entities could produce and use electricity cooperatively. In this case, synergies with farmers can be seen, with small farms becoming members of such energy communities.

Asset managers can contribute to energy transformation in two ways. In one case, they can develop solar panels on the roofs of existing buildings or on unused land. In the other case, they can harness surplus electricity, which can be used to charge cars using special equipment. This would make better use of existing resources, as the car charging facility would not need to increase its electrical capacity. Instead, the existing power input would be used during the off-hours at the site.

All these cross-cutting measures allow for the development of a comprehensive energy transformation model with a regional focus (Fig. 5.3). The model is based on the development of localized energy systems that will allow decentralized energy production. This will ensure security of supply, as energy production will be carried out by reducing the influence of centralized production. This situation will increase the resources available for the security of energy transmission and distribution systems. The regional energy transformation will have the most significant impact on the electricity, heating, and cooling sectors. In addition, there will be an opportunity to develop green transport through the treatment of highly polluting organic waste. The diagram in Fig. 1.1 suggests that the large-scale development of the energy sector within the regions will create the conditions for the emergence of new businesses, improvement of environmental quality, and energy self-sufficiency.

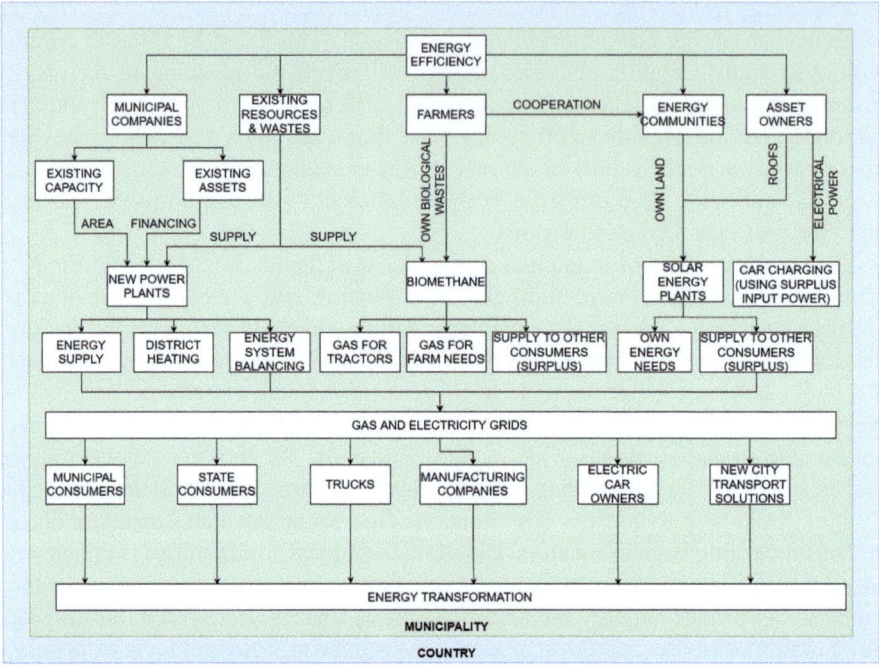

Fig. 5.3 Energy transformation modeling at municipal level

The models and assessments presented in this paper can be used immediately as they are universal. They can be applied to a region or part of a region, depending on its size. The concepts presented in the paper are valuable because of the compatibility between theoretical and practical aspects, as well as the assessment of synergy effects. The material presented allows to fill the gaps in the scientific field concerning short-term energy transformation solutions. The proposal to exploit synergies saves both financial and time resources, while generating positive environmental and economic impacts.

References

1. Boros, A., Lentner, C., Nagy, V., & Tőzsér, D. (2023). Perspectives by green financial instruments – A case study in the Hungarian banking sector during COVID-19. *Banks and Bank Systems, 18*(1), 116–126.
2. Ourahou, M., Ayrir, W., Hassouni, B. E., & Haddi, A. (2020). Review on smart grid control and reliability in presence of renewable energies: Challenges and prospects. *Mathematics and Computers in Simulation, 167*, 19–31.
3. Sirin, S. M., & Yilmaz, B. N. (2021). The impact of variable renewable energy technologies on electricity markets: An analysis of the Turkish balancing market. *Energy Policy, 151*, 112093.

4. Gan, L., Jiang, P., Lev, B., & Zhou, X. (2020). Balancing of supply and demand of renewable energy power system: A review and bibliometric analysis. *Sustainable Futures, 2*, 100013.
5. Opperman, J. J., Carvallo, J. P., Kelman, R., Schmitt, R. J., Almeida, R., Chapin, E., et al. (2023). Balancing renewable energy and river resources by moving from individual assessments of hydropower projects to energy system planning. *Frontiers in Environmental Science, 10*, 1036653.
6. Lazdins, R., Mutule, A., & Zalostiba, D. (2021). PV energy communities—Challenges and barriers from a consumer perspective: A literature review. *Energies, 14*(16), 4873.
7. Ciupageanu, D. A., Barelli, L., & Lazaroiu, G. (2020). Real-time stochastic power management strategies in hybrid renewable energy systems: A review of key applications and perspectives. *Electric Power Systems Research, 187*, 106497.
8. Chiş, A., Rajasekharan, J., Lunden, J., & Koivunen, V. (2016, August). Demand response for renewable energy integration and load balancing in smart grid communities. In *2016 24th European signal processing conference (EUSIPCO)* (pp. 1423–1427). IEEE.
9. Stadler, I. (2008). Power grid balancing of energy systems with high renewable energy penetration by demand response. *Utilities Policy, 16*(2), 90–98.
10. Shimbar, A., & Ebrahimi, S. B. (2020). Political risk and valuation of renewable energy investments in developing countries. *Renewable Energy, 145*, 1325–1333.
11. Egli, F. (2020). Renewable energy investment risk: An investigation of changes over time and the underlying drivers. *Energy Policy, 140*, 111428.
12. Khan, Z., Badeeb, R. A., & Nawaz, K. (2022). Natural resources and economic performance: Evaluating the role of political risk and renewable energy consumption. *Resources Policy, 78*, 102890.
13. Wang, Q., Dong, Z., Li, R., & Wang, L. (2022). Renewable energy and economic growth: New insight from country risks. *Energy, 238*, 122018.
14. Lowitzsch, J., Hoicka, C. E., & van Tulder, F. J. (2020). Renewable energy communities under the 2019 European Clean Energy Package–Governance model for the energy clusters of the future? *Renewable and Sustainable Energy Reviews, 122*, 109489.
15. Reis, I. F., Gonçalves, I., Lopes, M. A., & Antunes, C. H. (2021). Business models for energy communities: A review of key issues and trends. *Renewable and Sustainable Energy Reviews, 144*, 111013.
16. Caramizaru, A., & Uihlein, A. (2020). *Energy communities: An overview of energy and social innovation* (Vol. 30083). Publications Office of the European Union.
17. Tarhan, M. (2015). Renewable energy cooperatives: A review of demonstrated impacts and limitations. *Journal of Entrepreneurial and Organizational Diversity, 4*(1), 104–120.
18. Yildiz, Ö., Rommel, J., Debor, S., Holstenkamp, L., Mey, F., Müller, J. R., et al. (2015). Renewable energy cooperatives as gatekeepers or facilitators? Recent developments in Germany and a multidisciplinary research agenda. *Energy Research & Social Science, 6*, 59–73.
19. Lu, Y., Khan, Z. A., Alvarez-Alvarado, M. S., Zhang, Y., Huang, Z., & Imran, M. (2020). A critical review of sustainable energy policies for the promotion of renewable energy sources. *Sustainability, 12*(12), 5078.
20. Koperski, L. (2017). Why the renewable energy credit market needs standardization. *Washington Journal of Law, Technology & Arts, 13*, 69.
21. Finocchi, E. (2020). Standardizing a unique renewable energy supply chain: The SURESC model. *F1000Research, 9*.
22. Conkling, T. J., Loss, S. R., Diffendorfer, J. E., Duerr, A. E., & Katzner, T. E. (2021). Limitations, lack of standardization, and recommended best practices in studies of renewable energy effects on birds and bats. *Conservation Biology, 35*(1), 64–76.
23. Sovacool, B. K., Turnheim, B., Hook, A., Brock, A., & Martiskainen, M. (2021). Dispossessed by decarbonisation: Reducing vulnerability, injustice, and inequality in the lived experience of low-carbon pathways. *World Development, 137*, 105116.

24. Sundberg, P., Hermansson, S., Tullin, C., & Öhman, M. (2018). Traceability of bulk biomass: Application of radio frequency identification technology on a bulk pellet flow. *Biomass and Bioenergy, 118*, 149–153.
25. Hoang, A. T., Nižetić, S., Olcer, A. I., Ong, H. C., Chen, W. H., Chong, C. T., et al. (2021). Impacts of COVID-19 pandemic on the global energy system and the shift progress to renewable energy: Opportunities, challenges, and policy implications. *Energy Policy, 154*, 112322.
26. Patel, S., & Parkins, J. R. (2023). Assessing motivations and barriers to renewable energy development: Insights from a survey of municipal decision-makers in Alberta, Canada. *Energy Reports, 9*, 5788–5798.
27. Breyer, C., Khalili, S., Bogdanov, D., Ram, M., Oyewo, A. S., Aghahosseini, A., et al. (2022). On the history and future of 100% renewable energy systems research. *IEEE Access, 10*, 78176–78218.
28. Ceglia, F., Esposito, P., Marrasso, E., & Sasso, M. (2020). From smart energy community to smart energy municipalities: Literature review, agendas and pathways. *Journal of Cleaner Production, 254*, 120118.
29. Shafiullah, M., Ahmed, S. D., & Al-Sulaiman, F. A. (2022). Grid integration challenges and solution strategies for solar PV systems: A review. *IEEE Access, 10*, 52233–52257.
30. Baranauskienė, J. (2024). Evaluation of public projects in the light of sustainability. *Management Theory and Studies for Rural Business and Infrastructure Development, 46*(2), 174–182.
31. Elavarasan, R. M., Shafiullah, G. M., Padmanaban, S., Kumar, N. M., Annam, A., Vetrichelvan, A. M., et al. (2020). A comprehensive review on renewable energy development, challenges, and policies of leading Indian states with an international perspective. *IEEE Access, 8*, 74432–74457.
32. Fahlquist, J. N., & Roeser, S. (2015). Nuclear energy, responsible risk communication and moral emotions: A three level framework. *Journal of Risk Research, 18*(3), 333–346.
33. Friederich, S., & Boudry, M. (2022). Ethics of nuclear energy in times of climate change: Escaping the collective action problem. *Philosophy & Technology, 35*(2), 30.
34. Kang, J. N., Wei, Y. M., Liu, L. C., Han, R., Yu, B. Y., & Wang, J. W. (2020). Energy systems for climate change mitigation: A systematic review. *Applied Energy, 263*, 114602.
35. Ukoba, K., Medupin, R. O., Yoro, K. O., Eterigho-Ikelegbe, O., & Jen, T. C. (2024). Role of the fourth industrial revolution in attaining universal energy access and net-zero objectives. *Energy, 360*, 100002.
36. Uwaoma, P. U., Eboigbe, E. O., Kaggwa, S., Akinwolemiwa, D. I., & Eloghosa, S. O. (2023). Ecological economics in the age of 4IR: Spotlight on sustainability initiatives in the global south. *International Journal of Advanced Economics, 5*(9), 271–284.
37. Cowie, P., Townsend, L., & Salemink, K. (2020). Smart rural futures: Will rural areas be left behind in the 4th industrial revolution? *Journal of Rural Studies, 79*, 169–176.
38. Özgül, S., Koçar, G., & Eryaşar, A. (2020). The progress, challenges, and opportunities of renewable energy cooperatives in Turkey. *Energy for Sustainable Development, 59*, 107–119.
39. Qadir, S. A., Al-Motairi, H., Tahir, F., & Al-Fagih, L. (2021). Incentives and strategies for financing the renewable energy transition: A review. *Energy Reports, 7*, 3590–3606.
40. Bisaga, I., Parikh, P., Tomei, J., & To, L. S. (2021). Mapping synergies and trade-offs between energy and the sustainable development goals: A case study of off-grid solar energy in Rwanda. *Energy Policy, 149*, 112028.
41. Christensen, J. L., Hain, D. S., & Nogueira, L. A. (2019). Joining forces: Collaboration patterns and performance of renewable energy innovators. *Small Business Economics, 52*, 793–814.
42. Brink, T. (2017). Innovation collaboration in the renewable offshore wind energy sector. *International Journal of Energy Sector Management, 11*(4), 664–680.
43. Aleixandre-Tudó, J. L., Castelló-Cogollos, L., Aleixandre, J. L., & Aleixandre-Benavent, R. (2019). Renewable energies: Worldwide trends in research, funding and international collaboration. *Renewable Energy, 139*, 268–278.

References

44. Mu, C., Ding, T., Qu, M., Zhou, Q., Li, F., & Shahidehpour, M. (2020). Decentralized optimization operation for the multiple integrated energy systems with energy cascade utilization. *Applied Energy, 280*, 115989.
45. Mishra, P. C., Kishore, S., & Shivani, S. (2018). The role of information technology for knowledge management: An empirical study of the Indian coal mining industry. *Journal of Global Information Technology Management, 21*(3), 208–225.

Open Access This chapter is licensed under the terms of the Creative Commons Attribution-NonCommercial-NoDerivatives 4.0 International License (http://creativecommons.org/licenses/by-nc-nd/4.0/), which permits any noncommercial use, sharing, distribution and reproduction in any medium or format, as long as you give appropriate credit to the original author(s) and the source, provide a link to the Creative Commons license and indicate if you modified the licensed material. You do not have permission under this license to share adapted material derived from this chapter or parts of it.

The images or other third party material in this chapter are included in the chapter's Creative Commons license, unless indicated otherwise in a credit line to the material. If material is not included in the chapter's Creative Commons license and your intended use is not permitted by statutory regulation or exceeds the permitted use, you will need to obtain permission directly from the copyright holder.

References

1. Bazan-Krzywoszańska, A., Skiba, M., Mrówczyńska, M., Sztubecka, M., Bazuń, D., & Kwiatkowski, M. (2018). Green energy in municipal planning documents. In *E3S web of conferences* (Vol. 45, p. 00006). EDP Sciences.
2. European Commission. (2020). *Proposal for a regulation of the European Parliament and of the council establishing the just transition fund; COM/2020/22 final*. European Commission.
3. Popescu, C., Hysa, E., Kruja, A., & Mansi, E. (2022). Social innovation, circularity and energy transition for environmental, social and governance (ESG) practices—A comprehensive review. *Energies, 15*(23), 9028.
4. Piccinetti, L., Rezk, M. R. A., Kapiel, T. Y., Salem, N., Khasawneh, A., Santoro, D., & Sakr, M. M. (2023). Circular bioeconomy in Egypt: The current state, challenges, and future directions. *Insights into Regional Development, 5*, 97–112.
5. Pilusa, T. J., & Muzenda, E. (2014, April 15–16). Municipal solid waste utilisation for green energy in gauteng province-South Africa: A review. In *Proceedings of the International Conference on Chemical, Integrated Waste Management & Environmental Engineering (ICCIWEE'2014), Johannesburg, South Africa*, pp. 174–179.
6. Zulkifli, A. A., Mohd Yusoff, M. Z., Abd Manaf, L., Zakaria, M. R., Roslan, A. M., Ariffin, H., et al. (2019). Assessment of municipal solid waste generation in Universiti Putra Malaysia and its potential for green energy production. *Sustainability, 11*(14), 3909.
7. Johari, A., Ahmed, S. I., Hashim, H., Alkali, H., & Ramli, M. (2012). Economic and environmental benefits of landfill gas from municipal solid waste in Malaysia. *Renewable and Sustainable Energy Reviews, 16*(5), 2907–2912.
8. Cała, M., Szewczyk-Świątek, A., & Ostręga, A. (2021). Challenges of coal mining regions and municipalities in the face of energy transition. *Energies, 14*(20), 6674.
9. Anthony Jnr, B. (2020). Smart city data architecture for energy prosumption in municipalities: Concepts, requirements, and future directions. *International Journal of Green Energy, 17*(13), 827–845.
10. Bogdanov, D., Ram, M., Aghahosseini, A., Gulagi, A., Oyewo, A. S., Child, M., et al. (2021). Low-cost renewable electricity as the key driver of the global energy transition towards sustainability. *Energy, 227*, 120467.
11. Guarieiro, L. L., Anjos, J. P. D., Silva, L. A. D., Santos, A. Á., Calixto, E. E., Pessoa, F. L., et al. (2022). Technological perspectives and economic aspects of green hydrogen in the energetic transition: Challenges for chemistry. *Journal of the Brazilian Chemical Society, 33*(8), 844–869.
12. Adawiyah, W. R., Rahajuni, D., & Kadarwati, N. (2022). Economic growth and environmental degradation paradox in ASEAN: A simultaneous equation model with dynamic panel data approach. *Environmental Economics, 13*(1), 171.

13. Makarenko, I., Bilan, Y., Štreimikienė, D., & Rybina, L. (2023). Investments support for sustainable development goal 7: Research gaps in the context of post-COVID-19 recovery. *Investment Management and Financial Innovations, 20*(1), 151–173.
14. Boros, A., Lentner, C., Nagy, V., & Tőzsér, D. (2023). Perspectives by green financial instruments – A case study in the Hungarian banking sector during COVID-19. *Banks and Bank Systems, 18*(1), 116–126.
15. Tsaurai, K. (2022). Effect of foreign direct investment on domestic investment in BRICS. *Investment Management and Financial Innovations, 19*(4), 260–273.
16. Al-Faryan, M. A. S. (2022). Nexus between corruption, market capitalization, exports, FDI, and country's wealth: A pre-global financial crisis study. *Problems and Perspectives in Management, 20*, 224–237.
17. Tite, O., Ogundipe, O. M., Ogundipe, A. A., & Akinde, M. A. (2022). Analysis of foreign capital inflows and stock market performance in Nigeria. *Investment Management & Financial Innovations, 19*(4), 51.
18. Dar, J. A., & Asif, M. (2018). Does financial development improve environmental quality in Turkey? An application of endogenous structural breaks based cointegration approach. *Management of Environmental Quality: An International Journal, 29*(2), 368–384.
19. Ike, G. N., Usman, O., Alola, A. A., & Sarkodie, S. A. (2020). Environmental quality effects of income, energy prices and trade: The role of renewable energy consumption in G-7 countries. *Science of the Total Environment, 721*, 137813.
20. Streimikiene, D. (2022). Renewable energy technologies in households: Challenges and low carbon energy transition justice. *Economics and Sociology, 15*(3), 108–120.
21. Streimikiene, D. (2022). Energy poverty and impact of COVID-19 pandemics in Visegrad (V4) countries. *Journal of International Studies, 15*(1), 9–25.
22. Endri, E., Hania, B. T., & Ma'ruf, A. (2022). Corporate green Sukuk issuance for sustainable financing in Indonesia. *Environmental Economics, 13*(1), 38.
23. Bertrand, N. A. S., & Etienne, K. L. (2022). Increasing the productivity of manufacturing firms in Cameroon in a sustainable way: Renewable or non-renewable energy? *Environmental Economics, 13*(1), 28.
24. Kirikkaleli, D., & Adebayo, T. S. (2021). Do renewable energy consumption and financial development matter for environmental sustainability? New global evidence. *Sustainable Development, 29*(4), 583–594.
25. Alsmadi, A. A., Alrawashdeh, N., Al-Gasaymeh, A., Al-Malahmeh, H., & Moh'd Al-hazimeh, A. (2023). Impact of business enablers on banking performance: A moderating role of Fintech. *Banks and Bank Systems, 18*(1), 14–25.
26. Lantara, D. (2022). Indonesian Islamic banks: A review of the financial state before and after the COVID-19 pandemic. *Business Perspectives, 17*(4), 12–24.
27. Naumenkova, S., Mishchenko, V., & Mishchenko, S. (2022). Key energy indicators for sustainable development goals in Ukraine. *Problems and Perspectives in Management, 20*(1), 379–395.
28. Ginevičius, R. (2022). The efficiency of municipal waste management systems in the environmental context in the countries of the European Union. *Journal of International Studies, 15*(4), 63–79.
29. Štreimikienė, D. (2021). Externalities of power generation in Visegrad countries and their integration through support of renewables. *Economics and Sociology, 14*(1), 89–102.
30. Hys, K. (2015, June 4–5). Respect index stock exchanges in Poland as the corporate social responsibility tool. In *Proceedings of the International Scientific Conference, Nitra, Slovakia*, pp. 119–126.
31. Sarangi, G. K. (2021). *Resurgence of ESG Investments in India: Toward a sustainable economy*. Asian Development Bank Institute.
32. Zioło, M., Bąk, I., & Spoz, A. (2023). Incorporating ESG risk in companies' business models: State of research and energy sector case studies. *Energies, 16*(4), 1809.

References

33. Baran, M., Kuźniarska, A., Makieła, Z. J., Sławik, A., & Stuss, M. M. (2022). Does ESG reporting relate to corporate financial performance in the context of the energy sector transformation? Evidence from Poland. *Energies, 15*(2), 477.
34. Xie, C. L. (2020). *Institutional investors, shareholder activism, and ESG in the energy sector* (Wharton research scholars). University of Pennsylvania.
35. Alsayegh, M. F., Abdul Rahman, R., & Homayoun, S. (2020). Corporate economic, environmental, and social sustainability performance transformation through ESG disclosure. *Sustainability, 12*(9), 3910.
36. Behl, A., Kumari, P. R., Makhija, H., & Sharma, D. (2022). Exploring the relationship of ESG score and firm value using cross-lagged panel analyses: Case of the Indian energy sector. *Annals of Operations Research, 313*(1), 231–256.
37. Kuzmina, J., Atstaja, D., Purvins, M., Baakashvili, G., & Chkareuli, V. (2023). In search of sustainability and financial returns: The case of ESG energy funds. *Sustainability, 15*(3), 2716.
38. Cohen, L., Gurun, U. G., & Nguyen, Q. H. (2020). *The ESG-innovation disconnect: Evidence from green patenting*. National Bureau of Economic Research.
39. Domanović, V. (2022). The relationship between ESG and financial performance indicators in the public sector: Empirical evidence from the Republic of Serbia. *Management: Journal of Sustainable Business and Management Solutions in Emerging Economies, 27*(1), 69–80.
40. Liu, G., & Hamori, S. (2020). Can one reinforce investments in renewable energy stock indices with the ESG index? *Energies, 13*(5), 1179.
41. Saygili, A. T., Saygili, E., & Taran, A. (2021). The effects of corporate governance practices on firm-level financial performance: Evidence from Borsa Istanbul Xkury companies. *Journal of Business Economics, 22*, 884–904.
42. Lithuanian District Heating Association (LDHA). (2021). *Šilumos Tiekimo Bendrovių 2020 Metų Ūkinės Veiklos Apžvalga*. Lietuvos Šilumos Tiekėjų Asociacija.
43. Klevas, V., Biekša, K., & Murauskaitė, L. (2014). Innovative method of RES integration into the regional energy development scenarios. *Energy Policy, 64*, 324–336.
44. Štreimikienė, D. (2016). Review of financial support from EU structural funds to sustainable energy in Baltic States. *Renewable and Sustainable Energy Reviews, 58*, 1027–1038.
45. Sliogeriene, J., Turskis, Z., & Streimikiene, D. (2013). Analysis and choice of energy generation technologies: The multiple criteria assessment on the case study of Lithuania. *Energy Procedia, 32*, 11–20.
46. Štreimikienė, D., Šliogerienė, J., & Turskis, Z. (2016). Multi-criteria analysis of electricity generation technologies in Lithuania. *Renewable Energy, 85*, 148–156.
47. Katinas, V., & Markevicius, A. (2006). Promotional policy and perspectives of usage renewable energy in Lithuania. *Energy Policy, 34*(7), 771–780.
48. Government of the Republic of Lithuania. (2018). *National energy independence strategy*. Government of the Republic of Lithuania.
49. Hauberg, J. (2011). Research by design: A research strategy. *Revista Lusófona de Arquitectura e Educação, 5*, 46–56.
50. Martins, F., Felgueiras, C., Smitkova, M., & Caetano, N. (2019). Analysis of fossil fuel energy consumption and environmental impacts in European countries. *Energies, 12*(6), 964.
51. Luderer, G., Pehl, M., Arvesen, A., Gibon, T., Bodirsky, B. L., De Boer, H. S., et al. (2019). Environmental co-benefits and adverse side-effects of alternative power sector decarbonization strategies. *Nature Communications, 10*(1), 5229.
52. Environmental Projects Management Agency. *Saulės Elektrinės Namų Ūkiuose*. https://www.apva.lt/saules-elektriniu-irengimas-namu-ukiuose/
53. NordPool Group. *Market data*. https://www.nordpoolgroup.com/en/Market-data1/Dayahead/Area-Prices/ALL1/Hourly/?view=table
54. BNS. *Vandens Įmonėms Prakalbus Apie Nuostolius, Jo Tiekimas Vartotojams Brangs*. https://www.bns.lt/topic/1912/news/66233633/

55. Genys, D., & Pažėraitė, A. (2022). Mapping Lithuanian transition towards sustainable energy: Sociological account on a waste-to-energy case. *Entrepreneurship and Sustainability Issues, 10*(2), 527.
56. Vilniaus Apšvietimas. *Vilniuje—Pirmosios Elektromobilių Įkrovimo Stotelės Nuo Apšvietimo Stulpo.* https://naujas.vilniausapsvietimas.lt/vilniuje-pirmosios-elektromobiliu-ikrovimo-stoteles-nuo-apsvietimo-stulpo-2/
57. Lithuanian Geological Survey. *Geoterminės Energijos Tyrimai.* https://www.lgt.lt/index.php?view=article&id=344:geotermines-energijos-tyrimai&catid=233/
58. Connolly, D., Lund, H., & Mathiesen, B. V. (2016). Smart energy Europe: The technical and economic impact of one potential 100% renewable energy scenario for the European Union. *Renewable and Sustainable Energy Reviews, 60*, 1634–1653.
59. Gielen, D., Boshell, F., Saygin, D., Bazilian, M. D., Wagner, N., & Gorini, R. (2019). The role of renewable energy in the global energy transformation. *Energy Strategy Reviews, 24*, 38–50.
60. Bartholdsen, H. K., Eidens, A., Löffler, K., Seehaus, F., Wejda, F., Burandt, T., et al. (2019). Pathways for Germany's low-carbon energy transformation towards 2050. *Energies, 12*(15), 2988.
61. Nazir, C. P. (2019). Solar energy for traction of high speed rail transportation: A techno-economic analysis. *Civil Engineering Journal, 5*(7), 1566–1576.
62. Duro, J. A., & Padilla, E. (2011). Inequality across countries in energy intensities: An analysis of the role of energy transformation and final energy consumption. *Energy Economics, 33*(3), 474–479.
63. Frondel, M., Ritter, N., Schmidt, C. M., & Vance, C. (2010). Economic impacts from the promotion of renewable energy technologies: The German experience. *Energy Policy, 38*(8), 4048–4056.
64. Gielen, D., Gorini, R., Wagner, N., Leme, R., Gutierrez, L., Prakash, G., & Renner, M. (2019). *Global energy transformation: A roadmap to 2050.* International Renewable Energy Agency (IRENA).
65. Dvořák, P., Martinát, S., Van der Horst, D., Frantál, B., & Turečková, K. (2017). Renewable energy investment and job creation; a cross-sectoral assessment for the Czech Republic with reference to EU benchmarks. *Renewable and Sustainable Energy Reviews, 69*, 360–368.
66. Akella, A. K., Saini, R. P., & Sharma, M. P. (2009). Social, economical and environmental impacts of renewable energy systems. *Renewable Energy, 34*(2), 390–396.
67. Bulavskaya, T., & Reynès, F. (2018). Job creation and economic impact of renewable energy in the Netherlands. *Renewable Energy, 119*, 528–538.
68. Sharma, R., Shahbaz, M., Kautish, P., & Vo, X. V. (2021). Analyzing the impact of export diversification and technological innovation on renewable energy consumption: Evidences from BRICS nations. *Renewable Energy, 178*, 1034–1045.
69. Haseeb, M., Abidin, I. S. Z., Hye, Q. M. A., & Hartani, N. H. (2019). The impact of renewable energy on economic well-being of Malaysia: Fresh evidence from auto regressive distributed lag bound testing approach. *International Journal of Energy Economics and Policy, 9*(1), 269–275.
70. Elia, A., Kamidelivand, M., Rogan, F., & Gallachóir, B. Ó. (2021). Impacts of innovation on renewable energy technology cost reductions. *Renewable and Sustainable Energy Reviews, 138*, 110488.
71. Szpor, A., & Ziółkowska, K. (2018). *Transformation of the polish coal sector.* International Institute for Sustainable Development.
72. Wang, Q., Dong, Z., Li, R., & Wang, L. (2022). Renewable energy and economic growth: New insight from country risks. *Energy, 238*, 122018.
73. De Arce, R., Mahía, R., Medina, E., & Escribano, G. (2012). A simulation of the economic impact of renewable energy development in Morocco. *Energy Policy, 46*, 335–345.
74. Inglesi-Lotz, R. (2016). The impact of renewable energy consumption to economic growth: A panel data application. *Energy Economics, 53*, 58–63.

References

75. Sibuea, M. B., Sibuea, S. R., & Pratama, I. (2021). The impact of renewable energy and economic development on environmental quality of ASEAN countries. *AgBioforum, 23*, 12–21.
76. Lithuanian District Heating Association (LDHA). (2023). *Šilumos Tiekimo Bendrovių 2022 Metų Ūkinės Veiklos Apžvalga*. Lietuvos Šilumos Tiekėjų Asociacija.
77. NordPool Group. *Market data*. https://www.nordpoolgroup.com/en/Market-data1/Dayahead/Area-Prices/ALL1/Hourly/?view=table
78. Governance Coordination Centre. *List of MOEs*. https://governance.lt/en/apie-imones/svi-sarasas/
79. State Forestry Service. *Lietuvos Miškų Rodikliai*. https://amvmt.lrv.lt/lt/atviri-duomenys-1/lietuvos-misku-rodikliai/
80. Agricultural Data Center. (2023). *Lietuvos Respublikos Žemės Fondas 2023 m. Sausio 1 d*. Žemės ūkio Duomenų Centras.
81. Official Statistics Portal. *Indicators database*. https://osp.stat.gov.lt/statistiniu-rodikliu-analize#/
82. Litgrid. Renewable Energy Integration Centre. https://www.litgrid.eu/index.php/renewable-energy/renewable-energy-integration-centre/32092
83. LŽŪMPRIS. *Ekologinių Ūkių Statistika*. https://www.vic.lt/zumpris/statistine-informacija/
84. Capece, G., Cricelli, L., Di Pillo, F., & Levialdi, N. (2010). A cluster analysis study based on profitability and financial indicators in the Italian gas retail market. *Energy Policy, 38*(7), 3394–3402.
85. Chen, J., Qi, X., Chen, L., Chen, F., & Cheng, G. (2020). Quantum-inspired ant lion optimized hybrid k-means for cluster analysis and intrusion detection. *Knowledge-Based Systems, 203*, 106167.
86. Sari, I. P., Al-Khowarizmi, A. K., & Batubara, I. H. (2021). Cluster analysis using K-means algorithm and fuzzy C-means clustering for grouping students' abilities in online learning process. *Journal of Computer Science, Information Technology and Telecommunication Engineering, 2*(1), 139–144.
87. Brigham, E. F., & Houston, J. F. (2001). *Financial management* (8th ed., p. 39). Erlangga.
88. Yunusa, D. A., & Prasetyob, K. (2020). Company type, asset structure and capital structure listed on LQ-45 index. *International Journal of Innovation, Creativity and Change, 13*(8), 1251–1261.
89. Mukhtarov, S., Aliyev, J., Borowski, P. F., & Disli, M. (2023). Institutional quality and renewable energy transition: Empirical evidence from Poland. *Journal of International Studies, 16*(3), 208.
90. Štreimikienė, D. (2021). Externalities of power generation in Visegrad countries and their integration through support of renewables. *Economics and Sociology, 14*(1), 89–102.
91. State data agency. *Official statistics portal*. https://osp.stat.gov.lt/
92. Eurostat. *Portal of statistics*. https://ec.europa.eu/eurostat/
93. Agricultural Data Center. *Data from the agricultural sector*. https://zudc.lt/statistika/
94. Lithuanian Energy Agency. *Data*. https://www.ena.lt/aktuali-aei-statistika/
95. d'Amore-Domenech, R., Santiago, O., & Leo, T. J. (2020). Multicriteria analysis of seawater electrolysis technologies for green hydrogen production at sea. *Renewable and Sustainable Energy Reviews, 133*, 110166.
96. Bortoluzzi, M., de Souza, C. C., & Furlan, M. (2021). Bibliometric analysis of renewable energy types using key performance indicators and multicriteria decision models. *Renewable and Sustainable Energy Reviews, 143*, 110958.
97. Şahin, M. (2021). A comprehensive analysis of weighting and multicriteria methods in the context of sustainable energy. *International Journal of Environmental Science and Technology, 18*(6), 1591–1616.
98. György, O. (2024). Cluster grouping of EU member states according to some economic performance and circular economic indicators. *Management/Vadyba (16487974), 40*(1).

99. Hermesmann, M., & Müller, T. E. (2022). Green, turquoise, blue, or grey? Environmentally friendly hydrogen production in transforming energy systems. *Progress in Energy and Combustion Science, 90*, 100996.
100. Capurso, T., Stefanizzi, M., Torresi, M., & Camporeale, S. M. (2022). Perspective of the role of hydrogen in the 21st century energy transition. *Energy Conversion and Management, 251*, 114898.
101. Baquero, J. E. G., & Monsalve, D. B. (2024). From fossil fuel energy to hydrogen energy: Transformation of fossil fuel energy economies into hydrogen economies through social entrepreneurship. *International Journal of Hydrogen Energy, 54*, 574–585.
102. Coy, D., Malekpour, S., & Saeri, A. K. (2022). From little things, big things grow: Facilitating community empowerment in the energy transformation. *Energy Research & Social Science, 84*, 102353.
103. Igliński, B., Kiełkowska, U., Pietrzak, M. B., Skrzatek, M., Kumar, G., & Piechota, G. (2023). The regional energy transformation in the context of renewable energy sources potential. *Renewable Energy, 218*, 119246.
104. Ding, W., Du, J., Kazancoglu, Y., Mangla, S. K., & Song, M. (2023). Financial development and the energy net-zero transformation potential. *Energy Economics, 125*, 106863.
105. Kikuchi, Y., Nakai, M., Kanematsu, Y., Oosawa, K., Okubo, T., Oshita, Y., & Fukushima, Y. (2020). Application of technology assessments to co-learning for regional transformation: A case study of biomass energy systems in Tanegashima. *Sustainability Science, 15*, 1473–1494.
106. Beck, S., Jasanoff, S., Stirling, A., & Polzin, C. (2021). The governance of sociotechnical transformations to sustainability. *Current Opinion in Environmental Sustainability, 49*, 143–152.
107. Pickering, J., Hickmann, T., Bäckstrand, K., Kalfagianni, A., Bloomfield, M., Mert, A., et al. (2022). Democratising sustainability transformations: Assessing the transformative potential of democratic practices in environmental governance. *Earth System Governance, 11*, 100131.
108. Sovacool, B. K., Hook, A., Sareen, S., & Geels, F. W. (2021). Global sustainability, innovation and governance dynamics of national smart electricity meter transitions. *Global Environmental Change, 68*, 102272.
109. Hoppe, T., & Miedema, M. (2020). A governance approach to regional energy transition: Meaning, conceptualization and practice. *Sustainability, 12*(3), 915.
110. Knodt, M., Ringel, M., & Müller, R. (2020). 'Harder' soft governance in the European energy union. *Journal of Environmental Policy & Planning, 22*(6), 787–800.
111. Taylor, M. (2020). *Energy subsidies: Evolution in the global energy transformation to 2050* (pp. 10–14). International Renewable Energy Agency.
112. Shao, Y., & Chen, Z. (2022). Can government subsidies promote the green technology innovation transformation? Evidence from Chinese listed companies. *Economic Analysis and Policy, 74*, 716–727.
113. Wang, Z., Li, X., Xue, X., & Liu, Y. (2022). More government subsidies, more green innovation? The evidence from Chinese new energy vehicle enterprises. *Renewable Energy, 197*, 11–21.
114. Ginevičius, R. (2022). The efficiency of municipal waste management systems in the environmental context in the countries of the European Union. *Journal of International Studies, 15*(4), 63–79.
115. Svazas, M., Navickas, V., Paskevicius, R., Bilan, Y., & Vasa, L. (2023). Renewable energy versus energy security: The impact of innovation on the economy. *Rynek Energii, 1*, 60–71.
116. Caineng, Z. O. U., Xiong, B., Huaqing, X. U. E., Zheng, D., Zhixin, G. E., Ying, W. A. N. G., et al. (2021). The role of new energy in carbon neutral. *Petroleum Exploration and Development, 48*(2), 480–491.
117. Lund, H., & Mathiesen, B. V. (2009). Energy system analysis of 100% renewable energy systems—The case of Denmark in years 2030 and 2050. *Energy, 34*(5), 524–531.

References

118. Farhangi, H. (2009). The path of the smart grid. *IEEE Power and Energy Magazine, 8*(1), 18–28.
119. Jing, H., Zhu, P., Zheng, X., Zhang, Z., Wang, D., & Li, Y. (2022). Theory-oriented screening and discovery of advanced energy transformation materials in electrocatalysis. *Advanced Powder Materials, 1*(1), 100013.
120. Chu, S., & Majumdar, A. (2012). Opportunities and challenges for a sustainable energy future. *Nature, 488*(7411), 294–303.
121. Harrison, K. W., Remick, R., & Martin, G. D. (2010). *Hydrogen production: Fundamentals and case study summaries*. National Renewable Energy Laboratory (NREL).
122. Yasmeen, R., Zhang, X., Tao, R., & Shah, W. U. H. (2023). The impact of green technology, environmental tax and natural resources on energy efficiency and productivity: Perspective of OECD rule of law. *Energy Reports, 9*, 1308–1319.
123. Igliński, B., Kiełkowska, U., Pietrzak, M. B., Skrzatek, M., Kumar, G., & Piechota, G. (2023). The regional energy transformation in the context of renewable energy sources potential. *Renewable Energy, 218*, 119246.
124. Güler, İ., Atan, M., & Adalı, Z. (2024). The effect of economic growth, investment, and unemployment on renewable energy transition: Evidence from OECD countries. *Environmental Science and Pollution Research, 31*(39), 52001–52016.
125. Bali Swain, R., Karimu, A., & Gråd, E. (2022). Sustainable development, renewable energy transformation and employment impact in the EU. *International Journal of Sustainable Development & World Ecology, 29*(8), 695–708.
126. Xu, Y., Liu, A., Li, Z., Li, J., Xiong, J., & Fan, P. (2023). Review of green supply-chain management diffusion in the context of energy transformation. *Energies, 16*(2), 686.
127. Chomać-Pierzecka, E., Sobczak, A., & Urbańczyk, E. (2022). RES market development and public awareness of the economic and environmental dimension of the energy transformation in Poland and Lithuania. *Energies, 15*(15), 5461.
128. Sánchez García, J., & Galdeano Gómez, E. (2023). What drives the preferences for cleaner energy? Parametrizing the elasticities of environmental quality demand for greenhouse gases. *Oeconomia Copernicana, 14*(2), 449–482.
129. Chudy-Laskowska, K., & Pisula, T. (2022). An analysis of the use of energy from conventional fossil fuels and green renewable energy in the context of the European Union's planned energy transformation. *Energies, 15*(19), 7369.
130. Mohamed, M., & El-Saber, N. (2023). Toward energy transformation: Intelligent decision-making model based on uncertainty neutrosophic theory. *Neutrosophic Systems with Applications, 9*, 13–23.
131. Pietrzak, M. B., Olczyk, M., & Kuc-Czarnecka, M. E. (2022). Assessment of the feasibility of energy transformation processes in European Union member states. *Energies, 15*(2), 661.
132. Kiciński, J. (2021). Green energy transformation in Poland. *Bulletin of the Polish Academy of Sciences. Technical Sciences, 69*(1), 136213.
133. He, L., Wang, B., Xu, W., Cui, Q., & Chen, H. (2022). Could China's long-term low-carbon energy transformation achieve the double dividend effect for the economy and environment? *Environmental Science and Pollution Research*, 1–17.
134. Hughes, T. P. (2011). *Networks of power: Electrification in Western Society, 1880-1930*. JHU Press.
135. International Atomic Energy Agency. (2022). *Advances in small modular reactor technology developments*. IAEA: Advanced Reactors Information System (ARIS).
136. Fearnside, P. M. (2014). Impacts of Brazil's Madeira River dams: Unlearned lessons for hydroelectric development in Amazonia. *Environmental Science & Policy, 38*, 164–172.
137. Jonek-Kowalska, I. (2022). Assessing the energy security of European countries in the resource and economic context. *Oeconomia Copernicana, 13*(2), 301–334.
138. U.S. Department of Energy. (2021). *Annual energy outlook*. U.S. Department of Energy.

139. Janssens-Maenhout, G., Crippa, M., Guizzardi, D., Muntean, M., Schaaf, E., Dentener, F., et al. (2019). EDGAR v4. 3.2 global atlas of the three major greenhouse gas emissions for the period 1970–2012. *Earth System Science Data, 11*(3), 959–1002.
140. Chovancová, J., & Tej, J. (2020). Decoupling economic growth from greenhouse gas emissions: The case of the energy sector in V4 countries. *Equilibrium. Quarterly Journal of Economics and Economic Policy, 15*(2), 235–251.
141. Pavlov, G. K., & Olesen, B. W. (2012). Thermal energy storage—A review of concepts and systems for heating and cooling applications in buildings: Part 1—Seasonal storage in the ground. *HVAC&R Research, 18*(3), 515–538.
142. Dincer, I., & Rosen, M. A. (2015). *Thermal energy storage: Systems and applications*. Wiley.
143. Speece, R. E. (1996). *Anaerobic biotechnology for industrial wastewaters*. Archae Press.
144. Demirel, B., & Scherer, P. (2008). The roles of acetotrophic and hydrogenotrophic methanogens during anaerobic conversion of biomass to methane: A review. *Reviews in Environmental Science and Bio/Technology, 7*, 173–190.
145. European Biogas Association (EBA). *EBA's vision for renewable gas in the green transition*. https://www.europeanbiogas.eu/wp-content/uploads/2018/09/EBA-Vision-for-Renewable-Gas.pdf
146. National Renewable Energy Laboratory (NREL). *Hydrogen production: Natural gas reforming*. https://www.nrel.gov/hydrogen/proj_production_nat_gas_reforming.html
147. U.S. Department of Energy (DOE). *Hydrogen basics*. https://www.energy.gov/eere/fuelcells/hydrogen-basics
148. Rashidi, N. A., Chai, Y. H., & Yusup, S. (2022). Biomass energy in Malaysia: Current scenario, policies, and implementation challenges. *Bioenergy Research, 15*(3), 1371–1386.
149. Cengel, Y. A., & Boles, M. A. (2014). *Thermodynamics: An engineering approach*. McGraw-Hill Education.
150. Gimelli, A., & Luongo, A. (2014). Thermodynamic and experimental analysis of a biomass steam power plant: Critical issues and their possible solutions with CCGT systems. *Energy Procedia, 45*, 227–236.
151. Santos, V. O., Queiroz, L. S., Araujo, R. O., Ribeiro, F. C., Guimarães, M. N., da Costa, C. E., et al. (2020). Pyrolysis of acai seed biomass: Kinetics and thermodynamic parameters using thermogravimetric analysis. *Bioresource Technology Reports, 12*, 100553.
152. Yang, W., Pudasainee, D., Gupta, R., Li, W., Wang, B., & Sun, L. (2021). An overview of inorganic particulate matter emission from coal/biomass/MSW combustion: Sampling and measurement, formation, distribution, inorganic composition and influencing factors. *Fuel Processing Technology, 213*, 106657.
153. Hiloidhari, M., Sharno, M. A., Baruah, D. C., & Bezbaruah, A. N. (2023). Green and sustainable biomass supply chain for environmental, social and economic benefits. *Biomass and Bioenergy, 175*, 106893.
154. Heywood, J. B. (2014). *Internal combustion engine fundamentals*. McGraw-Hill Education.
155. Xu, Q., Wu, J., Guo, Z., Xue, X., & Li, X. (2022). Analysis of optimal intermediate temperature and injection pressure for refrigerant injection heat pump systems with economiser. *Applied Thermal Engineering, 210*, 118361.
156. Åström, K. J., & Murray, R. M. (2010). *Feedback systems: An introduction for scientists and engineers*. Princeton University Press.
157. Karki, S., Kulkarni, M., Mann, M. D., & Salehfar, H. (2007). Efficiency improvements through combined heat and power for on-site distributed generation technologies. *Cogeneration and Distributed Generation Journal, 22*(3), 19–34.
158. Bauen, A. (2010). *The economic potential of CHP in the European Union*. International Energy Agency (IEA).
159. Valente, A., Iribarren, D., & Dufour, J. (2017). Life cycle assessment of hydrogen energy systems: A review of methodological choices. *The International Journal of Life Cycle Assessment, 22*, 346–363.

160. Toklu, E. (2017). Biomass energy potential and utilization in Turkey. *Renewable Energy, 107*, 235–244.
161. Popp, J., Kovács, S., Oláh, J., Divéki, Z., & Balázs, E. (2021). Bioeconomy: Biomass and biomass-based energy supply and demand. *New Biotechnology, 60*, 76–84.
162. Favero, A., Daigneault, A., Sohngen, B., & Baker, J. (2023). A system-wide assessment of forest biomass production, markets, and carbon. *GCB Bioenergy, 15*(2), 154–165.
163. Zetterholm, J., Bryngemark, E., Ahlström, J., Söderholm, P., Harvey, S., & Wetterlund, E. (2020). Economic evaluation of large-scale biorefinery deployment: A framework integrating dynamic biomass market and techno-economic models. *Sustainability, 12*(17), 7126.
164. Gribbons, B., & Herman, J. (2019). True and quasi-experimental designs. *Practical Assessment, Research, and Evaluation, 5*(1), 14.
165. Anderson, V. L., & McLean, R. A. (2018). *Design of experiments: A realistic approach*. CRC Press.
166. Wen, C., Zhang, Y., Wang, C., Xue, D., Bai, Y., Antonov, S., et al. (2019). Machine learning assisted design of high entropy alloys with desired property. *Acta Materialia, 170*, 109–117.
167. Karimifard, S., & Moghaddam, M. R. A. (2018). Application of response surface methodology in physicochemical removal of dyes from wastewater: A critical review. *Science of the Total Environment, 640*, 772–797.
168. Behera, S. K., Meena, H., Chakraborty, S., & Meikap, B. C. (2018). Application of response surface methodology (RSM) for optimization of leaching parameters for ash reduction from low-grade coal. *International Journal of Mining Science and Technology, 28*(4), 621–629.
169. Chelladurai, S. J. S., Murugan, K., Ray, A. P., Upadhyaya, M., Narasimharaj, V., & Gnanasekaran, S. (2021). Optimization of process parameters using response surface methodology: A review. *Materials Today: Proceedings, 37*, 1301–1304.
170. Tataraki, K., Giannini, E., Kavvadias, K., & Maroulis, Z. (2020). Cogeneration economics for greenhouses in Europe. *Energies, 13*(13), 3373.
171. Barron-Gafford, G. A., Pavao-Zuckerman, M. A., Minor, R. L., Sutter, L. F., Barnett-Moreno, I., Blackett, D. T., et al. (2019). Agrivoltaics provide mutual benefits across the food–energy–water nexus in drylands. *Nature Sustainability, 2*(9), 848–855.
172. Sampson, G. S., Perry, E. D., & Taylor, M. R. (2020). The on-farm and near-farm effects of wind turbines on agricultural land values. *Journal of Agricultural and Resource Economics, 45*(3), 410–427.
173. Taibi, E., Gielen, D., & Bazilian, M. (2012). The potential for renewable energy in industrial applications. *Renewable and Sustainable Energy Reviews, 16*(1), 735–744.
174. Kougias, I., Szabo, S., Monforti-Ferrario, F., Huld, T., & Bódis, K. (2016). A methodology for optimization of the complementarity between small-hydropower plants and solar PV systems. *Renewable Energy, 87*, 1023–1030.
175. Pukšec, T., & Duić, N. (2010). Biogas potential in Croatian farming sector. *Strojarstvo, 52*(4), 441–448.
176. Scarlat, N., Dallemand, J. F., Monforti-Ferrario, F., & Nita, V. (2015). The role of biomass and bioenergy in a future bioeconomy: Policies and facts. *Environmental Development, 15*, 3–34.
177. Aydoğan, B., & Vardar, G. (2020). Evaluating the role of renewable energy, economic growth and agriculture on CO2 emission in E7 countries. *International Journal of Sustainable Energy, 39*(4), 335–348.
178. Liu, X., Zhang, S., & Bae, J. (2017). The nexus of renewable energy-agriculture-environment in BRICS. *Applied Energy, 204*, 489–496.
179. Jebli, M. B., & Youssef, S. B. (2017). The role of renewable energy and agriculture in reducing CO2 emissions: Evidence for North Africa countries. *Ecological Indicators, 74*, 295–301.
180. Chel, A., & Kaushik, G. (2011). Renewable energy for sustainable agriculture. *Agronomy for Sustainable Development, 31*, 91–118.
181. Park, J., & Kim, Y. (2019). The effects of renewable energy in agricultural sector. *Journal of the Korea Academia-Industrial Cooperation Society, 20*(1), 224–235.

182. Martinho, V. J. P. D. (2018). Interrelationships between renewable energy and agricultural economics: An overview. *Energy Strategy Reviews, 22*, 396–409.
183. Rahman, M. M., Khan, I., Field, D. L., Techato, K., & Alameh, K. (2022). Powering agriculture: Present status, future potential, and challenges of renewable energy applications. *Renewable Energy, 188*, 731–749.
184. Bardi, U., El Asmar, T., & Lavacchi, A. (2013). Turning electricity into food: The role of renewable energy in the future of agriculture. *Journal of Cleaner Production, 53*, 224–231.
185. Singh, A. K., Pal, P., Rathore, S. S., Sahoo, U. K., Sarangi, P. K., Prus, P., & Dziekański, P. (2023). Sustainable utilization of biowaste resources for biogas production to meet rural bioenergy requirements. *Energies, 16*(14), 5409.
186. Olatunji, O. O., Adedeji, P. A., Madushele, N., Rasmeni, Z. Z., & van Rensburg, N. J. (2024). Evolutionary optimization of biogas production from food, fruit, and vegetable (FFV) waste. *Biomass Conversion and Biorefinery, 14*(11), 12113–12125.
187. Jara-Rojas, R., Russy, S., Roco, L., Fleming-Muñoz, D., & Engler, A. (2020). Factors affecting the adoption of agroforestry practices: Insights from silvopastoral systems of Colombia. *Forests, 11*(6), 648.
188. Raihan, A. (2024). The potential of agroforestry in south Asian countries towards achieving the climate goals. *Asian Journal of Forestry, 8*(1).
189. Datta, P., & Behera, B. (2024). India's approach to agroforestry as an effective strategy in the context of climate change: An evaluation of 28 state climate change action plans. *Agricultural Systems, 214*, 103840.
190. Montagnini, F., & del Fierro, S. (2024). Agroforestry systems as biodiversity islands in productive landscapes. In *Integrating landscapes: Agroforestry for biodiversity conservation and food sovereignty* (pp. 551–588). Springer.
191. Pascaris, A. S., Schelly, C., Burnham, L., & Pearce, J. M. (2021). Integrating solar energy with agriculture: Industry perspectives on the market, community, and socio-political dimensions of agrivoltaics. *Energy Research & Social Science, 75*, 102023.
192. Ramalingannanavar, N., Nemichandrappa, M., Srinivasa Reddy, G. V., Dandekar, A. T., Kamble, J. B., & Dhanoji, M. M. (2020). Design, development and evaluation of solar powered Aeroponic system—A case study. *International Journal of Current Microbiology and Applied Sciences, 9*, 3102–3112.
193. Al-Omair, A., Djavanroodi, F., Yahya, E., Yahya, G., Yahya, O., & Jassim, E. (2023). Aeroponic tower garden solar powered vertical farm. *Materials Research Proceedings, 31*, 287–298.
194. Ukoba, K., Yoro, K. O., Eterigho-Ikelegbe, O., Ibegbulam, C., & Jen, T. C. (2024). Adaptation of solar power in the global south: Prospects, challenges and opportunities. *Heliyon, 10*, e28009.
195. Li, X., Cao, Y., Yu, X., Xu, Y., Yang, Y., Liu, S., et al. (2022). Breeze-driven triboelectric nanogenerator for wind energy harvesting and application in smart agriculture. *Applied Energy, 306*, 117977.
196. Winikoff, J. B., & Parker, D. P. (2024). Farm size, spatial externalities, and wind energy development. *American Journal of Agricultural Economics, 106*(4), 1518–1543.
197. Mu, Q., He, W., Shan, C., Fu, S., Du, S., Wang, J., et al. (2024). Achieving high-efficiency wind energy harvesting triboelectric nanogenerator by coupling soft contact, charge space accumulation, and charge dissipation design. *Advanced Functional Materials, 34*(2), 2309421.
198. Glasberg, D., Stratila, S., & Malael, I. (2024). A numerical analysis on the performance and optimization of the Savonius wind turbine for agricultural use. *Engineering, Technology & Applied Science Research, 14*(1), 12621–12627.
199. Gutiérrez, A. S., Eras, J. J. C., Hens, L., & Vandecasteele, C. (2020). The energy potential of agriculture, agroindustrial, livestock, and slaughterhouse biomass wastes through direct combustion and anaerobic digestion. The case of Colombia. *Journal of Cleaner Production, 269*, 122317.

200. Bell, S. M., Barriocanal, C., Terrer, C., & Rosell-Melé, A. (2020). Management opportunities for soil carbon sequestration following agricultural land abandonment. *Environmental Science & Policy, 108*, 104–111.
201. Wysokiński, M., Domagała, J., Gromada, A., Golonko, M., & Trębska, P. (2020). Economic and energy efficiency of agriculture. *Agricultural Economics/Zemedelska Ekonomika, 66*(8), 355.
202. Ramzan, M., Razi, U., Usman, M., Sarwar, S., Talan, A., & Mundi, H. S. (2024). Role of nuclear energy, geothermal energy, agriculture, and urbanization in environmental stewardship. *Gondwana Research, 125*, 150–167.
203. Alexander, S., Yang, G., Addisu, G., & Block, P. (2021). Forecast-informed reservoir operations to guide hydropower and agriculture allocations in the Blue Nile basin, Ethiopia. *International Journal of Water Resources Development, 37*(2), 208–233.
204. Wang, J. (2014). Decentralized biogas technology of anaerobic digestion and farm ecosystem: Opportunities and challenges. *Frontiers in Energy Research, 2*, 10.
205. Holm-Nielsen, J. B., Al Seadi, T., & Oleskowicz-Popiel, P. (2009). The future of anaerobic digestion and biogas utilization. *Bioresource Technology, 100*(22), 5478–5484.
206. Gas Infrastructure Europe (GIE). https://www.gie.eu/press/record-breaking-year-for-biomethane-production-shows-eba-gie-biomethane-map-2021/
207. Gas Infrastructure Europe (GIE). https://www.gie.eu/press/new-record-for-biomethane-production-in-europe-shows-eba-gie-biomethane-map-2022-2023/
208. Thrän, D., Schaubach, K., Majer, S., & Horschig, T. (2020). Governance of sustainability in the German biogas sector—Adaptive management of the renewable energy act between agriculture and the energy sector. *Energy, Sustainability and Society, 10*, 1–18.
209. Ben Jebli, M., & Ben Youssef, S. (2017). Renewable energy consumption and agriculture: Evidence for cointegration and granger causality for Tunisian economy. *International Journal of Sustainable Development & World Ecology, 24*(2), 149–158.
210. Paris, B., Vandorou, F., Balafoutis, A. T., Vaiopoulos, K., Kyriakarakos, G., Manolakos, D., & Papadakis, G. (2022). Energy use in open-field agriculture in the EU: A critical review recommending energy efficiency measures and renewable energy sources adoption. *Renewable and Sustainable Energy Reviews, 158*, 112098.
211. Ali, S. M., Dash, N., & Pradhan, A. (2012). Role of renewable energy on agriculture. *International Journal of Engineering Sciences & Emerging Technologies, 4*(1), 51–57.
212. Panwar, N. L., Kaushik, S. C., & Kothari, S. (2011). Role of renewable energy sources in environmental protection: A review. *Renewable and Sustainable Energy Reviews, 15*(3), 1513–1524.
213. Boltianska, N. I., Manita, I. Y., & Komar, A. S. (2021). Justification of the energy saving mechanism in the agricultural sector. *Engineering of Nature Management, 1*(19), 7–12.
214. Sreekrishnan, T. R., Kohli, S., & Rana, V. (2004). Enhancement of biogas production from solid substrates using different techniques—A review. *Bioresource Technology, 95*(1), 1–10.
215. Gorjian, S., Kamrani, F., Ebadi, H., Samanta, S., & Savoldi, L. (2022). Applications of renewable energy sources in agriculture from a complementarity perspective. In *Complementarity of variable renewable energy sources* (pp. 615–647). Academic Press.
216. Nordberg, E. J., Caley, M. J., & Schwarzkopf, L. (2021). Designing solar farms for synergistic commercial and conservation outcomes. *Solar Energy, 228*, 586–593.
217. Pavičić, J., Novak Mavar, K., Brkić, V., & Simon, K. (2022). Biogas and biomethane production and usage: Technology development, advantages and challenges in Europe. *Energies, 15*(8), 2940.
218. Dale, B. E., Bozzetto, S., Couturier, C., Fabbri, C., Hilbert, J. A., Ong, R., et al. (2020). The potential for expanding sustainable biogas production and some possible impacts in specific countries. *Biofuels, Bioproducts and Biorefining, 14*(6), 1335–1347.
219. Sinsuw, A. A. E., Wuisang, C. E., & Chu, C. Y. (2021). Assessment of environmental and social impacts on rural community by two-stage biogas production pilot plant from slaughterhouse wastewater. *Journal of Water Process Engineering, 40*, 101796.

220. Ali, Q., Raza, A., Narjis, S., Saeed, S., & Khan, M. T. I. (2020). Potential of renewable energy, agriculture, and financial sector for the economic growth: Evidence from politically free, partly free and not free countries. *Renewable Energy, 162*, 934–947.
221. Rehman, H., & Bashir, D. F. (2015). Energy consumption and agriculture sector in middle income developing countries: A panel data analysis. *Pakistan Journal of Social Sciences (PJSS), 35*(1), 479–496.
222. Chandio, A. A., Jiang, Y., Rauf, A., Mirani, A. A., Shar, R. U., Ahmad, F., & Shehzad, K. (2019). Does energy-growth and environment quality matter for agriculture sector in Pakistan or not? An application of cointegration approach. *Energies, 12*(10), 1879.
223. Sebri, M., & Abid, M. (2012). Energy use for economic growth: A trivariate analysis from Tunisian agriculture sector. *Energy Policy, 48*, 711–716.
224. Rokicki, T., Perkowska, A., Klepacki, B., Bórawski, P., Bełdycka-Bórawska, A., & Michalski, K. (2021). Changes in energy consumption in agriculture in the EU countries. *Energies, 14*(6), 1570.
225. Paramati, S. R., Apergis, N., & Ummalla, M. (2018). Dynamics of renewable energy consumption and economic activities across the agriculture, industry, and service sectors: Evidence in the perspective of sustainable development. *Environmental Science and Pollution Research, 25*, 1375–1387.
226. Ragazou, K., Garefalakis, A., Zafeiriou, E., & Passas, I. (2022). Agriculture 5.0: A new strategic management mode for a cut cost and an energy efficient agriculture sector. *Energies, 15*(9), 3113.
227. Kazimierczuk, K., Barrows, S. E., Olarte, M. V., & Qafoku, N. P. (2023). Decarbonization of agriculture: The greenhouse gas impacts and economics of existing and emerging climate-smart practices. *ACS Engineering Au, 3*(6), 426–442.
228. Saha, C. K., Nandi, R., Rahman, M. A., Alam, M. M., & Møller, H. B. (2024). Biogas technology in commercial poultry and dairy farms of Bangladesh: Present scenario and future prospect. *Biomass Conversion and Biorefinery, 14*(7), 8407–8418.
229. Kusz, D., Kusz, B., Wicki, L., Nowakowski, T., Kata, R., Brejta, W., et al. (2024). The economic efficiencies of investment in biogas plants—A case study of a biogas plant using waste from a dairy farm in Poland. *Energies, 17*(15), 3760.
230. Gadirli, G., Pilarska, A. A., Dach, J., Pilarski, K., Kolasa-Więcek, A., & Borowiak, K. (2024). Fundamentals, operation and global prospects for the development of biogas plants—A review. *Energies, 17*(3), 568.
231. Brahmi, M., Bruno, B., Dhayal, K. S., Esposito, L., & Parziale, A. (2024). From manure to megawatts: Navigating the sustainable innovation solution through biogas production from livestock waste for harnessing green energy for green economy. *Heliyon, 10*(14), e34504.
232. Borusiewicz, A., Skibko, Z., Romaniuk, W., Pietruszynska, M., Milewska, A., & Marczuk, A. (2024). Agricultural micro biogas plants as a factor in farm development—A case study.
233. Catalano, G., D'Adamo, I., Gastaldi, M., Nizami, A. S., & Ribichini, M. (2024). Incentive policies in biomethane production toward circular economy. *Renewable and Sustainable Energy Reviews, 202*, 114710.
234. Dal Magro, A., Lovarelli, D., Bacenetti, J., & Guarino, M. (2024). The potential of insect frass for sustainable biogas and biomethane production: A review. *Bioresource Technology, 131384*, 131384.
235. Panda, S., & Jain, M. S. (2024). Assessment of the biomethane potential of commingled farm residues with sewage sludge and its techno-economic viability for rural application. *Biomass Conversion and Biorefinery*, 1–14.
236. Muñoz, P., González-Menorca, C., Sánchez-Vázquez, R., Sanchez-Prieto, J., & Del Pozo, A. F. (2024). Determining biomethane potential from animal-source industry wastes by anaerobic digestion: A case study from La rioja, Spain. *Renewable Energy, 235*, 121175.
237. Oliveira, H. R., Kozlowsky-Suzuki, B., Björn, A., Yekta, S. S., Caetano, C. F., Pinheiro, É. F. M., et al. (2024). Biogas potential of biowaste: A case study in the state of Rio de Janeiro, Brazil. *Renewable Energy, 221*, 119751.

238. Klimek, K., Kapłan, M., Syrotyuk, S., Bakach, N., Kapustin, N., Konieczny, R., et al. (2021). Investment model of agricultural biogas plants for individual farms in Poland. *Energies, 14*(21), 7375.
239. Pappalardo, G., Selvaggi, R., & Pecorino, B. (2022). Biomethane production potential in southern Italy: An empirical approach. *Renewable and Sustainable Energy Reviews, 158*, 112190.
240. Koonaphapdeelert, S., Aggarangsi, P., & Moran, J. (2019). *Biomethane: Production and applications*. Springer Nature.
241. Fan, W., Huang, L., Tan, Z., Xue, F., De, G., Song, X., & Cong, B. (2021). Multi-objective optimal model of rural multi-energy complementary system with biogas cogeneration and electric vehicle considering carbon emission and satisfaction. *Sustainable Cities and Society, 74*, 103225.
242. Dalpaz, R., Konrad, O., da Silva Cyrne, C. C., Barzotto, H. P., Hasan, C., & Guerini Filho, M. (2020). Using biogas for energy cogeneration: An analysis of electric and thermal energy generation from agro-industrial waste. *Sustainable Energy Technologies and Assessments, 40*, 100774.
243. Manganelli, B. (2014). Economic feasibility of a biogas cogeneration plant fueled with biogas from animal waste. *Advanced Materials Research, 864*, 451–455.
244. European Biogas Association. (2022). *Gas sector situation*. https://www.europeanbiogas.eu/SR-2022/EBA/
245. O'Connor, S., Ehimen, E., Pillai, S. C., Black, A., Tormey, D., & Bartlett, J. (2021). Biogas production from small-scale anaerobic digestion plants on European farms. *Renewable and Sustainable Energy Reviews, 139*, 110580.
246. Bielski, S., Marks-Bielska, R., Zielińska-Chmielewska, A., Romaneckas, K., & Šarauskis, E. (2021). Importance of agriculture in creating energy security—A case study of Poland. *Energies, 14*(9), 2465.
247. Styles, D., Gibbons, J., Williams, A. P., Stichnothe, H., Chadwick, D. R., & Healey, J. R. (2015). Cattle feed or bioenergy? Consequential life cycle assessment of biogas feedstock options on dairy farms. *GCB Bioenergy, 7*(5), 1034–1049.
248. Villarroel-Schneider, J., Mainali, B., Martí-Herrero, J., Malmquist, A., Martin, A., & Alejo, L. (2020). Biogas based polygeneration plant options utilizing dairy farms waste: A Bolivian case. *Sustainable Energy Technologies and Assessments, 37*, 100571.
249. Trypolska, G., Kyryziuk, S., Krupin, V., Wąs, A., & Podolets, R. (2021). Economic feasibility of agricultural biogas production by farms in Ukraine. *Energies, 15*(1), 87.
250. Yazan, D. M., Fraccascia, L., Mes, M., & Zijm, H. (2018). Cooperation in manure-based biogas production networks: An agent-based modeling approach. *Applied Energy, 212*, 820–833.
251. Porto, B. H. C., Soares, J. P. G., Rodrigues, G. S., Junqueira, A. M. R., de Azevedo Caldeira-Pires, A., Martinez, D. G., & Kunz, A. (2021). Socioenvironmental impacts of biogas production in a cooperative agroenergy condominium. *Biomass and Bioenergy, 151*, 106158.
252. Valle, B., Simonneau, T., Sourd, F., Pechier, P., Hamard, P., Frisson, T., et al. (2017). Increasing the total productivity of a land by combining mobile photovoltaic panels and food crops. *Applied Energy, 206*, 1495–1507.
253. Walston, L. J., Barley, T., Bhandari, I., Campbell, B., McCall, J., Hartmann, H. M., & Dolezal, A. G. (2022). Opportunities for agrivoltaic systems to achieve synergistic food-energy-environmental needs and address sustainability goals. *Frontiers in Sustainable Food Systems, 6*, 932018.
254. Okoroigwe, F. C., Okoroigwe, E. C., Ajayi, O. O., Agbo, S. N., & Chukwuma, J. N. (2020). Photovoltaic modules waste management: Ethical issues for developing nations. *Energy Technology, 8*(11), 2000543.
255. Levin, M. O., Kalies, E. L., Forester, E., Jackson, E. L., Levin, A. H., Markus, C., et al. (2023). Solar energy-driven land-cover change could alter landscapes critical to animal movement in the continental United States. *Environmental Science & Technology, 57*(31), 11499–11509.

256. Chikaire, J., Nnadi, F. N., Nwakwasi, R. N., Anyoha, N. O., Aja, O. O., Onoh, P. A., & Nwachukwu, C. A. (2010). Solar energy applications for agriculture. *Journal of Agricultural and Veterinary Sciences, 2*, 58–62.
257. Aroonsrimorakot, S., Laiphrakpam, M., & Paisantanakij, W. (2020). Solar panel energy technology for sustainable agriculture farming: A review. *International Journal of Agricultural Technology, 16*(3), 553–562.
258. Hajto, M., Cichocki, Z., Bidłasik, M., Borzyszkowski, J., & Kuśmierz, A. (2017). Constraints on development of wind energy in Poland due to environmental objectives. Is there space in Poland for wind farm siting? *Environmental Management, 59*, 204–217.
259. Majeed, Y., Khan, M. U., Waseem, M., Zahid, U., Mahmood, F., Majeed, F., et al. (2023). Renewable energy as an alternative source for energy management in agriculture. *Energy Reports, 10*, 344–359.
260. Campos, I., & Marín-González, E. (2020). People in transitions: Energy citizenship, prosumerism and social movements in Europe. *Energy Research & Social Science, 69*, 101718.
261. Baiano, A. (2020). Edible insects: An overview on nutritional characteristics, safety, farming, production technologies, regulatory framework, and socio-economic and ethical implications. *Trends in Food Science & Technology, 100*, 35–50.
262. Parajuly, K., Fitzpatrick, C., Muldoon, O., & Kuehr, R. (2020). Behavioral change for the circular economy: A review with focus on electronic waste management in the EU. *Resources, Conservation & Recycling: X, 6*, 100035.
263. Gorjian, S., Ebadi, H., Jathar, L. D., & Savoldi, L. (2022). Solar energy for sustainable food and agriculture: Developments, barriers, and policies. In *Solar energy advancements in agriculture and food production systems 2022* (pp. 1–28). Academic Press.
264. Salkuti, S. R. (2020). Challenges, issues and opportunities for the development of smart grid. *International Journal of Electrical and Computer Engineering (IJECE), 10*(2), 1179–1186.
265. Kulkarni, V., & Kulkarni, K. (2020, June). A blockchain-based smart grid model for rural electrification in India. In *2020 8th international conference on smart grid (icSmartGrid)* (pp. 133–139). IEEE.
266. Streimikiene, D., Baležentis, T., Volkov, A., Morkūnas, M., Žičkienė, A., & Streimikis, J. (2021). Barriers and drivers of renewable energy penetration in rural areas. *Energies, 14*(20), 6452.
267. Sen, S., & Ganguly, S. (2017). Opportunities, barriers and issues with renewable energy development–A discussion. *Renewable and Sustainable Energy Reviews, 69*, 1170–1181.
268. Weiss, C., & Bonvillian, W. B. (2013). Legacy sectors: Barriers to global innovation in agriculture and energy. *Technology Analysis & Strategic Management, 25*(10), 1189–1208.
269. Fashina, A., Mundu, M., Akiyode, O., Abdullah, L., Sanni, D., & Ounyesiga, L. (2018). The drivers and barriers of renewable energy applications and development in Uganda: A review. *Clean Technologies, 1*(1), 9–39.
270. Jan, I., & Akram, W. (2018). Willingness of rural communities to adopt biogas systems in Pakistan: Critical factors and policy implications. *Renewable and Sustainable Energy Reviews, 81*, 3178–3185.
271. Abd-Allah, Y. S., Ahmed, T. H., & Metwally, K. A. (2023). Evaluation of the drying process of paddy rice with a biogas continuous rotary dryer. *Misr Journal of Agricultural Engineering, 40*(1), 59–74.
272. Ourahou, M., Ayrir, W., Hassouni, B. E., & Haddi, A. (2020). Review on smart grid control and reliability in presence of renewable energies: Challenges and prospects. *Mathematics and Computers in Simulation, 167*, 19–31.
273. Sirin, S. M., & Yilmaz, B. N. (2021). The impact of variable renewable energy technologies on electricity markets: An analysis of the Turkish balancing market. *Energy Policy, 151*, 112093.
274. Gan, L., Jiang, P., Lev, B., & Zhou, X. (2020). Balancing of supply and demand of renewable energy power system: A review and bibliometric analysis. *Sustainable Futures, 2*, 100013.

275. Opperman, J. J., Carvallo, J. P., Kelman, R., Schmitt, R. J., Almeida, R., Chapin, E., et al. (2023). Balancing renewable energy and river resources by moving from individual assessments of hydropower projects to energy system planning. *Frontiers in Environmental Science, 10*, 1036653.
276. Lazdins, R., Mutule, A., & Zalostiba, D. (2021). PV energy communities—Challenges and barriers from a consumer perspective: A literature review. *Energies, 14*(16), 4873.
277. Ciupageanu, D. A., Barelli, L., & Lazaroiu, G. (2020). Real-time stochastic power management strategies in hybrid renewable energy systems: A review of key applications and perspectives. *Electric Power Systems Research, 187*, 106497.
278. Chiş, A., Rajasekharan, J., Lunden, J., & Koivunen, V. (2016, August). Demand response for renewable energy integration and load balancing in smart grid communities. In *2016 24th European signal processing conference (EUSIPCO)* (pp. 1423–1427). IEEE.
279. Stadler, I. (2008). Power grid balancing of energy systems with high renewable energy penetration by demand response. *Utilities Policy, 16*(2), 90–98.
280. Shimbar, A., & Ebrahimi, S. B. (2020). Political risk and valuation of renewable energy investments in developing countries. *Renewable Energy, 145*, 1325–1333.
281. Egli, F. (2020). Renewable energy investment risk: An investigation of changes over time and the underlying drivers. *Energy Policy, 140*, 111428.
282. Khan, Z., Badeeb, R. A., & Nawaz, K. (2022). Natural resources and economic performance: Evaluating the role of political risk and renewable energy consumption. *Resources Policy, 78*, 102890.
283. Wang, Q., Dong, Z., Li, R., & Wang, L. (2022). Renewable energy and economic growth: New insight from country risks. *Energy, 238*, 122018.
284. Lowitzsch, J., Hoicka, C. E., & van Tulder, F. J. (2020). Renewable energy communities under the 2019 European Clean Energy Package–Governance model for the energy clusters of the future? *Renewable and Sustainable Energy Reviews, 122*, 109489.
285. Reis, I. F., Gonçalves, I., Lopes, M. A., & Antunes, C. H. (2021). Business models for energy communities: A review of key issues and trends. *Renewable and Sustainable Energy Reviews, 144*, 111013.
286. Caramizaru, A., & Uihlein, A. (2020). *Energy communities: An overview of energy and social innovation* (Vol. 30083). Publications Office of the European Union.
287. Tarhan, M. (2015). Renewable energy cooperatives: A review of demonstrated impacts and limitations. *Journal of Entrepreneurial and Organizational Diversity, 4*(1), 104–120.
288. Yildiz, Ö., Rommel, J., Debor, S., Holstenkamp, L., Mey, F., Müller, J. R., et al. (2015). Renewable energy cooperatives as gatekeepers or facilitators? Recent developments in Germany and a multidisciplinary research agenda. *Energy Research & Social Science, 6*, 59–73.
289. Lu, Y., Khan, Z. A., Alvarez-Alvarado, M. S., Zhang, Y., Huang, Z., & Imran, M. (2020). A critical review of sustainable energy policies for the promotion of renewable energy sources. *Sustainability, 12*(12), 5078.
290. Koperski, L. (2017). Why the renewable energy credit market needs standardization. *Washington Journal of Law, Technology & Arts, 13*, 69.
291. Finocchi, E. (2020). Standardizing a unique renewable energy supply chain: The SURESC model. *F1000Research, 9*.
292. Conkling, T. J., Loss, S. R., Diffendorfer, J. E., Duerr, A. E., & Katzner, T. E. (2021). Limitations, lack of standardization, and recommended best practices in studies of renewable energy effects on birds and bats. *Conservation Biology, 35*(1), 64–76.
293. Sundberg, P., Hermansson, S., Tullin, C., & Öhman, M. (2018). Traceability of bulk biomass: Application of radio frequency identification technology on a bulk pellet flow. *Biomass and Bioenergy, 118*, 149–153.
294. Sovacool, B. K., Turnheim, B., Hook, A., Brock, A., & Martiskainen, M. (2021). Dispossessed by decarbonisation: Reducing vulnerability, injustice, and inequality in the lived experience of low-carbon pathways. *World Development, 137*, 105116.

295. Hoang, A. T., Nižetić, S., Olcer, A. I., Ong, H. C., Chen, W. H., Chong, C. T., et al. (2021). Impacts of COVID-19 pandemic on the global energy system and the shift progress to renewable energy: Opportunities, challenges, and policy implications. *Energy Policy, 154*, 112322.
296. Patel, S., & Parkins, J. R. (2023). Assessing motivations and barriers to renewable energy development: Insights from a survey of municipal decision-makers in Alberta, Canada. *Energy Reports, 9*, 5788–5798.
297. Breyer, C., Khalili, S., Bogdanov, D., Ram, M., Oyewo, A. S., Aghahosseini, A., et al. (2022). On the history and future of 100% renewable energy systems research. *IEEE Access, 10*, 78176–78218.
298. Ceglia, F., Esposito, P., Marrasso, E., & Sasso, M. (2020). From smart energy community to smart energy municipalities: Literature review, agendas and pathways. *Journal of Cleaner Production, 254*, 120118.
299. Shafiullah, M., Ahmed, S. D., & Al-Sulaiman, F. A. (2022). Grid integration challenges and solution strategies for solar PV systems: A review. *IEEE Access, 10*, 52233–52257.
300. Baranauskienė, J. (2024). Evaluation of public projects in the light of sustainability. *Management Theory and Studies for Rural Business and Infrastructure Development, 46*(2), 174–182.
301. Elavarasan, R. M., Shafiullah, G. M., Padmanaban, S., Kumar, N. M., Annam, A., Vetrichelvan, A. M., et al. (2020). A comprehensive review on renewable energy development, challenges, and policies of leading Indian states with an international perspective. *IEEE Access, 8*, 74432–74457.
302. Fahlquist, J. N., & Roeser, S. (2015). Nuclear energy, responsible risk communication and moral emotions: A three level framework. *Journal of Risk Research, 18*(3), 333–346.
303. Friederich, S., & Boudry, M. (2022). Ethics of nuclear energy in times of climate change: Escaping the collective action problem. *Philosophy & Technology, 35*(2), 30.
304. Kang, J. N., Wei, Y. M., Liu, L. C., Han, R., Yu, B. Y., & Wang, J. W. (2020). Energy systems for climate change mitigation: A systematic review. *Applied Energy, 263*, 114602.
305. Ukoba, K., Medupin, R. O., Yoro, K. O., Eterigho-Ikelegbe, O., & Jen, T. C. (2024). Role of the fourth industrial revolution in attaining universal energy access and net-zero objectives. *Energy, 360*, 100002.
306. Uwaoma, P. U., Eboigbe, E. O., Kaggwa, S., Akinwolemiwa, D. I., & Eloghosa, S. O. (2023). Ecological economics in the age of 4IR: Spotlight on sustainability initiatives in the global south. *International Journal of Advanced Economics, 5*(9), 271–284.
307. Cowie, P., Townsend, L., & Salemink, K. (2020). Smart rural futures: Will rural areas be left behind in the 4th industrial revolution? *Journal of Rural Studies, 79*, 169–176.
308. Özgül, S., Koçar, G., & Eryaşar, A. (2020). The progress, challenges, and opportunities of renewable energy cooperatives in Turkey. *Energy for Sustainable Development, 59*, 107–119.
309. Qadir, S. A., Al-Motairi, H., Tahir, F., & Al-Fagih, L. (2021). Incentives and strategies for financing the renewable energy transition: A review. *Energy Reports, 7*, 3590–3606.
310. Bisaga, I., Parikh, P., Tomei, J., & To, L. S. (2021). Mapping synergies and trade-offs between energy and the sustainable development goals: A case study of off-grid solar energy in Rwanda. *Energy Policy, 149*, 112028.
311. Christensen, J. L., Hain, D. S., & Nogueira, L. A. (2019). Joining forces: Collaboration patterns and performance of renewable energy innovators. *Small Business Economics, 52*, 793–814.
312. Brink, T. (2017). Innovation collaboration in the renewable offshore wind energy sector. *International Journal of Energy Sector Management, 11*(4), 664–680.
313. Aleixandre-Tudó, J. L., Castelló-Cogollos, L., Aleixandre, J. L., & Aleixandre-Benavent, R. (2019). Renewable energies: Worldwide trends in research, funding and international collaboration. *Renewable Energy, 139*, 268–278.
314. Mu, C., Ding, T., Qu, M., Zhou, Q., Li, F., & Shahidehpour, M. (2020). Decentralized optimization operation for the multiple integrated energy systems with energy cascade utilization. *Applied Energy, 280*, 115989.
315. Mishra, P. C., Kishore, S., & Shivani, S. (2018). The role of information technology for knowledge management: An empirical study of the Indian coal mining industry. *Journal of Global Information Technology Management, 21*(3), 208–225.

MIX
Papier aus verantwortungsvollen Quellen
Paper from responsible sources
FSC® C105338

If you have any concerns about our products,
you can contact us on
ProductSafety@springernature.com

In case Publisher is established outside the EU,
the EU authorized representative is:
**Springer Nature Customer Service Center GmbH
Europaplatz 3, 69115 Heidelberg, Germany**

Printed by Libri Plureos GmbH
in Hamburg, Germany